Lucienne, the Simple-Minded

Lucienne, the Simple-Minded: A Novel

Copyright © 2022 by Norman Beaupré

Published in the United States of America.

ISBN Paperback: 978-1-951901-82-0
ISBN eBook: 978-1-951901-83-7

All rights reserved. No part of this publication may be reproduced, stored in a retrieval system or transmitted in any way by any means, electronic, mechanical, photocopy, recording or otherwise without the prior permission of the author except as provided by USA copyright law.

Lucienne, the Simple-Minded

Novel

NORMAN BEAUPRÉ

[La Simple d'esprit: translation by the author]

*For my daughter, Diane,
so that she may remember with pride her
francophone heritage fundamentally
linked to Quebec and its culture*

By the same author

✻ ✻ ✻

An Artist of Daring Creativity
Micheline Bousquet, Analytical Biography, 2022.

• FIRST PART •

The story of Célie Lafortune Lanouette

Lucienne, the Simple-Minded

The Lanouettes came from a very small village east of *Trois Rivières/* Three-Rivers called Sainte-Geneviève-de-Batiscan. The Lanouettes were first day settlers of the Batiscan region. Batiscan owed its name to the chief of one of the First Nations, the Algonquins. The Lanouettes let no one forget their important role, said to be precious, in the surroundings where we preached every day the charm of belonging and being of the blood of the settlers. No one aspired to the loyalty of Quebec and to his own village like the Lanouettes. They were the most proud if not the most haughty of people. When one belongs, one never goes astray of his land and of his family, said the Lanouettes. Never would they have believed of seeing themselves transplanted elsewhere than Sainte-Geneviève-de-Batiscan.

Never would they have wanted to separate themselves from their own just like the Lavertus, the Lantagnes, and the Tousignants who had gone to the United-States in order to join so many Québécois who now worked in the factories over there that we called *les moulins/*the mills. Never would the Lanouettes even dream of this exploit that would have changed forever their identity as pure-blood settlers. The heritage of these people would have never tolerated this cultural breach, this treacherous act, leaving and dissociating themselves from one's village, one's country and one's culture would have been a sacrilege for them, these darned settlers, because they would certainly lose their religion and their cultural values once displaced, God knows where. "It's not done" did they usually say. The Lanouettes sang that all day long, "It's not done."

Marjolain Lanouette was of the fourth generation of the Lanouettes of Batiscan. He was recognized for his keen and penetrating intelligence. He had married Énevrine Bellavance from Victoriaville and the two of them had raised a family of several children, all of them in good health except the last child, Héloïse, for she had the bad luck of contracting a kind of infantile paralysis when she had attained the age of ten. It was the daughter-in-law, Célie, who had taken care of Héloïse for the mother could no longer take care of this child since she had reached the advanced age of sixty-seven. The mother was at the end of her rope and strength after having given birth to seventeen children. Raising them meant taking care of them, nourish, clothe, and teach them their prayers prescribed by the pastor of the parish called the *curé*, who was the leader of his flock. These orisons were given to her in religious confidence for she was the woman purveyor and faithful to her sense of duty as mother of the family. She allowed herself a bit of leisure at night after the dishes, sitting in a large rough by usage Chantung chair after putting the children to bed. It's then she could stretch her legs and let out a long sigh of relief. The daughter-in-law, Célie, had taken with warmth and joy the last child home with her because she could no longer stand the tiring supplications of her mother-in-law, Énevrine, who lamented day after day of having to take care of and encourage a little girl whom she found so bad lucky for having contracted such a sickness that she found pernicious and troubling in her way of seeing things. Why did God allow such a late birth in her life, Énevrine. Why a birth that she had not hoped for when being at a point in her life where everything appeared to flow toward death and eternal rest that she hoped for with tolerance and hope in spite of her aversion toward death. She suffered and accepted the tenacious trials of a life dedicated to sacrifices and misery although never would she tolerate inside herself the admission of misery. She did her duty and that was all. In spite of her husband's death, there were a few years Énevrine had abstained herself from blaming God and a fatality that came to her breadwinner and father of her children.

    As for Célie Lafortune, she had married Maurice Lanouette, son of Marjolain and Énevrine. She had been widowed for about ten years. Just like her mother-in-law, Célie Lafortune Lanouette had lost her husband in the lumber camp while working with the axe and the "godendard", this monster of a two-man saw. He had died from an accident in the forest alone and without help from the other lumberjacks who had found him bathing in his own blood, dead with the head split in half. They never knew the reason for his death. Moreover, they well knew that Maurice Lanouette was a scatterbrain. Why had they permitted him to work as a lumberjack, one never did find out why. Better in the forest than in the house or in the streets with people laughing at him, they said of him. His poor wife working her fingers to the bone doing housework for others as well as ironing loads of shirts and aprons of other households whose members had more money in their pockets than poor Célie. Célie was a woman of strong body and spirit. It was she who had saved enough money to buy a small farm. She had done it at the end of her strength and at the redness of her knuckles with the hard work of rubbing clothes with heavy yellow soap and soaking them in bleach. While saving her own pennies and nickles added to the little money earned by Maurice in the lumber camp, she had convinced her husband to purchase their own farm. That's why she would not sell her little farm for all the gold in the world although she often found herself alone and sometimes somewhat despairing since money wasn't coming in. Célie oftentimes found herself at rope's end. Meaning that she couldn't even pay herself a good meal when all she could afford were a few meager vegetables with some bread that she had made with some leftover flour. However, she never complained, too proud and too hard a determination fashioned by misery that she encountered quite often. She and her husband had not had the grace of having children. Yes, grace because both of them believed in the *Bon Dieu*, the Good God, who granted his goodness by divine grace. What can one do when grace is not granted. Well, one must suffer with your eyes shut tight and the heart twisted, used to say the Lanouettes, sons, wives, and in-laws.

    The children of the grandparents Lanouette, Edouard and Livinie, had all survived in spite of the sorrowful pains of the sicknesses that ravaged the newborns of the neighborhood. The Lanouettes had raised all of their eighteen children without noticing that they had had one breach only in their little Québécois lives next to the river Batiscan. The Good Lord had been very generous to them, the Lanouettes, whose great great grandparents were of the first settlers became known as distinguished at the sight of all the small but lively population of Sainte-Geneviève-de-Batiscan. Yes, the grandparents Lanouette had been blessed by God, it was said each time we spoke of them. We did not miss repeating at the appropriate time and place that their son, Marjolain, was one of the most gallant and most talented of the region. And, one did not cease remarking that these Lanouettes had the good luck of having Célie Lafortune as a member of the family. It was she who had honored them by her presence as wife by linking herself intimately with the name Lanouette. She bore this name with pride and fidelity ever since her marriage with one of their sons.

They had baptized Célie's husband, Joseph Maurice Henri Arthur Lanouette. He was often called Henri-le-bavardeur[Henri the talker] because he loved to talk a lot and utter stupidities. The parents did not want to admit that their son Maurice Henri was a bit scatterbrain. Célie, his wife, wanted at all cost to get away from this condition that her husband had since she could never accept that her Maurice was not like other men, healthy and intelligent of body and spirit. She had rather sheltered him and covered him entirely with care and affection and kept telling herself that one day her Maurice would come out of his head weaknesses. He never did. He died in his scatterbrain blunders. His wife had buried him with all of the humble honors that a wife can give to her defunct husband. There was a high mass with songs and music at Sainte Geneviève church. The church was decorated with the black banderoles usually accorded to its parishioners on the day of their funeral. Tall candles stood guard next to the catafalque over which had been placed the black mortuary cloth with the gold embroided cross. Célie had worn the prescribed black mourning clothes for an entire year and had then replaced it with the traditional not so dark colors, grey or purple. She had thirty masses sung for the repose of her husband's soul and she never missed the opportunity to recite a short prayer for him every night before going to bed. No one could say that she had not grieved her Maurice as it was prescribed by village traditions. However, she had taken down from the living room wall her husband's portrait since she could no longer face a husband who had annoyed her all their married life every time she went into the living room to do the dusting and cleaning. It was not that she wanted to ignore or even get rid of her husband's memory. No, she had had enough of him and his intellectual impotence, a terribly upsetting feeling that she had nourished in the very bottom of her heart, if not in her soul bruised for years. Célie was a woman crushed by the great sullen misfortune of a misalliance. She would not in any way reveal to anyone one way or another this heartache and trouble of conscience that she called her cross. The beautiful cross that a good Christian woman must carry in order to merit her salvation according to the pastor, Monsieur le curé Lapointe.

    This was also part of her Québécois heritage. Célie never deviated at any time from her heritage that she received from her parents and her ancestors. Even her in-laws lent her their support in this heritage whose cultural values were inevitably attached. Crestfallen, tempered by the little misery, and wearing the scars of her long interior struggles, Célie had sought refuge in resignation and the hope that one day things would be better. After all, it was her way of confronting her future for she did truly believe that a life well lived would obtain its merits some day. Day to day, month after month and year after year Célie waited for the nice days that would give her the happiness of having exercized the merit of a life where everything is sifted through duty. Célie is still waiting. Up to her death.

    The only benefit in Célie Lafortune Lanouette's life was the intimate link established between her, her mother-in-law and the little Héloïse, the youngest so often called by her brothers and sisters "the little one with her nose stuck everywhere". She was full of life and had a sense of daring that her brother, Hector, called wild. Yes, Héloïse had a head full of traffic, as they say, enough to fill the neighborhood streets and alleys. And, she was frightfully daring. Her imagination was filled with all kinds of plans and imaginings so that when she had the taste for it, she would fabricate other plans more intelligent and more daring than what people would have thought about her. People said here and there that she would never grow up with a well-ordered maturity. That she could never hold up a head well-screwed on her shoulders, as the neighbor Monsieur Dumouchel said of her. She was a rascal, an impish one at that, both nimble and sprightly when playing tricks on others, people said of her. Except Célie who found her lovable, a bit agitated, yes, but full of energy that made her exceptional and interesting in her eyes. Héloïse was the joy of her mature life, Célie told herself.

    Skinny, somewhat tall for her age, the eyes clear and somewhat bulging, the mouth wide with big reddish lips, the cheeks somewhat lacking color, with ears that sprouted on both sides of the head like mushrooms, and the nose a bit too long, Héloïse did not pretend at all that she was beautiful. She was the leftover of a crop of kids to which her mother had given birth, and she, Héloïse, had received nothing of the benefits that nature grants as far as grace and beauty are concerned. She didn't care. She used to tell herself that the other children enjoyed the goodness of nature while she had received, on the other hand, intelligence and the energy of a fairy/sprite. Héloïse had become the joy and the consolation of Célie, especially during the great and terrible sickness that Héloïse had suffered. Célie had convinced her mother-in-law, Héloïse's mother, that she would take care of, night and day, her little sister-in-law. Héloïse was only ten years old when she was struck down by a serious and debilitating malady. She had lost the agility and the movement of her two legs. The doctor had diagnosed her as either having infantile paralysis or another debility on which he could not exactly put his finger. Not a single desired precision allowed the doctor to satisfy his groping diagnostics. Thus they put the poor patient to bed for an entire year without getting up, without being able to satisfy her need to either run and play in the summertime fields of flowers or enjoy the snowbound prairies in the wintertime that she so loved. All that she could do was to rely on the goodness and the active imagination of her dear sister-in-law. Célie was truly good for Héloïse. She brought her *crêpes* with maple syrup and brown sugar in the morning. She served her good hot soup for lunch at noon and at night for supper, she often offered her a mixture of meat and vegetables sprinkled with a brown sauce with a hint of well-chosen spices. Célie deprived herself of nourishment so that she could, in a way, satisfy the hunger of her little bedridden girl. Never did she ever complain of her sacrifice nor did she show any signs of her personal privation.

One day, when she perceived that the provisions were getting very low, Célie went to the grocer to beg for some bread and two eggs in order to satisfy the little girl's demand for French toast. The grocer asked her to pay the sum she owed him and had not been paid for several weeks. She excused herself and admitted that she did not have the money to pay him. The grocer refused her order and the poor woman left empty-handed, in tears and with a hidden shame inside her chest. So Célie returned to her usual ingrate tasks of washing and ironing for more fortunate households. She must have experienced a conscience ravaged by the worries of a lack of money and energy that became more and more restrained due to her advanced age. In spite of all the heartbreaks in her attempts to satisfy her needs as well as those of the sick little girl, Célie came out of it proud and capable of surmounting the weaknesses of the day, for she had an iron will and an extraordinary capacity to regain her fortitude and determination in fulfilling her duty against all odds. After all, she held her courage by her hand, a settler's hand well resolved and well determined by her Québécois enhardened heritage.

Little Héloïse's mother came to visit from time to time in order to find out from Célie how her daughter was doing both physically and mentally. She found her daughter always gay and satified with her condition in spite of her lamentations of being nailed to a bed without too much capacity of movement outside her bed. However, Héloïse never complained about her plight for she loved the ambiance and solicitude created by Célie for her. Héloïse's mother had noticed on one of her visits that her daughter-in-law was losing weight from week to week and she had brought with her some provisions from her own kitchen in order to satisfy the nutritive needs of her daughter and her daughter-in-law. At first Célie had refused to accept Madame Lanouette's gift but the mother-in-law insisted that if she refused squarely her offering she would take her daughter back home and care for her there. So, Célie finally accepted the basket of food murmuring that it was so terribly painful living at other people's expense. The mother-in-law saying at a high voice, after all it was all part of the family and she did that because it was indeed family. Family is family, she said, and that family obligations are totally sacred and are an integral part of the heritage.

In order to fill the day often lacking interesting activities for poor Héloïse, Célie told her stories, stories of her ancestors, fairy stories, and tales of the Amerindians called the Algonquins. Célie knew so many stories for her grandfather Lafortune had filled her head with all kinds of stories that he loved to tell in the evening after supper. At first, Célie told the little girl bits and pieces of stories about the family starting with the settlers, the Lanouettes who had settled Sainte-Geneviève-de-Batiscan. They were Héloïse's ancestors, she said, and that was why she thought it was so important that she, Héloïse, got to know her own story. The settlers Lanouette came from France in the Normandy region. They had come with Samuel de Champlain, the explorer, cartographer and great founder of the city of Quebec. The Lanouettes were passengers on the second voyage of Champlain after he had come back to France after his first voyage to New France, *la Nouvelle-France*. Later in 1608, they accompanied Dupont, a friend of Champlain on the ship, *Lévrier*, that accompanied the *Don de Dieu* [Gift of God] the ship commanded by Champlain. Célie told Héloïse that she knew quite a bit about the Champlain history because she had frequented the little country school for two years followed by the parochial school Saint-Narcisse during the period of four years before being displaced with her parents to a place called Sainte-Geneviève-de-Batiscan. It was at the little country school where the teacher had taught her the "rules" that is mathematics and the letters which meant reaching the reading level, *"dictées"* and sometimes grammar. Later she would go to the nun's school where she learned *"l'histoire sainte"* [holy history], and the history of France and Canada. The reason behind her displacement was the loss of work at the little factory of scissor and knife blades at Saint-Narcisse. Moreover, there had been the finding of relatives long forgotten in the Batiscan region. What earned the esteem of the Lafortune parents was their contact with the managers of the agricultural company of the village which ended up with a stable job offer for the father, Pierre-Léon and son, Léandre, Célie's brother.

Célie continued the story of the Lanouettes while noticing the gleaming interest in Héloïse's eyes. The settlers Lanouette landed at Tadoussac on the shores of the Saint-Lawrence river. Only the men were allowed to board the three ships destined for the overseas soil that was declared New France. There were four Lanouette brothers, one became a trapper, another a *"coureur de bois"* {runner of the woods] and the other two farmers. It's later that a few descendants of the Lanouettes would find themselves brides upon the arrival of the *"Filles du Roi"* [daughters of the king] sent by his majesty King Louis XIV with a dowry. Célie told Héloïse that one of the sons of her great-grandmother had married one of them and her name was Hélène-du-Figuier of Saint-Berthélémi in Paris who got off the ship in Trois-Rivières. A little later, she got married to Jacques Fournier in Quebec and it was reported that His Grace François de Montmorency de Laval, apostolic vicar of New France and the first bishop of Quebec, was present at the wedding as one of the a witnesses. Having become a widow, Hélène-du-Figuier Fournier was later married to Jacques Lanouette, grandson of Pierre-André Lanouette.

Héloïse went wild over the story of her ancestors Lanouettes as related by her sister-in-law in the evening after supper of abstinence and sacrifice for Célie. But, what the young girl truly loved were the fairy tales that were strung together during long free afternoons by Célie. She told her the tale of "Beaury and the Beast", one of Célie's favorites, "Tom Thumb", "Cinderella", "Puss in Boots", "Snow White" that Héloïse begged Célie to repeat since she loved this tale so much, and a tale by George Sand, *"Ce que disent les fleurs"* [what the flowers tell], *"L'oiseau bleu"* [the blue bird], and *"La Petite fille aux allumettes"* [the little match girl] as well as many others. Célie knew so many tales locked up in the head of a woman vowed to dreams and the delights of a guardian of children she never had. Then in order of not forgetting the tales of fun of Quebec, Célie, from time to time, used to tell Héloïse tales and legends breathed by the genius of the good *Canayen* [Canadian] inventor and raconteur. There was the legend of *"La Dame Blanche"* [the white lady] that Célie loved to tell to instruct the little one about the history and the geography of the Montmorency Falls. Then came the tales of the *loups garous* [werewolves], of the *feux follets* [will o' the wisp], the *diablotins* [imps] and the phantoms. Héloïse always asked her what were the imps, and she always answered they were the little devils or the evil goblins who came to pull the shirt tails of naughty children. There was also the legend of the Corriveau woman, but Célie kept this tragic story for later. It was when Quebec was fighting the British bastards, for the story of the Corriveau woman hit some raw nerves if not the brain, had said Célie.

Célie was only fourteen when her father took off for the grand route, we knew not where, leaving his wife with six children alone to fend for herself in good times or bad times. His wife who was called Alphonsine, Célie's mother, wasted away day after day after having lost her husband to adventurous exploits when so many men took on the mentality of the *coureurs de bois*. We began to call them the eaters of moose tracks since the Algonquins often followed the moose tracks, this huge beast that served as nourishment for them. In any case, these spirited men were in the wild and they sought adventure without being preoccupied by their own at home, and that was said in the family and at the Saturday night *soirées*.

Célie started to tell her own story to Héloïse when this one asked her to do so. She even insisted on it. After several pleadings on her part, Héloïse slipped herself in the soft comfort of her big feather pillows so that she could listen with ease to Célie Lafortune Lanouette's own story, the lady of a thousand and one nights of tales and stories. First of all, Célie told the young girl that she, Célie, very rarely told her own story, never to everyone. Because it was a story of love and sorrows of the heart, she had told those who pressured her to tell the story of her young life. However, Célie had reassued herself that if she began her story that she, Héloïse, would keep a good memory of it and this would render her more sympathetic towards those who suffer in life. Célie would teach her also a bit of the cultural history of the Amerindians specifically the Algonquins. Why the Algonquins? Well, Célie had made a full experience with them while they were culturally and ethnographically part of the Batiscan region. So Héloïse stretched out her right arm to reach her little notebook on the table where she kept her notes. Célie asked her why she wanted the notebook.

—It's because I want to keep notes on everything you tell me about the Lanouette family.

—Why?

—Because I want to retain all the details of my story so that I can later tell them to my children.

—Oh, you think you will have children?

—Don't make fun of me, Célie. You know very well that my health will get better and that I'll become a good provider and woman of the countryside just like my mother. And, I will certainly have children.

—Yes, but you will first have to find a husband.

—Of course. I know that it will take a long time but I'm convinced that this will happen according to the goodness of the *Bon Dieu* who will answer my prayers. You know well enough like me that the *Bon Dieu* grants the prayers of the sick just like those who are healthy.

—Not all the time, my dear.

—But I have full confidence in him.

—So much the better. One must rather hope than despair.

—Well said my dear Célie. You are the proof of this hope that leads one safe and sound.

—Maybe my dear little sick one, maybe you are thinking upside down of things you do not know or knows bad.

—What do you mean by that?

—Let's leave things alone.

—If you want. But I don't understand what you mean by that.

—Maybe one day you'll understand.

—Well, don't delay. Tell me your story. I want to know all the details.

Célie continued her story where she had left off. Well before she got to know the Lanouette family especially by the means of Maurice, her husband, that she would marry later on, Célie met the love of her life in the person of a young Algonquin named, Timiskamengo. He came from the First Nation of Notre-Dame- du-Nord.

Célie warned Héloïse of remaining calm and without uttering a single word until she had ended her story. The young girl said yes, certainly, for she did not want in any fashion to miss a single word of Célie's story. Héloïse would then be able to ask her questions once the story was terminated. Inclined in her bed, with her back on her pillows, and the head in the hollow of her hands, Héloïse stared at the storyteller with sparkling eyes and at the same time eyes that were smiling that she had not had even when her sister, Fernande-Marie, tried to tell her bits of fairy tales or Québécois stories. Célie had a big smile on her face and she began her story.

Timiskamengo belonged to a family whose mother and father were persons of prowess and dignity without equal. They had raised their son with a sense of firmness, discipline, and *savoir-vivre* [know-how-to-live]. He had become the model of every child of the clan. No one could ignore the virtues of the young man who was growing up like a beautiful white birch tree, proud and reflecting the beauty of nature. But what distinguished him from other young men was his attitude towards young women of his age as well as those who had surpassed the years of maturity such as the oldest ones and the weakest often abandoned by the clan. Timiskamengo radiated with goodness and with grace so much was he loved by his parents. his brothers and sisters, and especially the old people such as the sorceress-healer, Ministratou.

One day, when Timiskamengo found himself in the surroundings of the White people next to the village of Sainte-Geneviève-de-Batiscan, he met one of his friends who dragged him to the parish hall where several young men of the parish were playing checkers. Timiskamengo hesitated at first, but he succumbed to the convincing demands of his friend,. He did not want to displease him and found in his after thought that his parents would allow him this little afternoon delight where all what one could do was to walk the streets and think what one could do in his spare time. After two hours of playing checkers, the young friend became annoyed and decided to leave the hall. While being cautious to go back home, Timiskamengo saw from afar a horse-drawn buggy that was going like hell, the dust of the road flying every which way. He asked himself who was making the horse go so fast. It was a young man accompanied by a young woman who was sitting next to him. She was covering her eyes with her two hands and seemed to shout to him not to go so fast. Timiskamengo hurried to run toward the buggy and the poor beast whose flancs were being beaten with uncontrolled whipping. Timiskamengo knew horses very well and he knew how to control them with an adroit and just hand. He jumped on the reins and pulled so hard that the horse slowed down, all nerved up and looking at the young man with a wild eye.

Célie felt that Héloïse wanted to ask her, at this moment, some questions, but she made a sign to wait and told her,

—It was me with my brother in the buggy. I was so afraid. Then she continued her story.

My little brother was called Josephat. He was a boy filled with energy and had a perspicacious intellect. He was never afraid of anything that one. He never cared for anything one way or another, not even for imminent danger. He made the mare galop in the middle of the main road just to show off. He loved to show off in front of others. I was truly scared, feeling the panic, and thanks to this young Amerindian that I did not know, but who showed his prowess and his skill with horses, that we came out of it safe and sound. My brother laughed with a racy kind of laughter. I tried to tell him to slow down but he seemed to mock me and laugh at me. Then, I told him just wait and that I would tell our parents what he had done. A real crazy nut.

Célie related how she had been struck by the dark and ardent eyes of the young Amerindian and that her heart started to beat fast so fast that she believed that she would lose consciousness and faint. The young man was only fourteen years old while she was seventeen, but she found him to be of an extraordinary maturity for his young age. It was she who asked him later on to meet her next to the bower and they had introduced each other and then the conversation started and lasted two hours that did not appear to be long at all for the young Célie. She found out what his name was and the name of his parents, as well as all the members of his family, including the names of the grandparents, uncles, aunts, and other close relatives who were part of the clan to which they belonged for the clan forms the essential part of an Algonquin family, said he. With the weeks and the months that had gone by so fast for these two young people, an affection touching upon an intimacy that had been willed by both had quickly slipped into their lives without their not fully noticing it. Célie insisted that she did not want that intimacy that sometimes comes and blurs the feelings of a heart yet too sensitive to the inopportune faltering. However, she could not get rid of it, this want, this need, sometimes troubling, to see Timiskamengo again without bringing to it discontentment or regret. She did not know what to do. He, on his part, insisted on seeing her again each day and integrate himself in her life like a balm that refuses to disappear. Célie's mother very soon noticed that her daughter was entertaining a volatile if not dangerous friendship for she did not appreciate her daughter's feelings linked with those of a young Amerindian. Too young for her, said the mother to her. As for the father, he was not preoccupied with his children's love liaisons. He had no concerns for them. Timiskamengo's grandmother advised him to think about it carefully for intimacy between a White Skin and a Red Skin too often brings unhappiness. The traditional and ethnic links fall apart and carry a shock to the cultural sensibilities as well as displeasure in each individual's life, she told him. However, she added that the intimacy between two people is very often worthwhile if they want to get along together, and that it is hoped that the White Skin be open to the Amerindian values and more precisely the Algonquin values.

So Célie started learning about the values of the Algonquins for she did not want to collide with this intimacy which was being formed, day to day, in their young lives. Timiskamengo taught her his values as well as those of his family including those of the grand family of the Algonquins that he kept as a treasure in his soul as a Red Skin. He told Célie that he did not like this term Red Skin used by the Whites but that he acceeded to the lack of know-how-to-say of those who ill-understood the ethnic values of the native people. Célie never again used the term Redskin after that. It was the start of Timiskamengo's teaching with Célie.

The young man taught her his values and his heritage with patience and conviction for he thought she would one day become his spouse and that both of them would found a healthy home filled with love where their children would grow up strong and intelligent. Célie could not help but to believe in him, Timiskamengo, his plans and his desires for he had somehow bewitched her by his nice and smooth words as well as his convictions. She had so easily fallen for this seeing that the nice and tender words had pierced her skin and bones and they even touched her heart. And she wanted, at all cost, to learn the values, the beliefs, and the history of the Algonquin people. She bent honestly before the dictates of her own will so as to become more and more sensitive to this people who had been not only neighbors but the ante-settlers, the very soul of the First Nations where the White man had settled.

First of all, Timiskamengo taught Célie the fact that the Algonquins were divided into bands, then into clans and after that many clans formed a tribe. The Algonquins had a mode of life that was nomad. Traditionally, they changed territory during the seasons so as to be able to survive, but with the leap of time nowadays, said Timiskamengo to Célie, it had become more and more stable and his clan had not changed territory for over thirty or forty years. The principal source of nourishment for the Algonquins was the moose. However, they lived with what they now bought, just like the Whites. An important part of the Algonquin lifestyle relied on sharing. Timiskamengo insisted that his people was charitable like all Christians should be. He and his family were converted to Catholicism many years ago but his clan still paid respect to the traditional spiritual values such as the Grand Creator and that everything had a spirit. There also was an evil spirit that created problems for human beings. Moreover, there was a very great respect and love for the earth because the earth gave them all they needed to live. And then, there were shamans. The shaman could help heal a sick one or give advice. He would use herbs taken from the virgin forest for their medicinal attributes. The shamans used all natural medicines in order to heal the less fortunate. Prayer was also a spiritual link very important for them.

Célie listened to everything that her young friend told her and she kept it in her benevolent heart for she wanted to learn it all from Timiskamengo. She had become his heart companion. Her mother insisted that she should not precipitate herself in an affair of the heart because chances were such an affair, especially with an Amerindian, dared to become unhealthy due to the differences of values and ethnic convictions. Célie had answered that she would surmount all obstacles and that she would convince everyone that she was right in her affair of the heart. The father told the mother to leave her alone and not to put her nose into what was not in her domain.

Célie continued her lessons of cultural values of the Algonquins by insisting in learning certain tribal legends and stories. Timiskamengo offered her many such as the legend of Nanabozho and of his own grandmother, Nokomis, the old sage- sorceress who raised him and used to tell him all the stories known in the tribe. Then, he mentioned Kuchi Manido the Grand Spirit and the Creator God totally divine not having the human shape at all. There was also Kichi-Odjig or the Great Fisher who slays monsters puts the seasons on their way and represents the Great Bear in the constellation of stars. Moreover, he spoke of Widjigo a bad spirit who ate men alive. Also, the little Algonquins learned when an Algonquin committed a sin especially egoism, gluttony or cannibalism they became a Widjigo as punishment. Timiskamengo saw very well that Célie had her eyes riveted on him and listened with great pleasure. She insisted that he tell her entire legends without being shortened so that she could taste the full savor of the Algonquin legends. It was then that her interlocutor related to her the legend of the Grasshopper and the Origin of Tobacco. It goes like this, said he.

—One day Mishabo, the grandson of Nokomis, another name for Nanabozho with the Algonquins, was walking very close to a high mountain when he smelled a very nice odor that seemed to come from a fissure in the steep slope. He got closer and found that the mountain was the living site of a Giant who was known as the keeper of tobacco. Mishabo found a cavern on one of the borders of the mountain and infiltrated into it while following a passage that led to the center of the mountain where the Giant lived. The Giant asked severely Mishabo what he wanted. This one simply wanted some tobacco, but the Giant told him that the spirits had just come to smoke together. Since the ceremony only occured once a year, the Giant told Mishabo to come back the following year. Mishabo found that hard to understand since he saw stacks and stacks of tobacco piled high in the cavern. So he grabbed a bag of tobacco and got away outside the mountain while pursued by the Giant. Mishabo reached the summit of the mountain and leaped from summit to summit. The Giant pursued him closely and when Mishabo arrived at the very border of the fissure, he fell on his belly and so the Giant jumped over and above the fissure and fell into the chasm.

The Giant was severely hurt but he was able to climb the fissure where he hung from the summit, all of his fingernails torn. Then Mishabo seized the Giant by the nape of his neck and threw him on the ground saying, "On account of your greediness, yes, you will be turned into a Grasshopper, and then everyone will recognize you by your stained mouth. You will become a little harmful beast and you will bother those who cultivate tobacco." So Mishabo carried out his tobacco and went home to his people and gave each one his portion. Moreover, he offered each one tobacco seeds so that they could sow and cultivate tobacco thus as an offering and benediction. " For us the natives, tobacco has a sacred character and often the smoke of tobacco serves either as a sacrament or as a healing agent. We could even say that everything that touches the ceremonies is sacred, declared Timiskamengo with firm conviction.

Célie found that the legend was of the childish brand, just like the tales of Perrault.

However, she told Timiskamengo that she understood why his ancestors remained attached to these stories, and that she did not blame them for having kept the stories and the legends of their past. Timiskamengo told her that the stories and the legends went much further than the memory and even the traditions of the tribe. They were part of their cultural identity that could not be eradicated even if one wanted to. It was as if these stories and these legends found themselves to be the marrow of their culture and their traditions. They were found to be the myth in which every culture be it Algonquin or other gets behind it to try and explain the phenomena of their existence. Timiskamengo insisted that the great myths of their culture were sacred and no intellectual or mental exigency could abolish or efface them from the memory be they Algonquins or other tribes. Célie tried to convince her friend that she would never want to make an effort to suppress the cultural value of these tales and legends, and that she wanted, at all cost, to preserve them in her heart and in her memory like the sweet precious cachets that are so unforgettable.

—What's a myth? interrupted Héloïse.

—Don't interrupt me like that. But I will tell you what a myth is because you do not know what it is. You're too young to understand that. A myth explains a phenomenon such as a rainbow or the creation of the world or an Amerindian clan. It's what is not explained in ancient times. I mean by human reason. So, we invented stories to give an explanation. At that time, science was not formed enough nor had it evolved. The Greeks had many of these myths to formulate a response to the phenomena of their time. I will talk to you about that later on. I must continue my story or rather Timiskamengo's story.

—I want to know what is a phenomenon. With all these words that you give me as an explanation, I don't understand everything, you know. I didn't have much schooling as they say back home.

—Well, phenomenon means what is not seized by the intelligence and especially by reason. There has to be another measure of comprehension such as a story that gives semblances of truth given by a more opened intelligence and a reason less reasoning.

—You've got me, my dear. All these words and all these long explanations tell me absolutely nothing.

—Myth has the power to opening our intelligence to stories that give us more clearly reasons or explanations for what is hidden from us. Like the creation of the universe that is opened to us by faith and by a long story in our first book of the Old Testament, Genesis. The creation is a phenomenon and almost all peoples as well as all the tribes on earth fabricate their stories of creation, such as that of the Amerindians and specifically the Algonquins. Myth is not a lie, it's a truth but a different kind of truth. It belongs to a legend or to a story, a mixture of intelligence and the imagination. A phenomenon although difficult to understand, is explained to us by means of stories. You get it?

—Now you're speaking and I get it better.

—No more interruptions if you want to get to know my story.

—No interruptions, I guarantee.

The links between Célie and Timiskamengo got tighter and became intimacy. Intimacy eventually became more and more close up until the two of them became lovers. It was totally evident that Célie loved Timiskamengo and he loved Célie. However, there were hitches in that love affair. Célie's mother, while not opposed to it, wasn't in agreement with her daughter as for this intimacy that the mother called an affair to make the cows bawl. For the mother did not in any way believe in a love affair between two beings of different races, said she to her daughter. As for Timiskamengo's parents, they found themselves embarrassed in giving their son permission to continue the links that already existed and they even counseled him to break them without delay. Célie was close to desperation while Timiskamengo encouraged her to persevere in their love. Célie knew very well that she was older than the young man, and that she should have a sense of maturity to know better, but she could not resist this affair of the heart. What to do?

There came without knowing the cause, a terrible malaise that afflicted the Algonquins. It was a contagious and cruel sickness for it brought death with it. Almost all of Timiskamengo's family was hit cruelly by this disastrous sickness. It was named scarlet fever that came to decimate the Algonquin tribe. Even the Whites were affected, but those there escaped better from it than the Red Skins who did not have enough resources to overcome the fever. Célie did not see Timiskamengo for weeks if not months. She was heartbroken and she was brought to tears so much that she could not stop thinking of him and his family in danger of death. The family Lafortune tried to encourage her but with no results.

Célie remained mournful and powerless in her distress. It was only after six months of suspense on her part that Célie learned that Timiskamengo's parents if not the entire family had perished which meant that the son found himself alone and without relatives. It was one of the worst situations for a native born.

Without relatives there was no help or benefits of the links and access to vital resources for a young man like him. He found himself like abandoned. What to do?

Célie learned of Timikamengo's fate and asked herself how could he get out of this bad luck. She asked her parents to offer her friend lodging and give him nourishment necessary to his health. They told her that this would be difficult to do for the family was already large and that the members of the family had had it with this young "Indian" and that having him among them would be an insult to their own family intimacy. Célie then thought of escaping and fleeing from them, if possible with Timiskamengo. But, where was he? Where had he sought refuge? Timiskamengo was staying with a cousin of his in another village and found himself separated from Célie by distance and by family embarrassment, the Lafortunes. Timiskamengo came to be able to finally get to meet Célie after so many absences and annoyances. Once both of them reunited for a few moments only, he admitted to Célie that he now belonged to no one and to nowhere. Célie tried to encourge him but nothing could suffice to the misery of abandonment and the broken soul. They separated without any hope of getting together one more time. Timiskamengo did not want to darken things with the Lafortune family for he knew well that they did not want him, a stranger and above all a Red Skin alone and abandoned by the tribe. Timiskamengo knew very well that his tribe had not abandoned him but people nourished in themselves malevolent rumors as it concerned Timiskamengo, the young man without relatives and without a home.

It happened that the government had just established a program of Indian boarding schools created and financed by the state. The veiled aim was to assimilate the native children in the eurocanadian culture. The Canadian government committed itself at all cost to an attempt in educating the young natives and integrate them into the Canadian society. These institutions were intimately linked to the Christian churches, and another goal was to convert these poor souls considered pagans. The implementation of the Law on the Indians of 1876 [*La Loi sur les Indiens de 1876*] permitted the authorities to force the recrutement of the young natives for these institutions since they saw that providing schooling to the population was a means of making the First Nations autosufficient on the economic plan. It's underlying objective was to diminish the dependency of the natives in regards to public funds. They said that this plan would suffice and for the public and for the Indian minorities who, both of them, deserved progressive attention from the government. They founded boarding schools in the Western Territories and later in northern Quebec.

It is then that one day without feeling vulnerable to the plans of the state in regards to his tribe and the young people, Timiskamengo found himself all of a sudden in the hands of three police officers who brought him to a boarding school far from his home with the cousin Little Bear. In spite of the tears and the loud cries of the cousin and in spite of the vociferations of the young man, they forced Timiskamengo to leave his home and join so many natives over there in an institution unwanted by them. Célie did not know anything about this displacement. She always told herself that her lover would return to marry her and bring her far from these troubles that came to harm her plans for a happy future and filled with promises.

After an entire year of silence on the part of Timiskamengo, Célie felt in her heart a sorrow of abandonment and she began to despair in spite of the assurances of her mother who tried to raise her morale. One day in September when the leaves started to show their fall colors, Timiskamengo surprised Célie by appearing all of a sudden at her home. She asked him where had he gone for such a long time without telling her. He told her the story of the boarding school and all the difficulties in which he found himself. That the food was frugal, the health care sparse, work was terribly hard, and the clothing used or too small or too big.

Moreover, there were frictions between the mistresses-teachers and the students because of certain jealousies and cultural embarrassments. They had forbidden them to speak not even communicate in writing in their own native language. The courses were given totally in French, a language that many did not speak. Fortunately, Timiskamengo spoke French but he found this shameful on their part to forbid the maternal language of these poor abandoned ones now captives under government control. What had troubled more Timiskamengo was the fact that the religious practices denigrated often altogether the traditions and the spiritual beliefs of the natives. He could no longer stand those beasts more savage than the savages, he told Célie. At the height of all those ordeals inflicted by the directors of those institutions was the abuse of sexual predators. Timiskamengo vowed that in spite of his disdain and his modesty as well as his prudence of being an Indian, that he was abused several times, and that he had submitted himself to them, these vilanous predators, so as not to receive the bad hittings and the very bad psychological punishments that were inflicted on him. After having suffered so much that he no longer wanted to live, he found a way of escaping. He hid himself in the bundles of sheets and pillowcases destined for the laundry in a truck that came every two weeks to take the laundry. No one had seen him, no one had even suspected him. One must believe that they had not even missed him, but he was scared that with time they would come to put him back in the boarding school with certainly the bearing of police officers, bitter and vengeful. Thus he told his dear Célie that he had to escape the surroundings of Quebec and go far, very far. Célie told him that she wanted to accompany him, but Timiskamengo refused that she take such a chance. It was dangerous, very dangerous. Hardships trailed him and he did not want to put her in danger. She begged him intensely but he did not budge. Finally they had to bend to the exigencies of fate as Timiskamengo said. He told her to hold on fast to the souvenirs of the past for he held good thoughts as well as a felicity of possible promises although restrained but those that consoled the heart and soul of a native and a misallied White. Célie never heard from Timiskamengo after that nor did she get any news after so many years.

—You never got one word from him? asked Héloïse.

—No, never.

—Yet, you loved him.

—Yes, I loved him enough to spend the rest of my life with him.

—You never abandoned him in your heart, that I know.

—Yes, never. Even today I feel his presence inside me in spite his long absence. The heart never abandons such an alliance of love. The souvenirs of the heart never default. Never.

—Poor you, poor little Célie.

—I'm neither poor nor little, dear little girl, my bedridden sick one.

—Tell me more about what happened after this adventure.

—You have to know everything?

—Yes, absolutely everything and don't try to forget or even don't erase by fault of not wanting to bring back to your mind that sometimes wants to hide the little sorrows that come and form piercing needles of regret.

—Piercing?

—Yes, that pierce. You know well what I mean.

—Well, here is the ending of this episode and the continuation of my story.

After Timiskamengo's flight, Célie told Héloïse that she felt like empty, rather numb and altogether incapable of generating any feeling that would permit her to want to produce in her any doubt about her capacities to love or being attached to a man who would give her a bit of hope for a future without melancholy, without regrets. She no longer felt like throwing herself into an adventure of love. Finished the adventures that lead to deceptions. Finished the hope that one day she could wish for a marriage that would be convenient and bring her a little love. A marriage without love would be for her a missed alliance if not a forgotten one. That's precisely what happened to her. She met Maurice Lanouette and in spite of what her heart told her, she vowed herself to marriage without knowing if this would bring her at least a bit of relief if not a bit of affection so much desired and so much wanted. Maurice was a gentle boy from a good québécois family and seemed to be sweet enough in words and in action so that Célie decided to take a chance on someone like him. It was a bit later that she noticed that Maurice was lamebrain and that he lacked some intelligence that usually comes to put together rationally customs and decisions in a person. Not that he was deranged nor a fool, but there was something lacking in him, "something on a branch" as they say back home. Maurice's mother warned Célie of her son's condition, but she told her that he would make a good husband in spite of his little lack of intelligence and *"savoir-faire"*, knowing how to do things and his lack of a well planted noggin, as she called it. Célie believed that she could well become accustomed to the small faults of a husband like Maurice and that she would be able to surmount the little sorrows of a mariage that would certainly bring children and a consolation to the only love in her young life, Timiskamengo. When one hopes beyond hope, one expects to have the best of chances in a broken life from the very start. Hope brings happiness but it also brings deceptions. Thus Maurice and Célie were married at the village church and established themselves in a little rent right next to the Lanouettes of Batiscan.

At the beginning, it was a household that was convenient for both spouses. They endured their fate so-to-speak. Célie did the everyday housework as well as the *grands ménages* [spring and fall cleanings]. Maurice went to work in the logging camp and came back home from time to time. Each day sufficed its hardship, as they say, *chaque jour suffit sa peine*. Maurice's absences intensified the worries and pains of a spouse who felt abandoned. Without wanting to and without making herself deliberately contemplate the past, Célie started to think of Timiskamengo and the happiness that she would have had with him. She was sure of it. Now that he had disappeared from her and she could not do otherwise than daydream about him, which squeezed the conduits of her heart as a woman. She resigned herself to passing the time away by saying short prayers in order to erode what forced her to endure the setbacks and heartbreaks of her inexplicable existence. She often told herself that she was going crazy by dint of enduring, of praying, and losing the bit of hope that remained.

Célie resigned herself to her fate more and more, that of living as a spouse and housekeeper. Heaven would certainly reward her for duty well accomplished in spite of the terrible hitches that wrenched her heart without end. How to get rid of these hitches without revealing to others a horrible struggle inside her person who was, after all, woman of spirit and body. Each time she started to make an effort to extract from her life the memory of Timiskamengo and his sweet words as well as his affection for her, Célie just could not ever erase the tender and loving face of Timiskamengo from her memory that never let go of the hold he had on her. Maurice did not say anything regarding affection and love. He was null for her. She who was woman and spouse, she deserved a bit of love from her husband, but love did not infiltrate in her life as a woman. Maurice was as if dead, without any spark and without a single moment of human warmth. Especially, he was a man of the logging camp, a logger who left and came back without any effort on his part to console his wife in her painful sorrows and her grief as a woman. He considered his absences as part of his work and then there was nothing he could do subtract himself from this lack of presence. He took everything as fate accomplished. He never questioned the why of his existence and his life as a spouse. Everything worked the way it should for him. No remorse no support with him. Célie started to hate him in her woman's heart. She hated him not because he was hateful but because he did not understand the heart of a woman and a spouse who feared of never receiving love so desired in a mariage. After a certain time and a long series of absences, Célie began hating herself. She hated that she was woman. Yet the other women were not haunted by such hardships given to those who dare to love and are cut down by a fate seemingly inevitable. This fate was mixed with a misalliance produced by a White Skin attached to a Red Skin who collided with different values and different stories that form the life of each one. Célie never believed that would happen between her and Timiskamengo, but she had to accept the facts of her love story with an Algonquin. It was the boarding school that had turned him upside down, Timiskamengo, if not it had thrown him into the fear of no longer possessing what he had all his life honored and acclaimed, his native Algonquin values. The abuse at the boarding school had shaken him profoundly if not pulled out his soul and had cast out the person that had been Timiskamengo. Then these stupefying things that Célie had never thought of, on top of it all, had turned upside down the things so much desired. She could no longer say that things would or could change. Things do not change. Never.

After Maurice's death at the logger's camp, and following the mourning period once accomplished, Célie started to think that things would get better a bit. Not that she had wished her husband's death, for she accepted that this decease was for her a relief and a grace for her and her husband, the lamebrain. Things were getting fixed little by little.

It was later that things appeared too sideways as aunt Louise D'antin of Roxton Falls would say. Yes, things do not always appear as one wants it. If Célie expected better days, well she would be disappointed. In Canada, *"il faut attendre la meule"* one must wait for the millstone, as people say. Meaning having to wait a very long time for things to happen. Things, things, what are things? They are not any old things. But what are they? No one knows except that things happen.

That's it.

After so many years and so many things, especially ills and worries, well there is for a person such as Célie an establishing of things together, an alliance between worries and the good times. A relief, a sit-still time, a space in a life when things become less stressing and better handled. The calming time, that's it. It's exacttly what happened to Célie when she saw herself alone and wihout heartaches. She had found her own time in life where everything is possible and acceptable. The heart is no longer troubled and the soul is at peace. The peace of a satisfying repose that's well deserved. That's when the souvenirs of a Timiskamengo, the memory of a lamebrain, and a happy time with Héloïse are blended together in a vague remembrance of a faraway past. All that's left is a memoir that vacillates between the past and a future that edges its way between the stitches of a *catalogne*, [an artisan style rug or blanket], well worked and well appreciated, the product of a life altogether devoted to labor and duty. Célie remains in her rocking chair and submits herself to the rocking movement of her old chair. One has to believe that she is happy after all of the miseries, big and small, in the life of Célie Lafortune Lanouette. Everything had muffled itself comfortably and she hardly felt the distress of yesteryear. She only had to accede now to the thread of a life in which a Timiskamengo slides in.

They found Célie dead in her rocking chair one Monday morning when her neighbor had worried about her since Célie was not out hanging her clothes washed and rinsed every Monday of the week. Célie was seventy-seven years old. The few relatives she had had just celebrated her birthday. She died with a smile on her face. Héloïse melted into tears when she heard the news. Célie Lafortune Lanouette did not have a funeral, only a *libera* because she had not done her religion for a long time, said the *curé*. However, through an exception of the established rule, they buried her in the Lanouette plot where the first Lanouette settlers slept under the Québec soil. After all, Célie belonged to the Lanouette tradition and she now lay in the arms of a past that could not be broken and lasted forever it seems. The ancestors were there, the in-laws were there, the husband was there, and Célie was there now. No Timiskamengo though.

• SECOND PART •

*The story of
Héloïse Lanouette Charbonneau*

The day was long, very long for Héloïse who now lived with her sister, Félicité Moreau, married to Ernest Moreau of Sainte-Justine- de-Kamouraska. Héloïse had distanced herself from her village and her relatives after the death of her mother and the death of Célie. She no longer had a supporting hand, she told herself. No more hand of a woman that she could reach out to, since her sisters were scattered here and there and even there were some who had left for the United- States. They had gone to join the people of the village and of the surrounding area who had fled from the dangers and the worries of the loss of a farm, the loss of work and especially the loss of close friends who they themselves were gone to earn their bread in the factories called *moulins*, the mills.

Héloïse was now seventeen. She wanted, at all cost, to earn a living without depending on someone. She did not think of relying on her sister nor on her brother-in-law not even on her aunt Frélipine who had been after her to come and live with her in Saint-Cyr-de-Lanière in order to share her board and room. Her aunt found her frail of health and spirit and had written to Héloïse, but, Héloïse had not answered that neither her health nor her spirit were frail for both had gone through a transformation after days, weeks, and months with her sister- in-law Célie. This one had taken very good care of her, night and day, and she had never stopped giving her an affectionate care so proper to her health. Héloïse with time had benefitted from the respite at Célie's home and her legs got better with a therapy applied by the tender and adroit hand of her sister-in-law. Héloïse could walk straight and solid in spite of a small limping of the left foot, especially when she was tired or overburdened with shopping errands for her sister. But she could do anything once she put her mind to it. Nothing stopped her from helping others while manifesting herself as agile and independent of body and soul. Héloïse had become lively and full of steam, as they say, and no one could possibly say that she could not accomplish her duty as a woman. But what was this duty of a woman that she heard in the pulpit, out of the mouths of women that she knew well and the refrains of men at the Saturday night *veillées*, those gatherings where everyone sang, danced and had fun. No one dared to define to her the duty of a woman even when she asked. "Well, the duty of a woman is to please her husband and raise her children," the men said. As to the women, they reported that the duty of a woman is to please God, satisfy the needs of the family and never *manger du prêtre* [never talk bad or against the priest]. They added that duty implied also charity to others. But what did the duty of a woman mean, insisted Héloïse. No clear answer, no assurance on the part of others.

Nothing but weak and colorless remarks and without any good sense, according to Héloïse. She got back to her own affairs that she knew very well without neglecting the duty of a woman. She moved energetically in her life as she concentrated on the future that the Good Lord in his will as Father and Creator would grant her. Héloïse had not gotten too much catechism in school since she hardly attended the nuns's school, but she knew enough to be able to get along in life, a Christian life vowed to the holy will of God. It was her mother and especially Célie who had taught her the rules of good Christian conduct based on the holy Bible and the Sunday gospels. Cêlie told her that she did not need school books and a catechism with questions and answers not inculcating sufficiently the true sense of Christian life. And so, Héloïse found herself to be a good Christian and a good Catholic as her mother had been as well as Célie in her good graces.

Héloïse got lost in the memory of the abuses at the boarding school and the scars left on the flesh and the soul of Timiskamengo. She would not have the love testified by Célie for her beloved, but she would never lose this feeling of vulnerability and conscience caught up with a past where the abuses and the hypocrisy of a government in collusion with the Church had almost erased the wanted and needed respect. With time, Héloïse had become, if not agnostic, at least doubtful of these rules and doctrines that come to baffle the spirit and tarnish the innocent and febrile soul like her. She could not understand this hypocrisy of those on whom she had relied, who, once put to bare, reveal the faults and the abuses committed. It was all due to the government, the politicians, religious authority, people that she knew well or even certain relatives. There were some everywhere and at every instant in life, she told herself. Who to believe? Whom to rely on? Héloïse promised herself that she would not insist on this point but that she would keep herself on guard about this hypocrisy that veiled the bad deals and especially the psychological, corporal and sexual abuses. She was at a point when she no longer lent an ear to politicians and set foot in a church. Her sister sometimes gave her hell for her lack of religion, she said, but Héloïse did not pay any attention to what her sister told her as to religion.

—But you're going to lose your soul, my dear, said her sister Félicité.

—No, I won't lose it. I probably lost my sense of direction in life. It seems to me that I no longer have a compass to guide me.

—Yet, you are not a ship that's sinking. You have us and especially religion if you want to use it right.

—Yes, it's exactly that. I would like to use it but there are too many hitches in the ideal conduct proclaimed by the Church and the reality of each day.

—What do you mean by that?

—I mean that what I expect of myself and what others expect of me is not always at the same level.

—At the same level?

—Yes, at the same level. I mean that the religion that I see and practice often has hitches of hypocrisy. It's the same thing with certain people like you.

—Don't you dare insult me with that. I do my best and I do it with a judicious heart and eye just like it was taught to me and according to our heritage. You're still too young to not accept the right way to live. Correctly.

—Correctly?

—Yes, correctly as it must be done. We must not eat of the priest, *manger du prêtre*, and the Church. We must not neglect one's duty as a woman and a young girl like you must know how to listen to grownups. We have the age of experience, we do.

—Yes, the experience that often leads to authoritarian discipline.

—What do you mean by that? That I'm bossy and mean?

—It's exactly that. You said it.

—I'm your sister and I only want your well-being and the salvation of your soul.

—My soul, leave it alone. It is well. Let it be.

—No, it's not well. You don't do your religion.

—Yes, I do it, but my way of doing it and not the way of certain priests and people who are snooty like you.

—I can take care of myself and I don't need you and your dirty advice.

—My advice is not dirty. It's simply reasonable and to the point.

—Yes, your advice comes out of your stubborn and shitful head and not from the heart of a compassionate sister.

—Stop calling me names and bad qualifiers that I don't deserve.

—You deserve them but you do not know or do not want to understand why you deserve them. You have a hard noggin and a heart that is even harder.

—You're terrible saying such things to your sister who loves you and who takes care of you and your needs.

—Excuse me. I spoke a little too frank and please excuse me. However, there are things that I refuse to swallow. I said them and it's over.

—You are terribly [*vachement*] insensitive towards me and to my desires of rebuttoning you and putting you on the right track. Really, I don't understand you.

—You mean that I'm unbuttoned?

—Don't start making puns.

—I want you to laugh a bit. Don't be always grouchy and unpleasant.

—Unpleasant? Grouchy?

—Yes, you don't realize that you act like a woman who often has bad blood.

—Never on your life, my dear, never on your life.

—In any case, I don't want to hurt you. I'm telling the truth without hypocrisy on my part.

—You never had your tongue in your pocket. *[ta langue dans ta poche]*.

—There you speak the truth.

—Try to put your tongue where it belongs.

—You want me to say nothing about what irritates me and makes me angry. That I hide everything that comes out of my mouth and especially my heart.

—Sometimes it's not good to say everything. One must learn to speak while keeping something inside. Like that you irritate no one and yourself.

—Are you irritated against me just because we are speaking as sisters?

—Not irritated but I ask myself where do you come from when you speak like that.

—From the same parents like you.

—Our mother would not have endured that you talk to me like that and that you talk badly about priests.

—Here she goes on the same tune, the same refrain, yes, the same story about priests.

—Yes, because it's true. Someone must correct you, my sweet. No one enters into heaven by speaking like that against priests and the Church.

—What I say is the truth and I'm not ashamed of saying it. I'm not hiding anything.

—Be careful about what you say and do. You'll regret it one day.

—I have nothing to regret. All that I hate is the hypocrisy of people and especially of priests and the religious men and women.

—You still have your heart hurting on account of the abuses in the boarding school and the story of this Indian lover. Who knows if he was tellinng the truth?

—Yes, he was telling the God-awful truth. I know it very well. I felt it in my soul and in my heart, this astounding truth. Timiskamengo was a person who was cruelly hurt by those who wanted him to be well and good, so they said, but who inflicted evil on him, poor man.

—One must get to know both sides of the coin, both sides of the story. That's all I have to say.

—Do you take me for a liar?

—You know that the love story of our sister-in-law, Célie, is only a beautiful adventure that she wove together herself. At least, from what I know, Célie knew how to spin a tale that has no facts and no reason behind it. As for me, I never believed her.

—You're bad speaking of her like that. She doesn't deserve that. You are truly cruel and bad. I know her story totally and I know she told the truth.

—Think the way you want. I think that she fabricated a story of love to attenuate the damage of her marriage with our brother Maurice. I believe that it was her who pushed him more intensely into the dizziness of a lamebrain.

—Maurice was not totally lamebrain. He lacked something but he was not a fool. He lacked good sense for a man his age. I believe that progressively Maurice got worse. It's absolutely not Célie who made him worse.

—I'm not saying that he was a fool. He certainly did not belong in an asylum for the mentally ill. However, there was something that went wrong in the marriage of Maurice and Célie.

—Don't start making up stories. You didn't know Célie very well, her troubles, her sorrows.

—You, you knew them?

—Better than you.

—Well stay with your so-called memories of your sister-in-law.

—She took very good care of me. I consider her not only my sister-in-law but a friend of my heart who truly touched the soul of a young girl growing up under her guidance.

—At that time you did not see clearly. You were too young. You will never see clearly on this fact. She really had you brainwashed.

—Stop scorning her. What you say is calumny.

—Well, take it and lump it if you think that way. I think that her story of Indians, boarding school, broken heart, and nuptial misalliance is all a chapter of miscontent and uneasiness in a life that does not satisfy all the desires of a woman too dumb to get rid of her faults and her damn sorrows.

—You lie, Félicité, you're lying. You've become really bad and evil. and I can't live here anymore. That would cause me terrible worries. Worse than staying with Marie-Anne Houde the horrible step-mother of Aurore Gagnon of Fortierville. She died in 1920 and we still hear about her even today. She was a woman that was debauched in her manners and in her *savoir-vivre*, know how to live.

—What?

—Yes, a woman who abused a child, corporal abuse and especially psychological abuse. There's nothing more pernicious than hatred and jealousy.

— Where do you get all of that?

—In the newspapers. We just could not help reading about her, poor little martyr.

—Well, I'll be darn. I never read about that in our lttrle journal.

—That's because our little journal likes to hide things that are said to be sordid. The editor is truly stupid. I read about it in *La Presse* of Madame Loignon, our neighbor.

—Don't you believe that if this story was true wouldn't we have read it in our little journal?

—I told you, our little journal does not print all the news especially if it's a matter of our dear Quebec and its traditional values. Apparently they don't want to tarnish our honor and our reputation.

—What's our reputation if not a reputation of strapping men and strong and brave women.

—Yes the reputation of drunken men and women chasers.

—Don't start talking against our people, these valiant defenders of our language and Canadian values.

—Don't you see our people's faults? Don't you read between the lines to find out the truth about things?

—No need to read between the lines because I see that you want to destroy the good reputation of our French-Canadians just to make trouble.

—It's not trouble that I want to cause. It's to bring to light the hypocrisy and the hidden abuses under the folds of our culture. We adore this culture a little too much just to make it an ideal and a portrait without faults.

—You, you're going to put the nation in peril with your forked tongue.

—The nation?

—Yes, our nation of French-Canadians tied to its traditions and fundamentally Catholic and proud of it.

—You mean we the Québécois.

—Yes we are the only ones that count.

—You're well honed in, my sister. You know how to cover up all the hypocrisy and the shame of our people with your dream of idealism. I could care less about all of that. I can't stand that hiding place of shit and blunders.

—Get away. Go, yes take your rags and go. I cannot stand you anymore since you disgust me with your cruel words and your shit-in-the-air look.

Héloïse remained frozen there standing on the floor without saying another word. She turned around and saw that she would not be able to bring her sister, Félicité, to her point of view. So, she went to her room and she stayed there all evening without even eating supper.

A certain breach had been reached between the two sisters that brought about a rift to a point that embarrassment and friction lifted up their ugly heads. Héloïse could not take it anymore. She could not take the cold and repugnant embarrassment to her eyes and to her heart. So she decided a few days later to leave once and for all. But, go where? She decided to go to Quebec city. However, she had a friend who was named Marie-Paule Bélanger who convinced her to go to Trois-Rivières where she had a cousin called Marie-Ange D'Auteuil. She told Héloïse that Marie-Ange loved welcoming people and that it would be a pleasure to give Héloïse a room if Marie-Paule asked her. Héloïse did not know what to say for she did not know this cousin and she would feel somewhat of a stranger in a house and a city that she did not know. But, she had to do something since she no longer had a place to stay and no familiar locale in Sainte-Justine-de-Kamouraska. Marie-Paule offered her to go with her by train up to Trois-Rivières if she accepted the offer. Héloïse accepted the kindness of her friend right away without hesitation.

Once in Trois-Rivières, the two friends went directly to the d'Auteuil's where they received a warm welcome without ceremony and without embarrassment.

Héloïse let out a long sigh of relief seeing this generosity given to her and her friend. Marie-Paule gave all the details of the fate of her friend Héloïse. Then she thanked her cousin Jean-Paul and his wife, the cousin Marie-Ange. Marie-Paule stayed with Héloïse three days and showed her the city of Trois-Rivières accompanied by Marie-Ange. This one explained to them that Trois-Rivières had had a fire, a real conflagration in 1908 and that a large part of the old colonial city was destroyed. However, she showed them the old Ursuline monastery and the Manoir De Tonnancour that had escaped the conflagration. The three women made the rounds of the inner city and they went inside the Cathedral of the Assumption of Mary since Marie-Ange asked them to. Héloïse did not dare refuse. Before entering the church, Héloïse noticed the very tall spire that appeared to her as very impressive. Once inside the cathedral, Marie-Ange signaled that the cathedral was of the neo-gothic style as well as the shape of the lancet arches and the bright stained-glass windows. In trying so very hard to stretch their necks to better view the details of the ceiling, the apse, and the arches, the three women felt a bit dizzy and so Marie-Ange invited her two companions to kneel down and say a few prayers. Héloïse said a short prayer asking the Virgin to come to her aid in her journey far from home. She told her that she had not always been faithful to her religion but that she had never forgotten nor had she abandoned her faith. She told her that she would keep inside her the memory of a mother from heaven never forgotten. Once they stood, the three of them went to take a break in a cafe and after an hour and a half, they wandered in the streets of Trois-Rivières. Marie-Ange talked to them about the one who had founded Trois-Rivières, the Sieur De Laviolette, and then she brought them to see a commemorative plaque of the founder. She mentioned the presence of the Algonquins at the very beginning of Trois-Rivières even before its founding by the French. There was a slight smile on Héloïse's lips. After a long promenade in the city, the three women went to the d'Auteuil residence where they collapsed in some soft lounge chairs where they spent the rest of the afternoon already far advanced.

On the third day of the visit to the cousin's house, Marie-Paule decided to go back home. She left early in the morning and advised Héloïse to stay at her cousin's house until she felt well enough to undertake another trip, probably this time even further. Héloïse remained undecided as to go either to Quebec or Montreal. All she knew was that she should not take advantage of the cousin Marie-Ange and that it would be inconceivable to abuse the welcome of someone like this dear lady whom she had just met. Marie-Ange tried to convince her that she was part of the family now, but Héloïse felt as a stranger and too much in debt to this cousin who really wasn't her own cousin. So then, Héloïse selected the city of Quebec as destination and Marie-Ange offered to bring her to the train station.

Lucienne, the Simple-Minded

Once in Quebec, Héloïse took Saint Jean street in the Vieux Québec, the old part, in order to go in the Basse Ville, the lower town, in order to explore the cradle of her heritage. She noticed Notre-Dame des Victoires, the oldest church in Quebec, the few shops that were around, and a little further the Saint Lawrence river. On the other side of the river there was an habitation that she did not know. People called it Lévis. She then deciced to go up the steep hill that led her to the esplanade called the Terrasse Dufferin. She leaned on the guardrail that overlooked the river and at a short distance was Lévis. She remained there a long time imagining the settlers who had come to found Quebec. Her imagination wandered and wandered so as to furnish her a series if images of what she knew about Quebec city. She did not know much but she swore she would get to know much more once established in this city of French heritage, her own heritage.

Héloïse recognized that she belonged to this culture for she appreciated the heritage of her people by way of the settlers Lanouette de Batiscan. This made it an integral part of the band of *Canayens*, she told herself. She belonged. After having spent a long time enjoying the scenery, and the good time as well as the nice wearher of the month of May, a young man came and sat on one of the benches next to Héloïse. He looked at her with a solicitude and remarkable interest. Héloïse turned her head and noticed the young man who was scrutinizing her with an ardent eye. She started blushing so uncomfortable felt she. She did not have the habit of inviting such a look on the part of a male

presence. She turned around and continued looking at the river. The young man got up and came right next to her without uttering one word. After a long moment of silence, he said.--

—*Bonjour, mademoislle*, my name is Edmond Lajeunesse. What's your name?

—Héloïse hesitated then not wanting to be impolite, she said,

—My name is Héloïse Lanouette from Batiscan.

She did not know why she had added the place of her origin. It was without a doubt by force of habit and pride for a beloved place.

—I come from Trois-Rivières, responded the young man.

—Ah! I just come from there. I spent a week with the cousin of one of my friends, and we visited several places.

—I know Trois-Rivières very well. I was born next to the cathedral.

—Your cathedral is beautiful. It astounded me with its architecture and its beauty of the neo-gothic interior.

—Yes, I have to admit that it's very beautiful.

—Why did you come here in Quebec? I don't want you to think that I'm nosy and all that but that interests me.

—Not at all, Madedmoislle. I came to Quebec more than six months ago to look for work. There's very little of it for me in Trois-Rivières.

—Oh, that's too bad.

—Yes, young people like me, we are forced to seek employment outside our city in order to get a job that would be convenient to us and would pay us well...enough to stop going hungry and sleep outdoors.

—I understand, Monsieur Lajeunesse.

—Please call me Edmond.

—I didn't want to be too familiar with you for after all we're strangers.

—No longer, Madmoislle Héloïse. We know one another better now than when the polite rules were done.

Both of them started to laugh

—Listen Mademoislle Héloïse, would you go for a little snack with me somewhere? Just to get to know one another better and especially because I don't know anyone here in Quebec.

Héloïse hesitated an instant then she said to him,

—I'm also alone and I know no one, absolutely no one, since I have just arrived here from Trois-Rivières. I too am looking for work and before anything else I'm loooking for a room somewhere in the city.

—Well let's go. I know of a little restaurant not too far from here. I went there last night. The food is good and the prices reasonable.

Once there at the little restaurant called **Chez Tantine**, Héloïse and Edmond took a table near a window and ordered their snack. It wasn't a snack but a meal, nothing too heavy but nourishing enough, a slice of *tourtière*, pork pie, and a piece of strawberry pie for Edmond, and a little bowl of pork and beans with homemade *cretons* for Héloïse. Both of them drank some hot tea at the end of the meal. The little conversation between the two new friends was pleasant and amicable. Héloïse who did not have her tongue in her pocket, as they say back home, stopped herself from being too talkative either by modesty or shyness, something she rarely did. As for Edmond, he talked and talked as if he had known the young woman before him for years. The social thawing started to transform itself into intimacy, at least on the part of Edmond. They came out of the restaurant then climbed up towards city hall. Edmond wanted to show his new-found friend the effigy of Louis Hébert done by the sculptor Alfred Laliberté on the occasion of the third centenary of the arrival of the first settler in Canada. He explained to her that this effigy was inaugurated only three years ago in 1918.

Following the sightseeing tour led by the young man, the two friends walked towards the Plains of Abraham where they sat on the freshly mown grass. The two of them talked and talked for an hour when Héloïse told Edmond that it was getting late and she truly wanted to find a room somewhere. Edmond reassured her that he knew a place where there were rooms at a good price. It was in the Basse Ville and he could easily tell her about renting a room there. He told her that the place was very modest and a bit bare in some places, but the people were the cleanest, clean as one would have it, and that the ambiance and the welcome were very kind.

—You'll see. It's not expensive and the rooms are simple but elegant by their cleanliness and their good settlers furniture, said Edmond.

So the two friends left for the Basse Ville. They met several people who walked with a brisk but slow pace. Héloïse was surprised by this movement of the people who were going somewhere but no one seemed to know where. Once they arrived at the Basse Ville, Edmond pointed with his finger a humble abode with a slate roof and worn out shutters.

The color had totally faded. Héloïse began to feel somewhat out-of-sorts and far from home. Edmond reassured her that the propriator, a Madame Sansoucis, was a goodhearted woman and her welcome warm and kind. Thus the two friends went to the small inn that had a sheet metal sign above the front door saying in frail letters, **Chez Albertine**. Héloïse was relieved.

Héloïse rented a room for the night, not wanting to commit herself for a longer period of time since she didn'ts know if she would find the room convenient and satisfying. Especially clean according to her taste. She stayed there two full weeks.. In between time, Edmond came to get her each day and bring her either for errands or for visits around town. Héloïse found herself more and more at ease with Edmond. She even told him about her little story with Célie, with the members of her family, and especially about the fight with her sister, Félicité.

Edmond found that fight dishonest stemming from ill contentment.

—Why dishonest? asked Héloïse.

—Because your sister did not have enough honesty to tell you that she loved you in spite of the little hitches of savoir-faire

—What do you mean by that?

—Well, I believe that by what you tell me, your patience is short and you have a tongue that is quite ready to tell somebody off. Am I right?

—Yes, but not totally. I'm not a bad person. I know that I don't have the patience of an angel. Also, I know I have a tongue that doesn't know how to be still.

—I don't say that you are bad. On the contrary, you're a good person. Frank and loveable too.

—Only if someone doesn't treat me as atrocious.

—You certainly are not atrocious Somewhat forbidding but that's understandable due to the fact that you have a daring sense, my dear. Not that you are overly bold.

—Yes, I know. I was born that way. You're not like that.

—What do you mean?

—Well, you are always well-behaved and you act like you were raised very well. I was raised properly but did not always follow the dictates of my being raised properly.

—Yet, you're not a beast nor even a kind of animal that's raised by farmers.

—I know that raising applies to animals but sometimes I feel like an animal raised on a farm who needs to be properly raised. My father used to tell me often that my behavior was that of a stubborn mare or an indocile bitch.

—*Dure à cuire* as they say, a tough one, or maybe untameable.

—It's exactly that. One can't tame a mare that rears up in front of any obstacle. It must obey and stop refusing the kindness of what is being offered.

—Have you often refused the kindness given to you by others?

—Sometimes. I have neither the tolerance nor the acceptance of a person bending over to the exigencies of others. I have rebelliousness in the blood. Just like this Louis Riel that I hear so often talked about.

—You know Louis Riel?

—No, but I hear some people talk about him. According to them, he's a true rebel.

—He fought for truth and justice for the disadvantaged. He was a half-breed who recognized hypocrisy in politicians and the spite of the Whites who used their miscontentment to assault people like him. It's true that he was recognized for his own spite and his fiery words oftentimes too incindiary, but what he said was the truth that touched people's hearts. That's all I know of him.

—He's really a man of conviction., a man who has *du casque*, as they say, tough and daring. No?

— Yes. A man who was recognized as a contemporary messiah. We hanged him after a long fierce trial.

—It's too bad that these people who are honest and brave like him are "sickled" down, as my father would say. Yes, we take the sickle and we cut the feet and the head like we cut the hay.

—Your pun is very colorful.

—It's not mine but my father's. He was a farmer at heart.

—You never became a farmer?

—No. *Pas de saint danger,* as we would say. Holy danger? Do you see me knee deep in cow manure and the swill in the sow's sty?

The two of them started to laugh.

After two weeks of coming and going, Héloïse started to think that she was going nowhere in her search for work and stability. She found herself alone and

disillusioned of having accomplished nothing in life. Her compass was only vacillating. She talked to Edmond about it who he, as well, found himself somewhat disappointed of having, in fact, not found work. In spite of the good rapport between them, Edmond did not find any warmth in his friendship with Héloïse, for she did not show any sign of affection and closeness that the young man expected. They were friends and that's all. Yet Edmond had given a sign of affection that could burst into a passionate love, but Héloïse had not answered his call. The time for a closeness that sees itself open up to love and intimacy had not arrived yet. Her heart had not yet been seized by feelings imbibed with the surges of the strength of love that a young girl feels for a young man. It wasn't Edmond. One could see that.

So the two friends met each other one Saturday morning to talk while having breakfast at **Chez Tantine**. Without having previewed it, this would be their last meal together. Edmond revealed to his friend that he was leaving for the United-States to join his brother, Benjamin, so that he could get work in the mills where his brother worked.

—It's not that I want to leave Quebec and separate myself from Canada and my co-citizens, but I must do something to establish myself in a place where there's a place for me and my dreams.

—What's your dream?

—It's to meet once and for all success in life. To really feel happy with a sense of belonging.

—Yet, you belong here in your country where your heritage and your culture vibrate.

—I know but heritage and culture don't put bread on the table.

—My ancestors used to say that separating from one's heritage and going far away to the States was llike losing one's identity and even one's soul.

—But there are so many of us French-Canadians who have left for the United- States in order not to starve. They found a place where they could live together

and they even created what is called *Petit Canada*, the Little Canada where they have kept the language and even our values of this heritage so proclaimed in a loud voice by our people. You see, I'm not going away to a strange country as such.

—But it's not our country.

—Yes, it is by the values brought over and by the transmission of these values for the next generation. These values are now rooted in a new soil. If Canada cannot sustain us and offer us the opportunity of opening ourselves to the much wanted success, then we must leave it to find a better life even if it means transplanting oneself elsewhere.

—It's hard when it means going away from home. Home means to us the essence of our lives and even our souls.

—The soul lives in the self, not in a country or a city.

—I know but, even though, it's terribly difficult for me to leave my ancestors' soil, abandon the soil of the Lanouettes.

—It must be done if one wants to continue living our dreams and our belonging. Success in life is certainly not in an impoverished farm that can no longer nourish its children. At the core of it all, we are country folks and we can no longer exist as such. We must live in the present and not default in a a restrained and colorless past.

—Edmond, you are truly the passion of words and of sentiments when comes the time to express yourself.

—Yes, it's because I have adopted a sense of conviction and audacity. I want to succeed at all cost.

—Bravo for you! I do not think about going away and leave the soil where I was born. I am, after all, a Lanouette. The Lanouettes are settlers, dyed-in-the-wool, and we do not fly away like birds that seek to displace themselves to look for any

kind of food. I don't want to eat strangers' food. I don't want a lost existence in a soil that does not give new life. I am *Canayenne pure-laine*.

—Remain Canadian but think of your future.

Edmond and Héloïse left each other that very morning and would not ever see themselves on *québécois* soil. Edmond made Héloïse promise that if ever she wanted to look for work in the States, that he would come to her help, and that he would accompany her to work once she gets there. She told him that she did not think of going there, but that she thanked him anyway for his efforts and especially for his indefatigable friendship. He gave her his brother's address in the States in case she would like to send him a letter.

The following day, Héloïse made her baggage and left for Sainte-Christine where she knew an old neighbor from Batiscan named Cora Lantagne.

Sainte-Christine was located at a far enough distance from Quebec city, but not too far from Drummondville and Saint-Hyacinthe, told her Madame Sansoucis. This lady had relatives in Saint-Hyacinthe and she assured her that her aunt Félicienne would certainly give her advice to go from Saint-Hyacinthe to Sainte- Christine. Long live family contacts, thought Héloïse. "Family is exactly that in Canada," said Héloïse to Madame Sansoucis. Belonging to the family was belonging to the womb of a mother, the lady told her.

Héloïse left Quebec city and headed for Saint-Hyacinthe. She had gotten assurances that the trip would not last more than three hours. However, the trip took seven hours on account of a misunderstanding between her and the driver of the bus. He had made the grand tour by passing through Nicolet and then up to Sorel where once there several passengers went out. Héloïse did not expect this long a ride almost in circles that made her late for the expected hour of arrival. Moreover, there were two flat tires that made the delay that more mortifying. Since Héloïse expected to arrive at the very beginning of the afternoon, she arrived at Saint-Hyacinthe at seventeen hundred hours. She was drained of her strength. She took a taxi in order to get to aunt Félicienne on Saint-Honoré street. After having paid the driver for the long trip, a Monsieur Saint-Simon, she realized that she had little money left. Too bad, she said, "I'll have to earn some more."

On the long porch with cut-out posts, there was a lady who was about in her sixties. She wore an apple green cotton dress on which she had put her apron with large pockets and very well ironed by hand. Everything looked extra clean and distinguished at this dear lady's domicile. She was waiting for her company with a good disposition and with a joyous smile on her lips, the smile of a woman who likes to welcome people just like one who welcomes relatives in Quebec or those who are considered rare visitors or not. Héloïse felt soft and a bit tense as surprised at the welcome of a woman that she didn't even know.

—Come through here, my girl, you must be tired from the trip. It took you a lot of time to get here from Quebec to Saint-Hyacinthe.

—Yes, Madame, the bus driver gave us a very long tour without my knowing it. It took hours and that's besides the flat tires. My poor back feels dead and my head is buzzing with all that wasted time on the road.

—Well, come and wash your face a little and your hands for we are going to eat supper in a few moments.

—You don't need to give me nourishment. I can go to a restaurant.

—No such thing, my girl. Here we are at home and we treat well family as well as friends of the family.

—*Grand merci, Madame, Madame* who?

—Madame Félicienne Vadeboncoeur. But call me aunt Félicienne like all the others. Even the neighbors call me aunt. I no longer have children and no more husband. Both of them died. I live alone, think about it. Alone but not abandoned. People from the area take care of me and I take care of them. Like that, time goes by and we stay busy with the kindness shared.

—You seem happy and so contented in your residence and your surroundings.

—It's the *Bon Dieu* who gives me the grace of growing old peacefully and without too many preoccupations. Well, let's stop chatting and let's get ready for supper. You like baked beans and some good homemade bread with some picallili?

—Oh, yes, Madame...aunt Félicienne. I have so much a taste for beans in my mouth when you mentioned to me this food, food of the country, we could say.

—You know that most of the families right here at home could not always pay themselves a sumptuous meal like nice pork roasts with browned potatoes as well as Sunday meals every day of the week, so we enjoyed what was cheaper like pork and beans. Those who have a big family with several children cannot certainly offer themselves luxurious meals. That's how I call them.

—You're right, Madame.

After supper, Héloïse helped her hostess with the the dishes and helped her clean the table, even though *tante* did not want help. "We do not oblige the visit to wash and dry the dishes," said *tante*. However, Héloïse took it upon herself as her duty to help the lady with a nice smile.

Having gotten the details for her trip to Sainte-Christine, Héloïse took to the road the following morning after her arrival at *tante* Félicienne. She found the little village intimate and charming at first sight. She tried to find her old neighbor's address but she could not find it. The address that she had received by mail in Batiscan was not the one where Cora Lantagne lived. She must have moved without telling Héloïse. What to do? Héloïse decided to pay a visit to the little cemetery of Sainte-Christine where there would certainly be québécois names.

To her geat surprise, Héloïse noticed that there were many Irish names in this place of etenal rest. She could not understand why so many strangers in this cemetery. It was because she did not know that the Irish were a few of the first settlers of the region. She spent a little bit of time in the cemetery and decided to go back to aunt Félicienne and ask her for help. She found her so sympatheric this lady with a nice smile.

Aunt Félicienne welcomed Héloïse with open arms and gave her a room on the second floor. She stayed there for two and a half weeks. In the meantime she and

tante exchanged the news of the day as well as the little stories of their lives. Aunt Félicienne told her guest that her life was full of little joys that a good marriage brings, Her husband, Adelbert, came fom Saint-Yves-de-Colbert high up in the forest and that he had exercized the skill of woodcutter up until the age of twenty-four. He left the workplace in order to go to what he called the heart of Quebec rather than remain in the vast green domain where one starved from human intimacy. There was certainly men who cut wood with him day after day, but it wasn't the intimacy that he desired. No women and no children in this territory. One could very well say that it had been abandoned by God, said he.

—I met him at a Saturday night *veillée* at the Labries. We were celebrating the engagement of my niece, Délima Hubert. Délima was the daughterr of my brother Hector. She was getting married to a handsome and gallant boy named Adelard Fontaine. Unfortunately, he died in an automobile accident on the highway betwen Drummondville and Montreal. Ever since that time, I've always been afraid of cars.

—Didn't you have a car when your husband was alive?

—Oh, sure. But after he died, I sold it.

—What did your husband die of?

—He died after three strokes. On top of that, he died young. He was only forty-six. Forty-six is young.

—How many children did you have?

—None, but we adopted a girl. We took her here at the nursery in Saint- Hyacinthe. Oh, she was so cute and gentle. However, God came to get her, she was only four years old. I cried so much over her. My husband wanted to adopt another one, but I told him that I could not support another sorrow like that. I suffered a broken heart for years although my friends and my neighbors filled me with benefits and especially love. That relieved the heart of a mother without a child like me.

—Poor you. What was your husband's job?

—He was a postman. Everyone loved him by his welcoming grace and by his good sense of humor. He was loved so much. I loved him to death. It's true. I made all of his favorite dishes. When he came home he would snif the odors from the kitchen and he would always tell me that it smelled good be it a roasted chicken, a piece of beef in the oven with browned potatoes and green beans splattered with a browned broth or a *pâté chinois*, shepherd's pie, with hamburger, mashed potatoes and cream style corn on top. He loved a nice pork roast with carrots and a little bit of spices. We Canadians, we love pork especially in our New Years's pork pies, don't we?

—Ah, you're making me drool.

Héloïse told her little story without mentionning the episode with her sister, Félicité. She did not forget the souvenirs of Célie woven in her memory and filled with memories and little unforgetable regrets.

—This Timiskamengo, did you ever meet him?

—No, it was well before my time.

—And Célie, what happened to her?

—Well she got married with one of my brothers. He was somewhat of a lamebrain, not crazy but a little off the track, as we say. He died in the loggers' camp. Célie died a few years ago after maman died. I went to stay with one of my sisters after that.

—And you, what's happening now?

—I don't know, *tante*, I absolutely don't know.

—Well, rest up here and we shall talk about it together later.

After a four weeks of visit at aunt's house, Héloïse decided to write to Edmond in the United-States for she had not been able to find stable work in Saint-Hyacinthe in spite of the urgent words of *tante* who reassured her that she would always be welcomed at her house. Héloïse told her that she no longer wanted to count on her good deed and that she wanted only to rely on herself and not on others.

—You must not be so independent, dear, said *tante*, to her. The nice days will come in time.

—I know but I must trace a future myself and for myself. That's not being independent. It's rather vital energy that makes us act as such. I'm full of daring and I'm going to trace my way in life whatever the difficulties and the hitches.

Aunt Félicité gave a letter from the United-States to Héloïse one Saturday morning after the mailman had delivered the mail. He had put the letter in her hands for he knew Madame Vadeboncoeur quite well enough to talk to her and be nice to her. Héloïse opened the letter and read Edmond's words who was assuring her of his good wishes and invited her to join him in Newmarket in New Hampshire. That she could take the train, the Grand Trunk, and be able to go to this industrial city, and that he would be waiting for her and see her when she arrived. Héloïse answered Edmond's letter the following day telling him that she had decided to go and join him in Newmarket once she had taken the details of the departure of the train. She would then write to him and give him the details.

Newmarket was south of the border of the state of Maine to get to the state of New Hampshire where was situated this municipality. It was a city where the Cushnoc mills towered the city. Hundreds of French-Canadian immigrants displaced from their *rangs*, rows, and their farms had established themselves to stay there and found a family outside of Quebec. In the very beginning, they really thought they would return to their native country, but with time and the habit of working and of a well deserved security, they found themselves anchored in another country than theirs in heritage. They would become Americans, hyphenated Americans, that is to say Franco-Americans.

Edmond came to the train station to greet Héloïse. She seemed happy and at the same time even somewhat depressed of having to leave Quebec. She told him that she felt out-of-sorts being away from her native country. He reassured her that once established in the neighborhood where he lived, she would find that she would feel welcomed and at home since most people there spoke French.

They were practically all from the province who had left Quebec in order to arrive at the "lighthouse of the bobbins" of the mills that awaited them.

—Do you work at the mills? asked Héloïse.

—Yes, I found myself a good job. I'm an apprentice loom fixer. The looms are huge machines for weaving in what is called the weave room. I'm learning fast and it pays well.

—Like that you have become a mill worker like most of our emigrés.

—Yes.

—I don't know if I'd like to work in a mill.

—It's a job like any other jobs. It's much better to work than starving over there on the farm that yanks our lives away by dint of a lack of food and hope. The Quebec soil is no longer giving. Not for down-and-out people like me and so many others who wrench their hands in despair.

—I don't know this misery of the farmer, but I can easily imagine how poor were the farm people on a farm that had become poor by the damage done by bad crops.

—Oh, how hard it was for everyone, not only for us the farmers, the sowers of seeds in a soil that does nor promise much. As well as those who weep for having worked so hard by the sweat of their brows for nothing. Absolutely nothing. You get it?

—Poor Edmond, you really knew misery.

—Not especially me, but people that I knew who had a good-size family of eleven, thirteen and even eighteen children. Those children had to be fed. Then, how does one hand down a farm that's exhausted when the father dies. It's all a reversal of fortune. Down and out. Yeah, the ancestors' farm was no longer promising. One must believe that the descendants had drained it or what.

—I did not know that. I was born in good circumstances and they took good care of me. My mother and my father never suffered from that experience of the poor farmer. We had good luck in deserving a life without ill ease and reversals.

—It wasn't the case of many among us. I don't know if it's bad luck, fate or something that goes wrong in our lives, we the farmers of Quebec, but it happened like *un cheveu sur la soupe*, arrive at a most awkward moment, my mother would say. We did not expect it. What do you want, things are going to fix themselves one way or another. I sure hope so.

—I believe in the future, a future woven with dreams of good omen.

—You're an optimist.

—I always was. It's my mark in life.

—Stay marked.

Both of them started to laugh.

Héloïse found herself a job in the mills and right from the start she began to make friends. She was made that way. Open of spirit, good perceptor of talents, and tenderhearted. She attracted to herself people who had no faults and certainly no great defects that come and violate friendship. Héloïse knew how to cultivate friendship. As soon as she felt alone and a just a bit apprehensive, she went to meet a newly made friend. She made a dozen friends in the first week of work at the Cushnoc. Among others, there was Sylvie Lapierre, Anita Bellerose, and Béatrice Montpas to name three. Sylvie became her closest friend, the one to whom she could confide her thoughts and her dreams. Yes, Héloïse was a dreamer. Dreams of success, dreams of love, and dreams of becoming one day the mother of a family that she so desired. Family, for her, was one of the values of heritage that she shared with her mother, her grandmother, and her great- grandmother as well as all the other mothers who came before her. A value deeply anchored in the very depth of the soul of the Lanouettes de Batiscan.

It was a traditional value that could not be erased, not any more than a birthmark.

Newmarket was in the midst of preparations for the celebration of its fifthieth anniversary and everyone in the municipality was invited to come and celebrate at the grand picnic of the month of July in order to coincide with the annual holiday of the American Independence. Every single millworker was on vacation for an entire week. Some had left for Quebec to go and pay a visit to relatives over there. Those whom they had let behind so-to-speak, in order to look for work in the States. There were some who fulfilled a promise to *la Bonne Sainte Anne* to go and pray in the sanctuary of the *Basilique de Sainte-Anne-de-Beaupré* for a favor received. These Québécois, although displaced, kept in their hearts fidelity to the great patroness of yesteryear. Héloïse remembered very well the many times her mother had fallen on her knees before the image of the Good Saint Anne in her bedroom to beg her to grant her some favor that she held in her mother's heart. On the other hand, Héloïse had lost fidelity to this saint and that hurt her heart. She could hardly pray to her and to other saints that she had at a certain time favored. Her soul wanted to become simple and devoid of all devotions of old. For her, the values linked to québécois devotions had lost strength over the years. She felt a certain emptiness in herself but she did not display any uneasiness of conscience. As for her, religious devotions had become vestiges of the past, a past where religion and tradition became melded together enough to take the heart of the farmer hostage so naive in his convictions. Now, Héloïse felt liberated from all constraints of duty, tradition, religion and even country once she found herself outside Quebec. However, Héloïse was faithful to her heritage, but not as solidly and upright as before. And then, the little hypocrisies and abuses of a Church at one time known as intransigeant in its honesty and firm in its teaching of virtues and dogmas had shaken her so that she could not return to the self that she was, the good and faithful Catholic that she had been. The great lack of conduct anchored in ethical values had like shocked her if not shaken her totally. Héloïse doubted if she would ever return to values dirtied by the hypocrisy of the Church as well as the hypocrisy of her country in which she had placed at a given time all her confidence. She would think about it.

The grand fourth of July picnic that year was one of the greatest annual celebrations given by the Cushnoc mills. There were Québécois, Polish, English, Albanian people and other ethnic emigrés in the large municipal park. Edmond was not there for whatever reason for Héloïse had not heard people talking about him nor had she met him anywhere, not in the mill not on the street. She had tried to go to his house but no response from him when she knocked at the door.

Someone told her that Edmond had left for good. She was surprised enough to fall into tears.

The Monday morning after vacation, Héloïse went to meet the first hand of the department where Edmond worked. He informed her that Edmond had left his job at the Cushnoc and cut off all attachments with anyone that he knew. It was precisely that the director had told Héloïse that day. She was totally upset for she did not understand why Edmond had left like that without warning her or even letting her know about his departure. It was the following week that she got a letter from him from California. He told her that his sudden departure was caused by his decision to flee the justice system since he was being pursued on account of an infraction of the civil code more precisely the law that covers thefts and vandalism. He told her that it wasn't him who had done it but one of his friends on whom he relied, but who had betrayed him in commiting this crime.

Unfortunately, this friend had implicared him in this act of vandalism and theft by giving Edmond's name to the mill security agents, and then to the police who followed the process of investigation. He no longer wanted to live in a place where his name would be ever tarnished. That was why he had to flee. Edmond asked Héloïse to pardon him for not having confided to her his fears and his moves, but he said he was throwing himself on the mercy of his friend and hoping that she would not do him harm by giving his information to others. He wished her success in her enterprise whatever it was, for he was sure she would succeed in any effort she would undertake.

Knowing that the words of Edmond would resonate endlessly in her head, Héloïse started to think of a fact that she had for a very long time simmered in her mind full of thoughts and little plots, the possibility of undertaking a little business that would be hers alone. She would make and sell food items well apppreciated by her *gens/* people, such as *tourtières* and sugar pies made with maple syrup. She knew very well that these would sell like little hot breads, as we say, *des petits pains chauds.* It's the phrase that people in Canada use so often. She told herself that it was even used now in the States with the transplanted French-Canadians. Héloïse began the following day to really think about what would be needed to start her enterprise of *bonne grand-mère*, good grandmother. Everything would be made with fresh ingredients bought at the corner store of the Duhamel brothers. She had great confidence in them and their produce. She knew that they would not cheat her in any way. "That's what we call good *Canayens*" she told herself.

Héloïse continued to work at the mill while making her culinary products that she had been contemplating. She worked up to twelve hours a day and even sometimes fourteen hours, but never on the Lord's day. Ever since Edmond's flight, Héloïse began to accept herself as a Christian and practicing believer little by little. She no longer wanted get away from the sacred rites of the Church, and she wanted to receive the Holy Eucharist that she had abandoned a long time ago. She claimed to be converted by virtue of the haunting of no longer being an adherant to the divine mysteries revealed by the Lord. Not that she pardoned the Church and its hypocrisy, but she learned to pardon by reciting the "Our Father" and by going further than she would have if she had remained in her state of intolerance and implacability. She took the necessary step to rejoin the prescribed values by her heritage and fidelity to the traditional religious convictions. Not that she had put aside her character of the rebellious mare, like her father used to

say about her. The renewed doubt about certain things that revolted her never ceased to be her motto of the day. Héloïse's conversion was not a conversion, but a transformation of heart and soul. She would never have completely abandoned her religious values. She had become less intolerant and more docile in matters of the acceptance of the failings of others. She was convinced that she had never abandoned her religious beliefs but it was the Church who had abandoned her with the game of implacability and underhanded deceitfulness. Not that she had a grudge against the Church as such, but against its directors who had no frankness nor tolerance of the heart. Just like the political leaders and without thinking of the well-being of those who relied on them. How many victims did they make by their shady compromises and their action bodering venality. The fate of Timiskamengo and so many other natives could not be erased from Héloïse Lanouette's memory. Yet, she would have liked not to be tormented by this despicable souvenir, but whatever she thought or did, the memory of these poor afflicted ones did not exit her head. Especially Timiskamengo. She would keep this souvenir until her death, she claimed. Engraved deeply forever.

Héloïse called her small enterprise, **Chez Tante Héloïse** for she knew that the word *tante* like *grand-mère (mémère* for some) was very well known and even venerated with a traditional reverence. She chose not *grand-mère* for the simple reason that she was not old enough for that. After eight months of double-time work, the mill and the enterprise, Héloïse decided to let go of the mill and devote herself entirely to her commerce of *tourtières* and sugar pies. Things were going very well for her, enough to gain a large profit once the debts were paid. Héloïse was proud of herself.

In June right before the July vacation, the mill and the textile workers suffered the scuffle of a strike that would last several months and perhaps the rest of the year. God, no! Héloïse was glad she was no longer associated with the mill, but she knew that this strke would pull away some clients and especially reduce those who worked so terribly hard from day to day, and had a large family, those would suffer from it. Each day was filled with complaints and dissatisfacion for not having enough to eat or no food at all. Many took sides with those who sought violence and we could see fist fights, kicking and squabble in the streets. What had become of this municipality that at one time was so quiet and so peaceful, the people of Newmarket asked themselves. Yet the emigrés from Quebec were not quarrelsome, everyone said. Consequently, they took the attitude that it was the other emigés who had sown discord and conflict in the streets. When hunger and thirst enter into the life of the jobless poor, that's when discord and irascibility of people raise their ugly heads. People hardly got along anymore. The children were in the grips of the discontentment of grown-ups, and they themselves became unwholesome, and the devil will be in the *cabane*, as people said who felt the misery getting into neighborhoods that once were so peaceful and happy. How does one get out of this? Héloïse started to give credit slips to the indigents who had no money in hand to pay for their puchases. She herself felt the fallout of the misery caused by this strike. She tightened the strings of her purse and cut in two the mouthful of nourishment that she took every day. She lost weight, and then she felt weakened by her daily privations. There were days when she felt depressed. She wanted at all cost to extirpate herself from the tentacles of depression for she did not want to abanadon the hope that one day she would fully succeed in her enterprise. Especially she did not want to abandon those whom she called her folks, the mothers, the fathers, and their children as well as the aunts, the uncles, the nephews and the nieces, not to mention the cousins. They all needed some hope in order to continue to live, and not simply exist. She gave them some every day and she would continue to do so as long as she could. She prayed to God to give them the courage and a bit of bread.

Especially work. The strike continued; the bad times continued. People asked how they could spend winter which can be as cruel in New England as in Quebec.

Héloïse started to worry her head off about her weakened enterprise and for the debts that were accumulating each week. She did not know if she could survive in business or not. The signs of failure were being felt more and more. She especially did not want to go bankrupt for that would cause her shame and scorn of herself. She was at a point where there was no exit, no hope that the mills would survive if the workers did not get along with the big guys of this textile industry. This is precisely what the directors told them at every meeting of worker representatives and master-proprietors of the mill. Finally the workers ceded to the demands of the company who augmented the hours of work and also cut the the wages in order to compete more advantageously with the other textile companies. That's what the big shots said when they got together for the last time in the bureaus in New York. "Take what we offer you or we close the mill. That's the eternal jobless on stike workers' answer to their problem by the high-placed ones in New York, so they bent down and swallowed the bitterness of defeat. Not a single one murmured his discontent openly. Everyone kept it in their heavy heart crushed by the pain and the feeling of having lost. It was another link in the chain of survival. Survival of the heritage, *la survivance*, of cultural values, of the language and so forth. Finally, it was the chitty fly specks of the devil on their heads, said those who could not stand this defeat.

Héloïse felt relieved upon hearing that the strike was finally over. She felt inside of her a certain joy of survival and durability of spirit and body. She paid all her clients' debts by telling them that all was erased. They were thankful and filled with gratitude for a woman who had the grandeur of heart and the largesse of spirit. It was said in a loud voice that she deserved their repect and their love for having supported them in the worst moments of their lives. Héloïse's business was growing from day to day so much so bigger was the accumulation of clients. She contemplated enlarging the establishment called **Chez Tante Héloïse**. That's what she did.

Chez Tante Héloïse became an accomplished establishment with a clientele from almost all of the surrounding neighborhoods and even distanced ones, and of every genre of people, not only Franco-Americans, that-is-to-say emigrés from Quebec. From time to time, Héloïse went out with friends and she went to Saturday night *veillées* once a month. She was too drained to do more. She hired a young man about her age called Alexis Charbonneau. He was from the Montreal region. He was a good worker and very good in math. Héloïse considered him valiant and meritorous of the confidence that she had in him. She loved his clairvoyance because he knew how to plan things. He was a man of an extraordinary probity and tolerance and she saw him as a leaning post. Héloïse felt attracted to him and his good qualities. When she thought of him, she could not help thinking of Timiskamengo.

Célie and Timiskamengo, there's two persons engraved in her memory. She saw again Célie who talked about him with a sweet tenderness and a sincere love. She loved her Timiskamengo and it showed.

Héloïse began to discover that she had feelings of affection for Alexis Charbonneau. Did he share her sentiments, she asked herself. She did not know what to think. She slowly rocked in her head the yeses and the nos of her decisions. She decided to go and meet him one Friday night when Alexis usually went for his walk in the park. He did that almost every night, rain or not. He was surprised when he noticed that it was she who was coming to meet him. He did not expect it. However, he noticed that Héloïse was audacious in her steps and daring in her words. She had "*du casque*", boldness. At least, that's what Alexis noticed.

—What are you doing here after work? asked Alexis.

—I came to meet you and talk about business.

—What kind of business?

—Well, affairs of the heart.

Alexis could not hide his astonishment. Héloïse could not abandon the thread of her thoughts nor the vigor of her words.

—I know that you are astonished by what I have just said, but I don't hide anything from you. I don't want any feeling of disdain on your part. Only a spirit that is frank with an open heart.

—I don't know what to tell you at this moment. You totally astouded me.

—That's what the surprise is all ablout. You have to take it when it comes.

—Sometimes it comes like lightning. It strikes like that. No time to think.

—Don't think. All that I ask of you is to listen. Then you can think about it. Can you do that?

—He muttered, Yes.

—I'm going to make you a proposition that will seem a little daring, but will carry profit for you if you accept.

Alexis started to answer her but she cut him short.

—Let me speak. I tell you that you please me a lot and that I love your diligence and your *savoir-faire*. I also love how you deal with people and especially with clients. You have the way of speaking to everybody. I like that. Moreover, there's something in you that I discover each time I see you and when we exchange words either during work or on the sidewalk or the street. You are reliable, a good worker and a very good friend. You never speak badly about people. You have a good heart.

—But...

—Wait until I'm done. For all these qualities and all your good deeds, I offer you half of my business.

—Not true. I thank you, but...

—Wait, I did not finish. Moreover, there's something else in this proposition.

—What?

—Wait, I told you. I propose that we get married so that we can build a good household and then have children that I will esteem like the plenitude of my life. I know that I'm not beautiful on the exterior, but I am in the interior, I swear. I must not forget either to tell you that I love you. It's damn true, Alexis Charbonneau. I love you with all my heart and with all my will to love. Here's my proposition. Good, I've opened up my heart once and for all. I don't do that with everyone, you know. Not everyone knows my hidden thoughts. Only you, Alexis Charbonneau, do I dare open up my heart. You're the only one and the first one.

Alexis did not know what to say at this moment of great dazzling of heart and spirit. He was as if congealed, congealed like the fat on a dish of *cretons*. He had blushed a bit and the glow remained on the face of a young innocent man without shame or confusion in his manner of seeing things. Héloïse smiled benignly at him and with a teasing air. As for him, he did not know much what to say or what to do at that moment. He began to express himself with words that did not want to come out of his mouth numbed with shyness and surprise.

—I don't fall for anyone not even the guys that are of my taste, said Héloïse. When I love someone. I tell him so. Not that I've already done it. I really loved Edmond but not a love that drives you crazy. Not at all. You, I love and that's all. That you love me or not, it's the same for me. Of course, I would like it if you had at least a little feeling of love for me, that I don't hide. We can have an understanding with each other and not go above and beyond the heart's true feelings. I'm transparent like glass well cleaned with water and vinegar. It's clear, my intention, and it offers a true and sincere view of what I think and say.

Alexis stayed there stunned just like a child that is being chided by his mother.

—Speak, *mon vieux*, it's time, said Héloïse.

—I don't know what to tell you at this moment.

—Take time to think about it and you can give me your answer tomorrow. I'm not one to have long discourses and wait a long time for an answer from somebody. My proposition is made and I will wait for your response when you're ready to give it to me. But don't take too long.

Héloïse would have prefered that Alexis give her his answer at the very moment it happened, right now, But, she knew very well that the young man could not digest a proposition like that at least for an evening. Even two evenings. She couldn't add another word, any argument why the two of them should get married. She would let love speak for her. It wasn't easy to love. It wasn't at all like starting an enterprise and watching it grow. It was more complicated than that. But she would try to stay away from all doubt and all jealousy that could infiltrate into her affair of loving. Doubt that he could not respond to her demand and of jealousy on the part of an employee like him who could put a wrench in the works. Would he be afraid of losing his job if he refused her proposition, asked Héloïse to herself. His employment was neither in doubt nor in peril, avowed Héloïse. It was just a simple proposition.

That was it. However, a proposition that was heavily important on her life. The life of Héloïse Lanouette.

The following morning, no Alexis for work at **Chez Tante Héloïse.** Héloïse asked herself if she had rubbed Alexis the wrong way or had she insulted him with the proposion of yesterday. She felt ill at ease all day long. She went to bed early and concluded that if Alexis did not want her proposition, well she would accept his refusal, and things would start anew without bitterness and even without a hint of vengeance. She would not have wanted him to leave his job for she needed him in her commerce. He was, after all, a very good worker. Even if she tried to tell herself that the night brings counsel. The fear of losing Alexis hit hard the heart and twisted her stomach. Suddenly she woke up at four in the morning and could not go back to sleep. So, she got up, took a cup of *café au lait*, ate a bite of toast with some jam and left for work. It was five thirty and the sky was hardly lit with rose and violet hues. While walking on the sidewalk, she noticed from afar the shadow of a man leaning against the wall of her enterprise. She hurried to join this man who was the figure of a handsome man ready to go to work.

—Alexis, what are you doing so early in the morning?

—I was waiting for you to give you my answer. I hope you will pardon my absence yesterday. It took me a long time putting my thoughts in order, and convince myself that your proposition was most reasonable and most sincere. So I come here to tell you that I accept.

—It's not the only thing that I want to hear from you. Do you love me at least?

—Yes I love you in my way of loving. You're a good person, a person with a kind heart, a little bit sometime daring and hard to understand, but a person who has frankness in the soul. You have *du casque,* ma belle but it's a *casque* of down and velours. Soft.

Both of them started to laugh with guffaws. They kissed and Héloïse got her first kiss of love from a man in her life. It's true that she had gotten pecks and little kisses from uncles and cousins, but this one was real and full of life, tenderness and love that she did not expect.

She felt soft and warm inside her. Never would she taste this felicitty again. Tears came to her eyes so much did she share in contentment of the flesh and feelings. Alexis, taking her by the arm, brought her to the enterprise **Chez Tante Héloïse**. There they made love, but it was a kind of a platonic love however rendered more corporal than ideal. Héloïse kept saying to Alexis, "Keep it safe and pure" although she found pleasure in Alexis' touch.

Héloïse had never "known" a man before, as some people say.

The wedding took place in the little chapel Sainte Véronique somewhat far from the center of town. Héloïse wanted it that way, since she had a particular devotion to the holy veil known as Veronica's veil. She admired the dignity and especially the compassion of Saint Veronica, the holy woman who had wiped the Lord's bleeding face. She was a woman who had *du casque*, boldness, to advance in front of the soldiers and offer her veil to her Lord, beaten and bruised under the weight of the cross. She was a woman not unlike her, Héloïse, who dared to make decisions and jump onto something that was not easy to maneuver. She dared and that was ideal to her, the woman who constantly dared.

Héloïse wanted the ceremony to be simple and humble. She did not want a white wedding dress nor a long veil not even a long list of invited guests. She told Alexis that she had always wished for a wedding that would be the simplest of weddings.

She wanted neither *fanfare ni trompette*, fanfare nor trumpet, she insisted. So the wedding was simple and without great ceremony. She wore a sky blue crêpe georgette dress, a hat that went well with her dress, and white gloves. She carried in her hands a little bouquet of flowers, lillies of the valley that she so loved. As for Alexis, he had on a dark blue suit, a white carnation in his boutonnière, and a large smile on his lips. Both of them seemed happy. After mass and communion, the priest gave them his blessing and the married couple walked slowly down the aisle in order to go out into the blueness of the day. The sky was lightly blue and the sun shone with a soft brightness. It was the beginning of May, the birds were singing, the noisy sound of automobiles mixed itself with the noise of the street, and we could see the children who were getting ready to go to school, walking and jumping in the street, and others on the sidewalk wasting time. Héloïse said to Alexis that this was an ordinary day but remarkable by the fact that she was now married. Alexis nodded his head in silent approbation. It was not a wedding with hundreds of invited guests sharing as usual a nuptial banquet with the Québécois. A few friends of the married couple joined Héloïse and Alexis in the little corner restaurant, **Charivari duFour**. They were eleven in all. The head server had prepared for them a host table next to the large window with écru lace curtains. They all took a drink and raised their glasses in salutation of the married couple. The meal was a very simple one but appetizing. After the meal, the head server brought over a two-layer cake with white frosting with yellow rosettes. He had placed two little cheap porcelain doll-like figures of a bride and groom on top of the cake."Just because it was the *fête des noces"*, the nuptial feast-day, said he. There was laughter and chatter for two hours while Jeanne d'Arc Larochelle, a worker at **Chez Tante Héloïse** took the time to wish a good married life to couple. She then sang her favorite song, *"On va-tu n'avoir du plaisir, On va-tu n'avoir d'agrément"* / Are we going to have fun, are we going to have pleasantness.

Alexis and Héloïse returned to Héloïse's single's apartment. It would now be the residence of the two spouses The pace of life for both Héloïse and Alexis hardly changed. Early in the morning, they got up, washed, and got dressed as usual. Héloïse tried to get up earlier so that she could serve a full breakfast to her new husband, poached eggs, bacon, and toasts with butter, jam and sometimes *cretons*. At certain times Alexis did not want to eat everything that she offered him. Héloïse got somewhat angry and tried to convince him that the most important meal of the day was breakfast. She told him that in Quebec we served more than that: potatoes, meat, bread with *cretons*, and a good cup of hot tea. Sometime we serve hot soup because the stomach needs to be warmed up, they said. They swallowed that with great hunger and thirst, for the night had been long and without nourishment. They needed to boost the energy level for the workday so often very hard. Alexis responded that he didn't have that kind of hunger and that he would sustain himself with the least nourishment possible.

She raised her shoulders and told him that he could do as he pleased but that she would have the good nourishment of a farmer's wife. Besides, she had always done that even though she found herself alone without others at her side. Héloïse kept her spirit of independence and her ability to rely on no one even if she was now married and lived with someone. Yes, a man that she loved and respected for his frank speech and his conduct with her. However, she would never fear of telling him her thoughts if the time came to do so. Also, she had no back door, as people said. Héloïse was Héloïse and that was all.

The enterprise was doing well, very well, until there came another strike around the month of March the beginning of April. "The devil was in the *cabane*" said those who got mad to see coming the haulting of wages and nourishment. Alexis and Héloïse didn't say much except to sympathize with the poor souls of the mill. Worse, this time was the stubborness of the mill directors about wages and the work hours. It was always the same story every time they instigated the workers to discord, insisted the workers. "They always want to cut wages and lengthen the work hours," said the mill people. They no longer wanted this *pataraffe*, this burst of words, of menaces and violence mixed with the possibility that the big wheels in New York would transfer the mill down south where the poor workers, docile and without great care of losing their jobs was not under the empire of the syndicate. So, they could not get involved with a teasing strike like that of the workers in Newmarket. That was precisely what tormented the workers at the Cushnoc. The "highmuckamucks", these big mouths greedy for profits in New York, not understanding the unhappy fate of their employees at the Cushnoc working over there in the misery and the insufficiency of it all. The big pocketbook of the stockholders was shut tight following the will of those who made decisions and who chewed the fat, that is to say, who had empty and vain talks without any conscience of their workers. Who would take care of the poor people suddenly thrown out in the streets to beg or possibly steal. No one wanted this fate, but destiny of the poor out of work only calls for black misery for them. The resolution of not fighting for what they had promised, an equitable and just wage, was taken with a painful resignation, difficult to take. Yet the directors of the mill had told them that they were holding firm in their decision to guarantee a just salary for those who worked honestly. So, why the digression of those who managed those enterprises called mills? Yet, the worker did not want any part of the strike that menaced his daily earning [avoir] and his sad life as bread-winner. "If only God would come and get involved and give us the chance to to win once", said those who believed in *le Bon Dieu* of the good old days.

Héloïse and Alexis tolerated well enough the reversals of the day. They continued to make pies and *tourtières* as long as people wanted them. The poor people wanted some but they found themselves incapable of buying some, not having any money. So the proprietors of **Chez Tante Héloïse** closed and locked their establishment for the first time. The little commerce started by Héloïse did not exist anymore. Héloïse was heartbroken; Alexis became morose with the lack of resources and hope. He collapsed facing the trial of the incapacity of providing like a man should, honestly and joyously. On top of that, Héloïse was pregnant.

Both spouses happened to lack electricity for they had not paid their bill. They launched themselves in a restrained economy and without luxury, not even the necessary things such as pies, carrots, cabbage, jams, eggs(only two per week), pork and beef roasts, pigs's feet *ragoûts*, all desserts so desired but often abandoned due to hard times. They ate soup seven times a week, a soup often watered down without the soup bone. Alexis suffered from having but soup to eat and so very often watered down. Héloïse telling him that she too suffered, but

the good times would come back. She was sure of it. However, they were not poor for they kept a high enough sum of money in their bank account, enough to guarantee the purchase of another enterprise later on when times would get more favorable. No to that time, they scrimped and saved and they got used to not bending before reversals and hitches that came sometimes to take away the little daily luxuries.

The neighbors, seeing that the nourishment that Héloïse offered herself was not sufficient for a pregnant woman, started to bring her what they thought was more sustainable and more convenient for her. First of all, Héloïse refused to accept their offer. "It's charity and I don't want it" said she. But the neighbors insisted and she consented in order to please them and her husband who found her a little too proud of accepting what people wanted to give her.

The days, the weeks, the months went by without great respite. The workforce remained without jobs. The unemployment drove its results very hard. Many left and returned to Quebec knowing well that work was not a guaranteed factor over there. The soil and the farms were not anymore giving than before. But what do you want these people to do? The *curés* wished them welcome with no promises of eking out an existence as a *habitant*. They would have to return to the unceasing labor of a farmer who knows how to till the soil but who also knows that the harvest will be sparse and probably even destroyed by the bad weather and the terrible drought of a hard and implacable summer that brings black misery. What do you want, say the man and the woman watchful of the return of possible good times and a future without contemplated misery.

Late one September afternoon, Héloïse cried out to her husband that she was bleeding from her vagina and that she did not know what was happening.

—Go fast and get Madame Sévigny the midwife. She'll know what to do.

—Do what? asked Alexis.

—Don't ask me questions like that. Hurry, go get her.

The midwife came right away and went into the kitchen and saw Héloïse there her legs covered with blood. She told her to go to bed right away so that she could examine and judge if it wasn't a miscarriage. Unfortunately, it was. Madame Sévigny took all of her precautions so as not to frighten Héloïse, she and her husband who was watching from the corner of his eye in the kitchen that was right next to the bedroom. She washed Héloïse the best she could and put her under the blankets in order to keep her warm and calm her down. Madame Sévigny ordered Alexis to go and pour a small glass of wine so she could give it to Héloïse and that would give the poor woman a bit of warmth in her body drained by a traumatic hemorrage. Héloïse started crying softly and groaned along with her tears that she was trying to hide in the folds of the blanket. Alexis came into the bedroom and tried to console his wife the best he could as a husband and father of the lost child, although just a fetus. He found her inconsolable, his Héloïse, who so wanted to have children. Then finding that Héloïse was stable and was sleeping profoundly, Madame Sévigny instructed Alexis how to take care of his wife when she awoke. Héloïse did not wake up right away. She slept until early morning. She perceived that Alexis was sitting right next to her in a big armchair that he had displaced from the livingroom. She jumped up surprised and started speaking to him.

—Do you know that I slept all night and that I don't remember a single thing, said Héloïse.

—But you don't remember the episode with Madame Sévigny?

—Not at all.

—But you must be aware a bit of what happened last night. It's impossible to forget.

—Impossible to forget what?

—Impossible to forget you had a bad delivery and that Madame Sévigny took care of you for hours. On top of it all, it's you who asked me to go and get her so that she could help out. Don't you remember?

—No, not a single bit.

Then all of a sudden Héloïse burst into tears.

—Did I lose my baby? Tell me that I didn't lose my first child. Tell me.

—Yes, You lost it without being your fault.

—But how is it that one can lose a child that's planted in your belly?

—I don't know. I don't really know.

—My God, to lose one's child even though he's still in the mother's womb of a mother who's waiting to have him safe and sound. My God, my God, I can't believe it. No.

—Calm down, my dear wife. Calm down for we can make more babies. You know that.

Héloïse smiled with a somewhat sad smile but showing a ray of hope that would come and relieve her once back to her real self.

—Héloïse never abandon the hope of having a family. You know that like you know the breaking of daylight.

—Yes, my husband. I hope that you're hoping as much.

—Yes, my dear little maman.

—I'm not little. After all, I'm thirty-three years old. It's late to start having a family, but I'm ready to launch myself into it. We begin tonight.

—Whoa, little mother, You must allow yourself time to get better before making love, you know.

—I agree, but we must not lose too much time. We have to go fast, *"aller sur le beau-père"* like aunt Rosée used to say [to go on the father-in-law].

—Yes, your aunt Rosée had nineteen children. Quite a *potée*, a hotpot.

—Tante Rosée must have exhausted her little husband, he who was but four feet six but who had the energy of a man six feet tall.

Héloïse burst out laughing. She couldn't help herself.

Once the strike was over, people started to breathe better again and go back to work. It was the seventh month of being out of work. Seven months without wages. Seven months of doubts, torments, worries, and misery. Seven months of twisting the heart and the noggin. Nothing had changed. The wages remained the same while the hours were discussed but not increased. The Cushnoc remained in New Market. So why this long period of a strike and fighting between the company and the union, asked the people. No response. No reasonable response possible either.

Héloïse and Alexis reopened the enterprise and people began crowding the place. They were happy to return to a *pâtisserie* that they knew well, and in which they had confidence. The two proprietors were overjoyed. They felt in heaven.

They counted the days when they would be able to enlarge not only the clientle but the enterprise. It would be an advantage for them and the children they would have. Héloïse and Alexis figured more and more a small family of three and even four children. Héloïse wanted at least eight, but Alexis told her that they had to start a little lower. For, after all, they had to feed those mouths. Moreover, the mother should not be drained of energy, after all, and dry up all of her energy and without *élan* to make love.

Three months later, Héloïse found herself to be pregnant again. She was ever so joyous and terribly happy. She told Alexis that this time she would carry the baby to full term. She asked herself if the baby would be a boy or a girl. However, this was of no importance for her. All she desired was a normal child in good health. Fortunately and unfortunately, the child was born but it had something that was wrong with the child. After three months, the parents noticed that the child did not respond to the sweet incitements of the parents. Assuredly the baby was not normal, said Héloïse to her husband. Alexis told her that a child grows up and later on demonstrates its capacities for communication and gestures. Héloïse answered that she did not like what was going on with little Lucienne. Yes, it was a girl and they baptized her Lucienne Marie in the church of the Holy Sacrament, now their parish church.

Little Lucienne grew up step by step like all children of her age. However, the more troubling warnings of the condition of retardation started to be in evidence when Héloïse noticed that the little one did not respond to maman's words and gestures. Her caresses were practically all neglected by the little girl. The father attempted to make her smile or say a few words, but little Lucienne did not want to or could not respond to his paternal advances. After a while, the parents decided to go and see a doctor. The doctor examined the little one and reassured them that the child had no physical faults, but that she had assuredly some mental and affective difficulties. He advised them to go and see a psychologist.

First of all, the parents hesitated to go and see this kind of doctor for they would have preferred rather to see a pediatrician well known in the city and the surrounding areas. The doctor, Doctor Roussin, advised both of them if they so chose, but that nothing would change in the child. Little Lucienne would remain a simple-minded child. The parents were surprised and even somewhat shocked by his declaration for they did not want at all to leave this brand or ticket of appellation fall on their little girl's head, never to be changed or erased. They had almost reached desperation when the neighbor, Madame Lajeunesse, told them that she had a sister who had a retarded child and the little one had grown up healthy and well developed and that his mental condition did not stop him to live a good life like all other children. Except that Charles, that was his name, did not have the qualities of a precocious child nor the full capacities for letters and math. He managed with what the *Bon Dieu* had given him, said Madame Lajeunesse.

Alexis and Héloïse went to see Doctor Émile Laprise, a pediatrician who announced to them that the little one certainly had symptoms of a retarded child and that he could do nothing to bring her to normalcy. Alexis and Héloïse found that Doctor Laprise was frank but a little too brutal in his approach. So they decided to go and consult with a psychologist in spite of their doubt and their fear. They didn't want to hear that their dear little one was not normal like other children. Parents do not like to be told that their children are not normal. The psychologist, Doctor McKinney, reaffirmed that the little girl had mental problems but that she should go through some examinations with him before he himself could pronounce officially and professionally his diagnosis of their little girl. "Everything takes time," said the doctor. "And money," said quietly Alexis to his wife.

—I don't care about the money and the expenses for little Lucienne. We must not back away from this trial, do you understand? said Héloïse to her husband.

—That's not what I said. It's simply that these expenses will have to come out of the savings that we have made, that's all.

—To hell, the savings. We'll make some more money with time. First we have to adhere to Doctor McKenney's advice. I want to start the treatments as soon as next week.

So little Lucienne, the little simple-minded, (Héloïse had never her called that), went with her mother to Doctor McKenney's office. He advised the mother to wait at least eight months before starting the first treatments when the little girl will have passably grown up and thus she would have a greater comprehension of things and a greater sense of reacting to the attempts of the doctor. Alexis did not want to go afraid of having cold feet because he didn't want to talk to a psychologist. He was afraid of him. He was afraid of finding himself without words and too many acute feelings in his veins. As a father, he did not want to face an unfortunate condition that would affect his little girl all of her life and bring to the family an unbearable malaise. He also nourished a feeling next to shame that people would laugh at him and his wife and plus his little daughter every time she would open her mouth to speak or even fall to pieces in her gestures. He felt cornered between the affection for his daughter and the repulsion for that malady of being retarded. Why did God afflict her with such a misfortune, he asked himself. The very first of his children, moreover.

After eight and a half months, Héloïse went to pay a visit to Doctor McKenney every week with the little girl. Following the mental treatments administered to the little girl during six and a half months, Héloïse and Alexis found that these implementations of care said to be therapeutic were nothing but a kind of valuable treatments but not very effective for the little girl who understrood nothing about what was happening. So, they decided to live with what they had, a little retarded girl but full of life and go-head for her age. Her body was fully healthy while her head lacked vigor.

The days, weeks, months rolled like a play ball and they noticed that little Lucienne was getting better as far as comprehension went and her gestures were more reasonable. She needed to be watched but that was simply to guarantee that her actions and her gestures did not default. This became a mode of everyday life that the parents accepted as such. They did not want to contradict the reality of things. Their fate in life did not ask less.

The following year, Héloïse found herself to be pregnant for the third time. Being pregnant for her was not a strange thing and then she did not succumb to the defaults of fear and doubts of beforehand. The waiting did not seem too long and the delivery almost immediate. Héloïse and Alexis were happy over these fortuitous events, and Alexis went with the godmother and godfather, Monsieur and Madame Labrecque from the neighborhood, to the baptismal fonts of Sainte-Anne-de-Beaupré church named after the basilica in Quebec. It was the Labrecques' parish for the Charbonneaus had not yet chosen a parish of definitive preference although they had belonged to the Saint-Sacrement parish before for a short time. It was another little girl and the parents had decided to call her Hermance after an old aunt in Canada. Alexis had known her and admired her for her pies and her homemade bread as well as for her benevolent ways accorded to the little Alexis when he went to visit her with his mother and father in Saint- Antoine-de-Langsford. Héloïse found the name a bit old-fashion but she accepted it since she had a feeling of belonging for Alexis's sake.

Hermance was the gayest and the most ravishing little girl based on her nice smile and beautiful disposition. She learned fast and her affective qualities showed forth very well in view of her liveliness and gaity compared to her sister, Lucienne. However, Hermance and Lucienne got along very well in disposition and in talents although those of Lucienne were not at the same level as those of Hermance. Little Hermance grew from day to day with the mobility and wisdom of a child when Lucienne did not sound too lively in her sentiments and her comportment as the older one. They should not be submitted to comparison, said the mother, to those who wished to do it. Héloïse took the two children as if they were two little mustard seeds that, with time, grow tall and strong. Anyways, the Sunday Gospels said so, proclaimed Héloïse.

The following year saw another child being born at the Charbonneau house. A little boy that they named Joseph-Arthur after a first cousin from Batiscan that Héloïse remembered being well endowed with a marvelous talent for music. She hoped that her son would grow up and show the same talents with which the first cousin from Canada was endowed by excellence and by birthright of the Lanouettes. She told her husband that little Joseph-Arthur would grow up with his talents anchored in the québécois heritage of Batiscan. She had never lost from sight this heritage that was fundamentally hers. Alexis told her that he also was part of this heritage by his side of the family Tremblay-Charbonneau of Saguenay/Lac Saint-Jean. He loved to tell his wife, who was always avid for stories and tales, about the family and that the Tremblay family was the most numerous in North America. That only one ancestor had carried the name Tremblay in Nouvelle-France: Pierre Tremblay of Randonnai in Normandy. He married Ozanne Achon. From this union would be born twelve children. Pierre Tremblay became a *habitant-fermier* and later on Msgr de Laval confided to him the exploitation of a farm in Baie-Saint-Paul. Alexis added that the Tremblays were equally numerous in New England.

—It's precisely why I want my son to carry the name that I bequeathed him, Tremblay-Charbonneau.

—You deserve to be proud of your history and heritage. We the Québécois we have a history that is worthwhile being transmitted to our children. However, we should not inflict upon the child a name with a hyphen. Charbonneau suffices.

—But it's important for me that the child have two names.

—It's not done, Alexis. It's much too much of high society that contraption.

So the little boy remained with only a one-name family name, Charbonneau. Tremblay would be for the heritage placed in suspension.

Alexis reassured Héloïse that he would never abandon his heritage which was that of his children. An integral part of this heritage was the language and Alexis started to tell his wife that language was one of the dearest and most important values for a Québécois. Héloïse answered him by saying:

—I do hope that it will not get lost with time and negligence of those who do not care for their language and their history. How many people, even today, do not rely on anything that is québécois, and they throw themselves in the English that is American. Our children shall speak French if I have anything to say about it, the spoken language of the Lanouettes and the Tremblay-Charbonneaus here in Newmarket in the States.

Alexis nodded his head while singing low a bit of a song that he had learned in Quebec. Also, he was proud of the appellation of the two names of the family that Héloïse had just mentioned.

As the days, the months, and the years went by like a thread that is unwound, the Charbonneau children neared the school age. It was the school of the nuns as the parishioners of Sainte-Thérèse-de-l"Enfant-Jésus parish called it. The family had just adopted this parish that was in the surroundings. The Canadians are *"déplaceux"* displacers, said Héloïse to her husband. "We displace ourselves from place and parish without being subjected to distressing consequences, continued Héloïse. Then she had found a new rent on Maple Street. Hermance and Joseph- Arthur adapted themselves well to the scholarly challenge for they both had an alert and lively intelligence and imagination. They learned fast without any difficulty. As for Lucienne, it was another story. She did not like school and balked every time her mother got after her to get ready for the school day. She did not like school because her intelligence level did not favorize her at all. She had great difficulty with the memorization of grammar rules, of responses of the catechism, and the French and English vocabulary. She told her that she did not understand at all what the nun tried to teach her. She got home late in the afternoon in tears chagrined of having spent an entire day in frustration of having learned nothing.

Her mother got in contact with the superior and tried to resolve her daughter's school problem that they had baptized as such in view of a reality too evident to ignore: *Lucienne-la-simple-d'esprit*, the simple-minded. Héloïse remained shocked when she heard that name spoken by the children and even the grown-ups who did not understand her daughter, this disadvantaged retarded one by a supposed lack of intelligence. However, Lucienne had a beautiful and great memory, a gift from heaven, as her father said. She could easily remember names, dates, and events that others did not remember at all. All those who knew her were left astounded by her finesse of memory. Her mother could not get over it, that her oldest to whom we had attributed the mark of retarded, was so brilliant as far as memory goes. Madame Lévesque, one of the neighbors, said to Héloïse that *le Bon Dieu* had compensated the lack of intelligence in Lucienne with a lucid and extraordinary memory. "The children said to be *mal-aimés*, ill-loved, of the *Bon Dieu* find themselves his *bien-aimés*, his beloved," said the neighbor to Héloïse who did not understand why her little Lucienne made so much progress in the domain of memories while she was so retarded in the matter of intelligence.

Alexis told his wife that the day would come when they would notice that Lucienne was more gifted with good qualities than many other children that were considered well balanced and without faults of the intelligence. Héloïse told him that he was dreaming and that he did not realize the fact that retardation of a child does not disappear. Once stained by that malady the child grows up like that. "It's like original sin but there is no baptism for that," added Héloïse. Alexis answered her that she was totally pessimistic and had no hope for the day when Lucienne would be healed. "There is no healing for that," declared categorically Héloïse. "You'll see, my dear wife, that things fix themselves like that."

Time had come for first communion and the children of the parish were prepared to receive the sacranent of the Eucharist. They had spent weeks and months learning their catechism before receiving the sacred host from the hands of the priest. They were all joyous but nervous if not giddy from the fact that they were going to receive the *Bon Dieu*, as the teaching religious nun had told them. The previous year, they had refused Lucienne for the second time her receiving this sacrament because she had not known the reponses of her catechism as

prescribed. They had to learn them by heart and then repeat to the teaching religious nun each response word for word without missing a single word. Even though Lucienne had learned all of the responses since her mother encouraged her to repeat them to her, when time came to recite them by heart to the teacher, Lucienne could not remember the responses that she had learned with her mother beforehand. She found herself as if congealed if nor frozen like an icicle in winter, incapable of moving and respond. Her mother was in despair. Alexis took over the task of teaching the catechism responses to Lucienne and she gave them to him word for word without fail. The parents did not understand why Lucienne could not do the same with the nun. "It's because I'm terribly scared of the nun," said the little girl. So Héloïse got together with the nun to agree in having a short séance of responses to the catechism with the mother present so as to guarantee a spirit of confidence in her daughter. Lucienne ended by giving all the right respones to all the quesrtions without missing a single one. So, Lucienne was allowed to participate in the first communion of children younger than she for she was not at the same learning level as they were. In the end, Lucienne did not go to school regularly because her maman taught her daughter herself at home under the direction of the religious teachers at a slower pace but much more advantageous for Lucienne.

The day of the first communion arrived and Lucienne had put on her white slip with the help of her mother, her beautiful white dress with lace around the neck and her pudgy little arms where the short sleeves ended. She was proud of her dress and happy to wear on her head a white veil with a little flat crown adorned here and there with little flowers. Lucienne appeared to be totally ravished and joyous of being the angel of the day as her mother called her. Héloïse was in her most maternal joys for she did not think of the disadvantaged fate of Lucienne.

She had a little retarded daughter but who had a very good memory, *une mémoire de chien*, as was said back home. Yes, the daughter and the mother were proud like peacocks that day. Héloïse would always remember the beautiful smile on Lucienne's red lips with the beatitude of the little retarded child when she walked down the aisle in rows in Sainte-Thérèse-de-l'Enfant- Jésus church. They celebrated Lucienne's first communion like they celebrate a family holiday. There was Hermance, her little brother Joseph-Arthur, Monsieur et Madame Lévesque, Madame Pontbriand, from the very end of town who knew Héloïse very well on account of the voluntary work they did together. They helped the miserable souls from the poorest corner of the municipality. There was also one of Alexis' cousins who lived not too far in the State of Maine., and who sometimes came to visit her cousin. Alexis was not really her cousin but a kind of kissing cousin, *un cousin de la fesse gauche,* said tante Éléonore from Thetford Mines. Included in this holiday were a few neighbors who lived next door such as the Vaillancourts, the Murphys, the Aubuchons, and others. Lucienne was in heaven and she enjoyed her gifts especially the little child missal with a cover genre mica on which was painted a little girl kneeling down before a Jesus-priest offering communion. She had also received a little cristal rosary with a silver cross. Seeing the rosary, Lucienne shouted, "But, 'man, I already have one." The mother telling her not to shout so loud, "*à pleine tête*, as they would say back home. But Lucienne dared to tell her mother that it was holiday time and she could say what she wanted in spite of the warnings from her mother. And the mother to say to her not to do her *fantasse*, impolite, in front of company. Alexis looked at Héloïse a little askance without saying a single word. The party continued until the wee hours of the night. The last one to leave was Mrs. Murphy who had drunk a little too much hard liquor brought over by Monsieur Lévesque. Apparently, it was a hard liquor that he himself had made. He had brought it with him in order to *faire la traite*, give a free drink to those who enjoyed drinking and have fun. He liked to rejoice people as he told each and everyone who wanted to hear him speak. Monsieur Lévesque had a very nice voice and he used it to tell his stories sometimes a bit dirty. That's when his wife would put her hand over his mouth while telling him to shut his trap. His wife blushed, the fact being that her husband dared to tell such stories in good company. He responded just like little Lucienne had said to her mother that it was a holiday and it was time to celebrate. Lucienne's parents went to bed way past eleven while Lucienne did not want to go to bed. "I'm not sleepy," said the little girl all the while letting go of a big yawn.

The following morning, Lucienne was awake early and she wanted to go to school. Her mother told her that it was neither time nor the occasion to go to school and that she should not beg her mother to go see the nuns when she knew that her mother herself would give her the required instructions as usual. Lucienne answered back severely tapping her foot on the floor loud enough for her father to come down to see what was happening.

—Don't be a bad girl, said Héloïse.

—But I want to go to chool like the other children.

—You're not like the others.

—I know, but I want to go to the nuns's school. Why the others and not me? I made my first communion like the others and that should be the sign that I'm ready to do like the other kids.

—But you're not like everybody else.

—Stop telling me that. I'm not a monster, you know. And the papa responding to her:

— No, you are certainly not a monster. You are Lucienne the little one with the memory of a dog(*la mémoire de chien*)..

—Why do we say *une mémoire de chien*?

—Because it's a saying from olden times when people made up all kinds of ways of saying things, a very colorful and lively manner.

—In France we say the memory of an elephant, adddded Héloïse.

—It's another animal, that's all, replied Alexis.

—Oh, I prefer the elephants, said Lucienne.

—But you've never seen an elephant, said the father.

—Yes, I've seen one in my image book.

—So you see my husband, Lucienne can read and she reads avidly and with great curiosity.

—It probably would be time to send her to school.

So, Lucienne started frequenting the nun's school at Sainte-Thérèase-de-l'Enfant- Jésus. She was placed in the third grade even though she belonged in a higher level, the fifth grade. She was twelve and a half. Lucienne progressed according to her retarded step of the way which did not allow her to advance too quickly alongside the other students. She sometimes faltered and that gave her stomach cramps, and so she generated a little tantrum, flushed red as a tomato and she tapped the floor with her foot. The nun would bring her out in the hallway and put her in a corner until she calmed herself down. Then she warned the parents about the tantrum episode in class. Héloïse wanted to keep Lucienne at home at all cost in order to give her her lessons rather than sending her to school every morning. Lucienne always promised not to have tantrums and adhere to the dictates of the nun. In the end Lucienne stayed at home because the nun no longer wanted her in her class. Lucienne cried day after day and turned obstinate with her mother each time that she saw her sister and her brother leaving for school each day. Héloïse had had enough of this school thing, and she took some information about sending Lucienne to a convent somewhere where they invited children like Lucienne. Alexis did not want to send the little retarded one far from the paternal home. "I'm the father and I'm the one who makes the decisions," he said to Héloïse. However, it was Héloïse who was the boss, or as they say, it was she who wore the pants in the family.

Lucienne left for a convent in the city of Saint-Hyacinthe in Canada. It was an establishment known for its discipline and its excellence in education for the retarded. The religious nuns of l'Anonciation-de-Marie had a reputation of being more sympathetic. They received Lucienne with aplomb and kindness, the kindness of women vowed to the rule and well formed by religious discipline. Also, they had the reputation of being good and generous guardians. Héloïse had gotten good information about this convent and about educative-leaders. She had gotten some very good testimonies. As for Alexis, he could not believe that such a change could provide for his daughter a good progressive education as well as a quality of enviable mores. "What can they do there that they can't do here? It's far over there in Canada, you know", said he. Héloïse told him that first of all it was not men but well-trained women in the domain of retardation and well-formed in matters of discipline. That the convent in Saint-Hyacinthe had the reputation of receiving children like Lucienne. Besides, Lucienne spoke French fluently and that she would have no difficulty to make herself heard and speak to the nuns.

—Are you sure that this is not a case of overdrawn discipline as was demonstrated by the Indian boarding schools of yesteryear when the government and the Church wanted to assimilate the native children in the Canadian culture? I read in the journals that there were inside there some abuses and denigration of values.

—Yes, I'm sure that this convent follows the rules and that the religious are absolutely responsible for their conduct for and their caring about abuses.

—Are you truly sure?

—I told you, yes.

—Well, as you want, my wife, as you want.

—I must have your support, Alexis. We must not have parents each on their side and opposing the decisions made. It will not work like that. We must not worry about anything either.

The trip was long, very long for Lucienne. She had not travelled so far in all of her little life. Her mother tried to persuade her that things would fix themselves and that the good days would come once installed in this convent where the good nuns would be attentive to her special needs.

—You'll see that things will be more pleasant at the boarding school, Héloïse told her.

The father made the remark that things are not always as beautiful even if we go far to ameliorate them. Héloïse told him to shut up and not discourage Lucienne who was already somewhat depressed and who had tears in her eyes. She promised her daughter that she would come often to visit her. Lucienne looked at her with a tamed smile on her lips.

So Lucienne entered the boarding school also called the convent, two weeks after the vacations in August because the religious wanted her entry occur three weeks before classes in September. She went timid and apprehensive but obedient to the persuasive dictates of her mother. She did not want under any circumstances to disobey the unconditional desires of her mother who took, after all, the steps to put her daughter in good hands. Which also meant that her gesture guaranteed to herself that what she did was for the well-being of her daughter and especially for the well-being of the family who was going through a crisis of psychological tension. The father, the other two children and she herself had suffered this tension that had put them in a watchful stage of miscontentment of Lucienne which was becoming more and more evident. They noticed that the retarded daughter who was Lucienne demontrated her repugnance for the condition in which she found herself without being her fault. She did not like who she was and on the other hand felt jealous of the normal condition of her sister and her brother. Héloïse had tried, so many times, to convince her that she was normal in her own condition, but that she would never be able to join her sister and her brother and even the other children seeing the level she was. She was who she was and that was that. She had to accept it. Lucienne the simple-minded did not tolerate well her mother's arguments. She simply wanted to be like the others. "Why did the *Bon Dieu* make me like that? asked poor Lucienne. Héloïse answered her, "I do not know, my dear Lucienne, I do not know. The *Bon Dieu* gives us children just as they are and we must accept them as they are. We can neither exchange them nor change them. That's all."

The weeks flowed one into another and Héloïse never missed going to visit Lucienne every two weeks. She found her well enough, alert and calm. The nuns told her that her little tantrums had diminished and were now rather rare. Héloïse was happy to hear that. She was hoping that her daughter would no longer throw herself in tantrums of anger. However, Héloïse noticed after two or three visits, Lucienne did not show good spirits. She even had the face of one who is pouting each time that her mother tried to ask her if she liked the convent or not. Héloïse felt a bit uneasy when the nun who always accompanied Lucienne in the parlor responded for her daughter. She corrected her when this one tried to admit to her mother that things did not always go well. The nun told Lucienne not to tell lies to her mother and to tell her always the truth what the little girl tried to do but was too often interrupted by the harsh words of the nun. Lucienne ended up always by keeping silence.

Héloïse asked the superior if her daughter could, from time to time, go and visit her home and family in Newmarket. The nun explained to her that it was better for a young girl like Lucienne with her problems of retardation not to go too far from the bosom of her therapeutic care. Once far from this immediate care, a young person like Lucienne becomes disoriented and even troubled. One must not go far from the attention and the good care that one gets here in the convent, said the religious.

—But a short visit home would reinforce, I am sure, a feeling of belonging and relief of being with her mother, her father, her sister and her brother and enjoy the family all together. Don't you think so?

—No, dear lady. Even a short visit can aggravate the situation of the dependence on the strong and able hand that we, the religious well educated and formed in the therapeutic care, give her to guarantee her moral and mental growth.

Héloïse did not know what to say and so she abandoned the idea of a visit to the bosom of the family.

The next visit, accompanied by the driver of the car, a Monsieur Sylvain of Newmarket, Héloïse greeted Lucienne outside on the lawn. She was playing ball with a young girl of about the same age. The other children were spread here and there while two of the religious were watching over the games and the children. Lucienne and her companion were a bit aside and when Lucienne noticed her mother, she hurried to go and greet her. The other girl followed her. The three of them were chatting when one of the two nuns approached them and started to send the companion away. Her name was Yvonne-Marie. Héloïse told the nun to leave the little girl with her and Lucienne so that she might better get to know her. First, the nun hesitated to let Yvonne-Marie talk with Madame Charbonneau of the United-States. When Héloïse learned that the companion came from the States also, she insisted that Yvonne-Marie remain with her. The nun nodded her head and assented to this proposal. The nun left the place where Héloïse, her daughter and her companion were seated. From time to time, the nun looked behind her so as to see what was happening with the three of them. Without doubt, she would have wanted to know what they were talking about. After a certain time, Héloïse started asking Yvonne-Marie where she came from in the United-States.

—I come from Lewiston, Maine, she said to her.

—Oh, I don't know that city. Are there people who speak French there?

—Yes, Madame. Many of them come from Quebec and their children were born in Lewiston.

—Ah, I understand. There must be several towns and villages where the immigrants from Quebec came to say.

—I don't know, Madame. All I know is that my parents came from Quebec. As for me, I was born in Lewiston. My father is a doctor and my mother is an artist, but retired from her music since my father did not want her to waste her time with that. He wanted her at home with the care of the children. I have one sister and one brother. Mathilde and Jean-François.

—Your father did not want your mother to make music? Why?

—My mother plays the violin and she is a very good musician. She interprets very well pieces of music enough to participate in an orchestra and even give concerts.

—Why doesn't she do it?

—Because my father does not allow her to do it.

—Really? I cannot believe that a man, a husband could do that.

—All I know is that my mother put away her violin in its case and then hid it under the couch in the living room so that it is no longer in sight. Only once did she take it to play Massenet's "Meditation." I found it charming that piece of music. My mother had tears in her eyes. After she finished, she went to put back her violin in its hiding place before my father came home from his office. It was we the children who had pleaded with her to play her violin.

—Yet, your mother's violin is not only an instrument of music but the instrument of competition as an artist. Why hide it?

—I don't know, Madame.

The surveillant nun came to announce that that the afternoon snack was being served. Héloïse, Lucienne and Yvonne-Marie got up, stretched their numbed legs and left for the snack. After this brief afternoon break, Héloïse invited Lucienne and her companion to sit outdoor on the big porch with tall white rails. The surveillant nun attempted to prevent Yvonne-Marie from accompanying them on account of the siesta required every afternoon. Yvonne-Marie looked at Héloïse in the eye pleading for permission to stay with her and Lucienne. The nun pulled the companion by the right arm while the little girl resisted leaving with her. Héloïse intervened and insisted that Yvonne-Marie remain with her. "After all", said she, "Yvonne-Marie, I'm sure, gets rarely any company from the States."

—It's true, added Yvonne-Marie.

The nun turned around and left somewhat offended. Héloïse and the two girls left to go and sit on the grass under a big oak tree.

—Tell me, Yvonn-Marie, why your parents do not come to visit you sometime. They are your parents. They must love you. You're their daughter.

—I don't know, Madame. All I know is that it was my father's idea to place me here. He said that I was over-excited and that he could not take it anymore. That I got on his nerves. That's all I know. My father comes once a year to settle my acount and to bring me a Christmas gift, usually some dried fruits. He says that those fruits are good for your health. I hate them. I give them to the nuns who eat them with delight and see them as delicacies.

—How about you mother?

—She never comes.

—My God, what a sad story is yours.

—Not sad but full of tension and strife.

—Do you like the convent here?

—You mean the boarding school? There's the nuns' convent and the boarding school for us children whose parents cannot handle them.

—But that's not the case for Lucienne. Not at all.

Lucienne, the Simple-Minded

Lucienne looked at her mother with a timid eye somewhat like that of a wild animal.

—Don't look at me like that, a wild animal caught in a trap. I'm a good mother, a very good maman. I only want your well-being and your educational accomplishment.

—Yes, that's your way of finding relief in the heart because you have a retarded child. All that you want for me is the opposite of what I want for myself.

—You certainly do not want to become a retarded and abandoned individual trapped in mental difficulties. That's what I want to prevent for you.

—I'm satisfied with what I shall become some day. I have enough of dreaming of total change when I become other than what I am. I already made that dream and it led me almost to despair. I was angry and jealous of what others had, the normal ones. I'm not abnormal and I'm not without intelligence enough to be a lost person, a person always dependent on the others. I am my own person and I want that others have confidence in me, myself and my qualities of a person who wants to act like a real person and not a retarded.

—Do you like it here, Lucienne? No response.

—Yet your father and I, we wanted to place you where you would get the best education possible and the best care possible. We never wanted to put you in a vulnerable and compromising situation. We want what is best for you. I love you, Lucienne, and so does your father. That's the only reason why we placed you in a convent.

—It's precisely what I don't like. It's to be placed. Like most young girls here, we're all placed and not engaged by our own will in a situation that is healthy and sympathetic. Sympathetic as it concerns not only the needs of the body but of the intellect and especially of the heart. We have feelings too. We are not over- excited or wild beings. We have a heart made of flesh and not of stone. It's the religious who have a heart of stone. Not all of them but most of them.

—Explain.

Not a single word except "I can't, maman'" came out of Lucienne's mouth.

—Let me tell you something, Madame Charbonneau, said Yvonne-Marie.

—Go ahead dear, I'm listening.

—Well here's the situation here at the sisters' convent and at the boarding school for the youths. Here the nuns are well nourished and well taken care of when the needs are asked for. As for us at the boarding school there's no appetizing nourishment. It's gruel and a piece of bread in the morning, soup with a small piece of fattened meat and a piece of boiled potato, and at night again soup and then some jam for dessert. It's always the same thing.

—Not more than that?

—Yes, Madame. Not more than that. It gets to be boring and "plate"

—Is that true, Lucienne?

—Yes, maman. She's telling the truth.

—Yet we give them a good sum of money for boarding here. It should suffice to nourish and lodge the school boarding members. I do not understand. What's happening here at the convent. I believed them more honest than that these religious.

—It's not all, Madame.

—What do you mean?

—Well, Lucienne is not as retarded as one would think and what the religious say. She has a very good vocabulary, better than mine and she has an excellent memory.

—I know about her memory but I thought of what the doctors had told me that my daughter was retarded and her mental condition would never change. So, we believed she had an abnormal mental condition. That's why we placed Lucienne here in a convent that treats the pensioners for their retarded condition. The convent enjoys a very good reputation.

—The reputation and what is done or not done by the nuns is not always on the same level of authenticity. It's not always "transparent" here their game. Between their mission and their vocation and its reality swim in false realizations. These ladies of the veil are not all humble and devoted to the service of their clientele, I assure you. I know because I see it even though they blame me of being a spy. I have eyes in front and behind the head. It's because I'm a suspicious person. My experiences with my father have given me the feeling of suspicion.

—I don't know what to say and what to do now.

—Moreover, there are abuses here. Not only physical abuses but psychological abuses.

—No!

—Yes, Madame. Lucienne is one example.

—Not so. Yet I was sure that she was well protected from all abuses, the convent.

—Lucienne show her your blue spots.

—No. I really don't want to.

—Show them to me, I beg you. I want to see the results of what is going on here.

Lucienne unbuttoned her blouse that uncovered some blue spots on her left shoulder.

—It's not the nuns who did this, maman. I fell in the stairs coming down.

—She's not telling you the whole truth, Madame.

—What is the truth then?

—Lucienne was pushed by someone in the stairs and the nuns did nothing for it. Not even punish the guilty one. I tell you, Madame, there are things that happen here that we hide and cover up. There's one nun who touches us where she should not. She has perverse fingers that one, I'm telling you. And she watches us with piercing eyes when we get undressed. I don't like her at all, that one, Sister Sainte-Bougrèse-de-Lamprai.

—Why did you not denounce her?

—And be told that I'm a liar and that I'm a spy and all that. No one wants to talk about it and no one listens to me and especially not my father.

—Why not?

—Because he wants to keep me here far from him and far from his conduct *of Monsieur le médecin* the high professional personage who walks with his head held high while saveguarding his reputation and would not want for all the gold in the world to have an over-excited daughter like me in his little world. You see, he wants to remake me, reform me, I think, transform me by means of a stern and sour-tempered discipline. That's why he placed me here in a boarding school far from Lewiston, Maine. However Yvonne-Marie does not bend. She doesn't want to associate with the hypocrisy of others either.

—I admire your candor and your independence. Like me you have some *casque.*

A religious arrives suddenly and holds the left arm of Yvonne-Marie and orders her to follow her somewhere with a veiled harshness of voice. Then she murmurs loud enough for Héloïse to hear her. "Stop telling your stories to strangers. You lie and you know it." Yvonne-Marie followed her, turned her back and gave Héloïse a sardonic smile.

Héloïse started thinking as in a nightmare about everything Yvonne-Marie had told her. She contemplated with doubt and exasperation all the steps she could take in order to extirpate her child from a precarious situation. She has to judge the situation with perspicacity and good judgement, she tells herself. But how can she not trouble her daughter and not fill her with worries who is becoming the prey of the difficulties provoked by the same situation. Héloïse does not absolutely want to put her daughter in danger whatever the decisions made in secret. She's afraid of alienating Lucienne and lose her once and for all. Losing your child is losing her confidence. She must not put her child in peril of eternalizing the anguish and the vestiges of retardation in spite of the conclusions of Yvonne-Marie. Is it possible that she is exaggerating things and does not diagnose the mental condition of Lucienne with the ability of an expert, Héloïse asks herself. All of this keeps milling around in her head and gives her a brutal headache. What to do, how to do it and then when to do it are questions she must resolve. In the end, what is the truth and where is it? Héloïse left with a heavy heart. Monsieur Sylvain was waiting for her in the parlor.

The next visit, Héloïse went to meet Lucienne in the parlor where her daughter was waiting. Lucienne was sitting down straight and without any motion on her part. She looked like an abandoned doll. One of the nuns was there surveilling her. Héloïse did not know her. Lucienne introduced her.

—Maman, this is Mère Sainte-Justine-de-Valois. She's a very good person who takes good care of me and she's the one who wipes my tears when I'm missing home.

Héloïse went to greet the nun.

—Thank you Mère for taking care of my daughter. Turning to her daughter, she told her with compassion,

—Is it true that you miss home sometimes?

—Sometimes.

—Do you want to come home with me?

—Right away?

—If you want.

—I don't know, maman.

—What do you mean, I don't know?

—It's because it's true that I don't always like the boarding school, but I like it most of the time. I don't care about the food that Yvonne-Marie talks about. She's a little bit disdainful. I like my little friends and I give them my affection when it tells me to do it. And I know that my intelligence is limited but it's certainly not invalid as a model of reasoning.

The religious turned towards her and threw her a glance of approbation and trust.

—So you want to stay here?

—Not forever but for a short while.

—You can stay here at the convent as long as you want, my dear little angel, said the nun.

—Well, that's well and done. I'll be back next week to see you. Addressing the nun, Héloïse told her, "I would like to see Yvonne-Marie before leaving for the States, please."

The nun brought her aside and confided to her with a tamed murmur,

—I doubt that you will be able to see Yvonne-Marie again because she ran away in the woods around here right after she left you. She escaped from the hands of the nun who was leading her in the boarding school. It's really severe this matter of evasion.

—Oh my gosh, Héloïse exclaimed. I would not have believed that she was capable of doing that and cause sorrow to all of you.

—Oh, it's not the first time that she causes us worries like that. She's a little misunderstood and misguided by her own vexations, as her father says Héloïse got closer to Lucienne and gave her a goodbye while hugging her. She gave her a big kiss and left with tears in her eyes because she had not found the way out of her predicament that of bringing Lucienne with her or leaving her with people that she could not trust totally. The trip from Saint-Hyacinthe to Newmarket was long, very long for her. Not a single word between her and Monsieur Sylvain and Héloïse were exchanged except for two or three yeses and four no's.

Once home, Héloïse told her husband that she was exhausted from her trip and that she was going to bed. Night would certainly bring her advice, she told Alexis, using the old French saying of *la nuit porte conseil*. He asked himself what had happened over there in Saint-Hyacinthe. Héloïse spent a very ravaged night, a night of villainous nightmares. She dreamt of all kinds of things like the nuns who haunted her dreams, Yvonne-Marie who had become an appeal to the needs of Lucienne and who strew her dream with bad conscience. Moreover, there was the presentiment that something was wrong in her mentalitty of woman and mother. Was she neglecting her other two children so as to satisfy the needs of the retarded Lucienne. Was her task of being a mother and a spouse compromised by the conviction that things would fix themselves once Lucienne's condition would be resolved. And then, she herself, Héloïse, didn't she totally give herself to the pressure of satisfying the needs of one only child in casting aside the two others and in neglecting her own needs as a woman. All was tumbled around in her head and in her heart as a woman. She felt alone and abandoned by a God who had thrown her an ungrateful fate.

The following day, Héloïse told her husband what had happened at the boarding school. She told him everything that she remembered in every detail. She did not want to miss anything, not a single detail. She told him about Yvonne-Marie who had talked about the boarding school and all the alleged abuses. Then, she told him that Lucienne had black and blue spots on her left shoulder because someone had pushed her in the stairs, and the nuns had not given any concern to it. On top of it all, Yvonne-Marie told her that Lucienne was, according to her, not so much retarded since she had acquired a very beautiful vocabulary and a very good memory, *une mémoire de chien*. That her intelligence rarely lacked being operational in spite of the diagnostics of so-called professionals.

—What does she know at her age this girl? asked Alexis.

—She's fourteen and she's very well endowed for her age, I assure you.

—But why is she at the boarding school?

—She's there because her father placed her there since he says she's an over-excited kid and she does not like to be told that she causes trouble for everyone. When we have no testimony of affection from anyone not even from the father, so we revolt and we become abandoned by family and relatives. That's the case for Yvonne-Marie.

—It's not Lucienne's case.

—So, what are we going to do with Lucienne? We leave her at the couvent or not? My heart feels torn with this affair of boarding school. I tell you Alexis, I can't anymore.

—Well, we're going to get her tomorrow. That's all. It's over with this come and go and the squabbling over our retarded child. Finished the disputes with the religious and the abnormal cases. We don't know where to put our heads with all of that.

—Alexis, we must not rub the religious the wrong way while thinking that we are doing some good to the one who deserves it, our Lucienne.

—Never mind about the troubles of conscience concerning the religious and their mission of therapeutic education. I don't like what is going on over there even though it's only a suspicion of abuse. Abuse is abuse whether it's minimal or not. I would not want that I as a father be responsible of any scratch on the person that is my daughter who is innocent and who relies on us her parents.

—I agree with you, my Alexis, tender father.

Alexis smiled with a nice and wide smile of a spouse and this father who is attentive to the needs of his family.

The day that the Charbonneaus left to go and fetch their daughter, the parents started to think that their Lucienne was a relief for the father and a tearing apart for the mother. The father was content while the mother was hurt of not having succeeded with her daughter at the boarding school. Héloïse and Alexis arrived at Saint-Hyacinthe around three in the afternoon when the sun poured down its rays of warnth on the emplacement of the convent-boarding school. Without too many words, the father and the mother went to the large white and silent house and they went directly to the parlor upon the formal invitation of the nun at the reception desk. They asked to see the superior to explain their aim of taking out their daughter from the boarding school without any warning. The superior was stunned and troubled by this decision on the part of Lucienne's parents. The superior tried to convince them to wait some time before separating Lucienne from her convent. It was Alexis who first started to speak and declared with insistance that they would not leave before recuperating his daughter. Héloïse did not utter a single word. The superior asked her the reasons for which Lucienne was being taken away from the convent. Alexis said that there was only one reason and it was that he and his wife were neither happy nor satisfied with the results of the their daughter's placement at the boarding school. The superior wanted to know more about that reason. Alexis cut her off and told her that the decision had been taken with determination and that it was that, no more. The religious turned toward Héloïse and begged her to respond to her demand.

Héloïse kept silent with her eyes lowered. The superior seeing that any demand on her part would not be met with a satisfactory answer for her, she told Alexis that the convent could not reimburse the money already put on the account for the stay at the boarding sdchool. Alexis responded that money already given did not mean anything to him and that he considered it as a donation to the community.

Alexis, Héloïse and Lucienne left around six o'clock to go towards Newmarket. There was a profound silence in the Charbonneau auto until Lucienne opened her mouth to ask her parents why they had pulled her out of the convent without asking her opinion on it. Alexis responded that he did not need her opinion. He added that he did it for her well-being and the well-being of the family. He was tired of this convent-boarding school affair, said he with a steely tone. Héloïse kept always silence. Lucienne curled herself up in a corner of the backseat without revealing too much evident emotion. but her heart was broken of having been pulled away from the only place where she had truly belonged with pride and confidence in herself. A broken heart is not so soon mended.

After having established herself at home following an absence of eight months, Lucienne tried to renew her friendships with the few friends that she had left behind. It was difficult for her to adapt to the day she had left and supplanted it with another. She needed time and patience of which she had very little. Her mother tried to encourage her, but Lucienne ignored her or contradicted her every time she knew that her mother wanted to give her advice. Héloïse did not understand this confusion of calculated conduct that made her hair stand on end. She could not stand to say and say again the words that would benefit her daughter, Lucienne, the simple-minded one. She regretted calling her that way for she never liked calling her that. One must believe that Héloïse could not do anything about the problem of intimacy and communication with her daughter.

Alexis sometimes found her crying. He tried to console her, but Héloïse did not want his advice. She too, it seems, had no more patience with him, just like she had hardly any patience with her daughter, the simple-minded one. Hermance and Joseph-Arthur used to ask themselves often what was troubling their mother usually so happy and so patient before. The two children drew away from her more and more due to a lack of warmth and intimacy as well as maternal feelings. A slight coldness established itself in the Charbonneau household. They felt ill at ease, even those who came to visit them. Something had to be done. But what?

Did the presence of a retarded one cause worries and even a breakdown of communication and intimacy that bond family ties? Yet, Héloïse had desired all her life to found a family, an intimate and generous family. A family that would generate love and well-being of one and all. However, all that she could see now was a family submerged by the pains of slipping away and hit by a certain tangible and breathtaking friction.

Week after week brought forth daily activities. Time went by and nothing changed. It was as if the days ended with interminable sighs of frustration and anguish. Something was bound to happen so as to put an end to it, Héloïse told herself. She arrived at convincing her husband that conjugal separation was the best thing that could happen. Alexis was completely frayed by his wife's declaration. He wanted to arrive at a compromise but Héloïse did not want any part of it. He wanted his wife to stay with the children and he would go and live with a friend for three or four days and he would then return home trying to reestablish normalcy in the family that existed before Lucienne's entrance in the boarding school. Was Lucienne the cause of this disruption, Héloïse asked herself. She concluded that it was not the daughter's fault but her fault, she Héloïse. Then she turned towards her husband to find the germ of this fault. This fault, she told herself, yes, this fault lay in the great lack of love that Alexis owed her. She could not help comparing the wanted love in her marriage to the shared love of Célie and Timiskamengo. Always the romance of love that comes to open up the heart and satisfy pushed away feelings. We accuse the one who is not really the cause of our annoyances but rather the one who gives his love that is frank and inexhaustible with full hands and an open heart. Romance only comes to muddle things and pale true feelings.

Alexis tried to come back home for good but Héloïse told him that she could not support the effort of winning back what reigned in the home long time ago, that is to say calm and understanding. She was convinced of it. Where to turn to? What to do when one feels alone and abandoned? Was the feeling of abandonment the cause of her worries? How does one get rid of spider webs that came to muddle a groping brain and an uncertain heart? Why so many worries and so much muddling in her life, she Héloïse? "*Dieu viens à mon aide*, God come tp my assistance, she cried out, but God was mute and sent her only silence. Héloïse started to drink and run around neighborhood bars trying to find peace in the heart that she so needed and that would render the promise of a future filled with sunshine that she was hoping for. Héloïse cradled often nice dreams of love known a long time ago by Célie and Timiskamengo. She firmly believed in dreams woven by the gift of an active and at times unreal imagination. As often she fell into the unhealthy miasma of dreams, she turned towards the stupor that was brought about by the alcoholic beverages that she swallowed with avidity. Alexis often found her sitting in a bar with a few drunken companions talking while under an unintelligible numbness. He took her by the arm and brought her home without disputing her, without warning her of the shame drinking to excess. He loved her, Héloïse, and he did not want to cause her pain, the pain of feeling abject and filled with remorse.

Seeing her so often drunk, not steady on her feet and especially in a state of public drunkeness, Alexis decided, one day, to place her at the center for detoxification in spite of his profound regret of doing what he had done with his daughter, Lucienne, placing her away from the view and esteem of others. He did not say it but he felt shame and he did not want at anytime and place to dishonor her in the children's eyes.

He had thought about it night and day, and there was no other solution to his problem than place Héloïse somewhere where she would get the needed if not required care. He told himself that it was a malady that was becoming a huge challenge for him. He had to face it with care and determination. However, he had a hard time doing it. He loved his wife and did not really want to place her but there wasn't any other choice. Placing for him meant putting someone in the hold of the tenacity and the implacability of a fault, such as alcohol, that pushes one to lose the will to reject that fault. The victimization of Héloïse by alcohol was seen clearly by Alexis. It was that that troubled Alexis to no end. Once the decision was made, Alexis took Héloïse to the center called **Center Louis Hubert, Establishment for Readaptation and Well-Being**. It was an institution run by Franco-Americans. At the beginning, Héloïse struggled not to go there and even resisted with violence for she sometimes hit Alexis with her boxing fists on his stomach so enraged against him was she. But Alexis told himself that it was against the sickness that she did that and not against him personnally. Finally, he succeeded to convince her that it was only for a short period of time and especially for her health and the well-being of her children that he had begun to stay away from her more often than possible. Héloïse left one Monday morning even before the sunrise because Alexis didn't want the neighbors to know they were leaving.

Héloïse left with *le taquet bas*, pouting, and dared not say a single word, because she knew in her heart that she was the only source of discontent for the children and especially of misery that she caused her husband who was walking next to her with his head low. She turned her head to say something but the words did not want to come out of her mouth. She wished she could have a glass of something, beer maybe, in order to calm her hands shaking and especially the fear that was rising and kept rising from her feet to her head. Alexis took her by the hand and they headed for the detoxification center. Both of them went inside the big red brick building and upon her arrival Héloïse wanted to turn back fast to leave this environment, outside in the fresh morning air. Alexis held her by the hand strong enough that she would not be able to separate from his strong and insisting grasp. Héloïse felt feeble but strong enough not to cede to the hold of her rebellious tendencies. They were greeted at the reception desk and the lady asked them to fill out the admision form for the rehabilitation patient. She did not mention the word intoxification which pleased Alexis. Once inside the center of the large room, where several men and women of every age were rocking themselves in rocking chairs, Héloïse began to cry. Alexis consoled her and held her right hand and told her not to be afraid that those who were responsible for treatment only wanted to put her back to a point of sobriety whereby she would be able to go home happy. That she would be able to enjoy being alive again like before. She smiled at him and nodded her head, yes.

Alexis went home confident that his wife would get very good care and that she would get to put herself back on her two feet once and for all healed from the folly of alcohol. He did not know that the taste of alcohol lasts a long time and does not cease to leave the victim tranquil and free to drink or not. That becomes a haunting, a terrible haunting that one cannot ever totally get rid of. Alcohol serves as a support to those who often clamor for this reliance. As for Héloïse, she spent the day praying and asking God and the Blessed Virgin Mary to grant her mercy and pardon for having offended them and her husband. Even her children. So Héloïse's rehabilitation started with prayers that she had so often abandoned. She thought herself to be unworthy of prayers and she had ceased praying to God since she hardly understood his will, so very intransigeant for her and for her family. First of all there was her daughter Lucienne, the simple-minded. She now recognized this expression attributed to her daughter. Then, she remembered the fate of poor Célie who had lost her beloved, Timiskamengo, fault of abuses and wickedness on the part of those responsible for wanting to assimilate the native children. Then she remembered her sister, Félicité, who had welcomed her to her home but who wanted to convert her to her way of seeing things. Félicité wanted to cover the faults of those responsible for the abuses and the shame while glorifying *"les nôtres"*, ours, since they were Canadians. Héloïse had refused to accept what was unworthy and disloyal to the values fundamentally human. She even accused God of this.

After five weeks of detoxification treatments, Alexis brought Héloïse home where the children were waiting with trepidation and some anguish in the heart. They did not know how to take their maman in hand and how to render her service as much as they could. Each of them had visited her at the center, each their turn, but now it was different for she was going to live with them from day to day. They had learned how to cook, and do household chores at the instigation of the father who now worked at the mill as second-hand. The Charbonneaus had lost their commerce **Chez Héloïse** for the clients had stopped coming and Alexis could not take care of it at all by himself. After all, it was Héloïse who was the very soul of the enterprise. She was the one who had conceived it, furnished it and given the people the beautiful and tasty *tourtières* and sugar pies. Alexis had been but the associate and master maintenance man.

Lucienne came to help her mother each time she saw her trembling and anxious. She asked her what to do and she did it without murmuring. Lucienne had learned to attenuate her little fits of anger and accept herself as a young girl with a few mental difficulties, but not with severity to make her incapable of learning something and communicate to others what she wanted to say. She always had this daunting memory and used it when someone asked her for a date, an event of the past, a certain name or the year when Sainte-Thérèse-de-l'Enfant-Jésus was built. Lucienne was now fifteen and a half years old and she had grown up with a certain maturity and wisdom to compensate for what she lacked in mental capacities. Lucienne was a beautiful girl although she did not admit it. She did not feel beautiful. Ordinary, she told people who wanted to compliment her for her feminine beauty.

Hermance was fourteen years old and Joseph-Arthur was twelve. Hermance had found a job at the Laverrière store where we sold hats and some nice jewelry to attract the ladies who could afford to spend money to show off that they had it and could spend it. She loved beautiful clothes and told her mother about all the small conversations in a small boutique ever busy with the sales by satisfied ladies who had the luxury of not having to work in the mills and have enough time to spend money on objects considered frivolous. Hermance had become a bit coquette and that worried her mother who tried to keep her humble and without inordinate pride. However, in spite of the worries and the counsels of her mother, Hermance insisted on being, one day, the grand lady of the theater. She could then enjoy a luxurious life up to now unknown to her. She would be able to flaunt herself in front of a world that appreciates the success of a star, she told her mother. Héloïse used to tell her that such a success is only for those who earn it and work hard to get it.

—You need talent to become a star, her mother told her.

—I have talent, mother of the star.

—Wel,l show it to me for I haven't discovered it at this point in your life.

—But, you don't have confidence in me at all. I'm telling you, I'll go far some day.

—Yes, up to the corner. That's all.

—To the corner of Hollywood and Vines. Hollywood the mecca of stars.

—What?

—The very center of dramatic activity in the United-States.

—You read too many magazines and impertinent reviews that make the head spin.

—You have no feeling for the theater and that's why you understand nothing about Hollywood Stars.

—As for that, you're right, but I know very well what it is to work hard and the perseverance that it takes. I have experience in that.

—Yes, and you fell into the trap of drinking and the flight from reality.

—You break my heart.....and Héloïse started to weep.

—I didn't want to make you cry, 'man. Forgive me. It's not what I wanted to do at all.

Héloïse went away from the kitchen so that she could wash her face, a face with wrinkles affected by the bite of time and misshapen ideals. She did not want to reveal the interior of the person she was fighting drunkeness and the doubts that embarrassed her if they started to raise their ugly heads. She did not want any of these faults badly appreciated. She loved her little family and she, in any case, did not want to cause it profound pain. She wished all of them a bright future filled with success and well-being, and she would work with all her might to assure that it happened. This renewed strength in her would compensate for the failures of the past. Héloïse could not understand how she had gone from a happy and productive life to that of a creature haunted by humming and hawing as well as shame, shame of not having succeeded with Lucienne. At least, she had not lost the gift of hope, the hope that one day Lucienne would end up finding her *niche* in life. It would be a nest filled with vigor and well-being in her own skin, Lucienne, the simple-minded. Héloïse recognized the value of words and their full sense such as simple-minded. Before, she did not want to hear these words in regards to her daughter. Proferred in regards to others than her, yes, but she had almost horror of this name when it meant retarded and designated her daughter, Lucienne. Moreover, Héloïse never wanted to admit that her daughter was retarded, simple and slow in her fashion of speaking and doing, but not retarded. Not at all abnormal. There were some who had even called Lucienne a *sans- dessein*. Yes, a *sans-dessein*. A *sans-dessein* is a person not too bright who did not invent the four-hole button, as our people say, thought Héloïse. A *sans-dessein* is one who is little inventive and without initiative, she told herself. Lucienne is certainly not a *sans-dessein*. She's probably a little limited in her intelligence, but she is not without initiative. No. Moreover, she enjoys a marvelous memory, she told herself. What would happen if Lucienne found herself alone and without parents. "I will leave some day and I will join my parents and my ancestors in the other world...but what will happen to the simple-minded without a parental post to lean on and without direction in life? she asked herself. "May *le Bon Dieu* not abandon her. No, with abandonment comes despair," murmured Héloïse.

Lucienne, the Simple-Minded

As for Joseph-Arthur, it was a case of happy and fortunate conduct. He was fine, his academic courses demonstrated an intelligence and an acuity of spirit almost extraordinary. "That one there takes after my father," said Héloïse to herself. Her father, Marjolain, had the intelligence of a dog (that's how people said it) just like Lucienne has a memory like a dog. Héloïse loved to think about her father in these terms. Yes, Marjolain Lanouette was gifted with a lively and penetrating intelligence. He could do anything with his habitant hands and think about everything and anything in order to come up with a solution whatever the difficulties perceived. He was so capable that people came to see him and ask him to fix a situation or repair anything be it a broken fence, a broken post, a door in a bad condition, a bridle whose blinkers and the [sous-gorge] were deformed by abandonment and lack of care, a butter churn fallen in disuse or a knife that had the need to be honed. He was truly a *touche-à-tout*, touch everything, as they say. Moreover, he was gifted with a talent of giving counsel to those who asked him.

Hermance, Lucienne and Joseph-Arthur did not need to have anyone watching over them like before. Certainly the parents needed to cast an eye on them but not to watch over them constantly like watching over small children. Lucienne especially did not like someone watching over her like one who watches over an unruly child. Hermance had disdain for restrained surveillance by a maman or a papa. She thought of herself as being too grown-up and too mature to be watched every moment and every time she decided to go somewhere. Joseph-Arthur did not pay any attention to surveillance if it existed or not. He went at his own regulated pace and at his own liking. He followed the counsels of his father and sometimes his mother. He was a big boy.

Alexis now worked at the mill as loom fixer. Hermance worked in a boutique that sold hats and nice jewelry. Lucienne found herself a part-time job in a small store that sold candy and choice goodies. Joseph-Arthur worked in a boutique that made and sold wooden sculptures, and Héloïse wanted to work in the mills because she only worked in her spare time in the kitchen. She believed she was without work and she could not support that. She was not raised that way, she told her husband. Her husband told her that he did not want her to go in the mills where women worked so much and so hard that water pissed down their backs and through their undergarments. They went home totally worn out and out of breath for having labored beyond their strength. The mill was only for those who really needed the work and who risked everything and without wages each week. Poverty elbowed misery in their case. Alexis insisted that he was going to take care of his family, his children and his wife. Héloïse tried to take the upper hand and succeeded finally in doing so by insisting and insisting until Alexis bent down to her wishes and told her to do what she wanted in spite of his warnings. "You have a hard head, my wife, just like the pigs. You have a *tête de cochon.*" Héloïse laughed up her sleeve. "No man will ever tell me what to do," she murmured.

Héloïse started walking toward the mill one Tuesday morning when the rain was coming down in buckets. However, she had no feelings of regret and she did not care about the rain. She called this her baptism of the mills. She went inside three large courtyards after having gotten some information about the office of admissions. They gave her a long form and she started filling out the form, Then the one in charge of the bureau asked her if she had experience in a mill. She told him she had none. He told her that was not necessarily a condition for employment at the mill. He had also discerned that she was not illiterate. She had a nice signature, he remarked. The man then told her that there were openings in the department of looms, more precisely, in the area of battery fillers. She told him that she did not want to work in that area. It came to her mind that Alexis worked there and she did not want to find herself where he worked each day. That would strike her nerves. So he proposed to her to work with the spinners, the ones who ran the spinning frames. She told him that she did not know how to spin. "So, you will learn, Madame, said he." Thus Héloïse became a spinner. When Alexis found out that she had been looking for work in the mills, he told her that he would not prevent her from working there. She answered that she would do it want to or not. He knew all too well that she always followed her headstrong wishes and would find out how hard was mill work.

The two spouses left for the mill early each morning five and a half days a week. Reassured that the children were in good hands, the two girls at work and Joseph- Arthur in school, Alexis and Héloïse went to work without too many worries. The days turned into weeks and the weeks into months until the year came to its full. The money came into the household and the Charbonneaus had no debts to pay. As for Héloïse, she often thought about her little commerce of *tourtières* and sugar pies and how she had forged it by herself. It had become the pride of the neighborhood and the bread winner of the Charbonneaus. She had enjoyed so much this enterprise conceived and executed by herself, a young woman that we would not have thought that she could have done such a coup. Héloïse had always enjoyed a head sitting well on her two shoulders and full of dreams and determination. She had never believed that she would fail in anything, and that she would attempt anything good times bad times. She was a good "*Canayenne*" in the process of demonstrating to others and especially the men that a woman could succeed if she wanted to junp into anything that came into her head for she had *du casque* and a spirit of independence. Her mother as well as Célie had always said to her that she would go far in life if only she managed to do things and went to work to fashion her own future.She had an elephant's confidence, Madame Verrier had told her, one of the neighbors in Batiscan.

"*Mon Dieu*, Batiscan. I miss it, this town with good people who shirk from nothing They're people from the land, people in whose veins flows the blood of the settlers. They're sometimes a difficult people to live with but they're generous with the favors they give freely and are wise in their advice. "People of the land I miss you," as Héloïse remembered them. She rarely got news from them except from an old neighbor who did write from time to time. It was Geneviève Labranche with whom she went to the nuns's school for a short time. Geneviève remembered her and Héloïse kept a good souvenir of dear Geneviève- the- mother-of-cats as she was called. She loved cats that one like one who loves her dearest friends. She spoiled them and caressed them as well as dress them and then put them in a little child's cart and walked them around every Sunday afternoon when the weather was nice. She did not get angry when the other kids used to tease her. She even talked to her cats as if they were real babies.

When it happened to be the night before Monday when the mill workers thought of their work for the first day of the workweek and people fell into a nostalgia of a free time accorded to them with a happy weekend, the mammas and the papas got organized by getting out their work clothes and putting them on the back of some chairs folded and, of course, clean. One and all got ready for the upcoming week. It was always the same routine. We did not think of *changer le mal de place*, change the pain from its place, as the old millhands used to say. Once the routine has settled in, it does not linger to remain in evidence. It was as if people were accustomed to the constant pace of the routine. They became like robots formed by the darn mill and its call every Monday morning. There was even a large clock whose bell rang the exact time of quarter to six every workday. There were some who had gone to bed late and had gotten up late with waxen eyes and dry mouths. Alexis often had the experience of that these days although he never made it a habit. Héloïse went to wake him up with words of rage mixed with tenderness. She had become a little too impatient with her husband. He forgave her impatience but he could not give her his good humor so early Monday morning.

After nine months of work at the mill, Héloïse decided to leave the spinning work and hunt for another job not as hard and that was worthwhile. She was sick of this robot work. She was at the end of her rope. Alexis told her,"I told you so." She shrugged her shoulders and left for Main Street in Newmarket where there were boutiques and large department stores like Fishman and Newberry. She noticed a hat boutique with a sign, **Chez Les Mademoiselles Maheu** and she decided to go in. She would have thought she was back home since the name was French. Not that she didn't like the other names such as McKenney, Feinberg, Wolonski, and Politano but she preferred a name representing her heritage, that of her ancestors. There was a certain measure of security in a French name for her, she who had left for another country but was not too far away to feel out of sorts. After all, Newmarket like many towns and villages where Québécois such as Héloïse and Alexis established themselves was home where a large part of the population spoke French. They got along very well. They went to Sunday mass and they built churches so as to guarantee that the language would be French.

The *curés* would be one of theirs, these Québécois who were transplanted in the United-States, told themselves. And, they would make sure that the young girls would marry a young man of their race, as said by Monsieur Lantagne from Lipton Street right next to where Héloïse lived.

Héloïse learned that two unmarried women owned and managed the boutique, a Mademoiselle Yvonne Maheu and her sister, Juliette.

They exuded warmth in their greeting and they greeted Héloïse with an exquisite charm. The three women entertained themselves talking during almost two hours while there were not any customers who came to buy hats. The Mademoiselles Maheu also offered some nice Chinese silk scarves or some *foulards* made of beautiful fine woven cotton and silken at the touch with bright color designs. Moreover, there were also necklaces, earrings, bracelets imitating gold, and pins garnished with stones not precious stones but they looked luxurious. Héloïse was ravished by this merchandise. She admitted to both proprietors that she would not have any difficulty selling the hats and the jewelry.

Everything pleased her infinitely."And you have very good taste for everything, I assure you," said she. The Mademoiselles Maheu were more than pleased with the charm of this woman who loved to talk. She would be a very good saleslady, they told one another. They hired Héloïse on the spot without asking her too many questions. The salary was minimal but she could earn more money with the commissions, assured the Mademoiselles Maheu.

Héloïse got home all out of breath and radiant for having found a job that pleased her enormously. She did not stop talking about it at supper to her children and her husband, Alexis. As for Hermance, she was not too much impressed by this, and Joseph-Arthur said simply to his mother that he was happy for her, while Lucienne was *aux anges*, in heaven. She praised her mother for having left the mill to find a job that would bring her an immense pleasure. Alexis said nothing.

Héloïse asked him why he had nothing to say at that moment. He responded that he preferred to let things go at this moment without saying anything for he had nothing to say about this news and that it would be nice to say nothing if he found nothing nice to say so as not to offend his wife.

—So, you don't like my news, asked Héloïse.

—I have nothing to say, that's all.

—I feel that you are angry and that you're hiding your anger concerning my new job.

—I'm not mad.

—But you're not pleased.

—I didn't say that.

—If you have nothing to say it's because you have no good words neither in your heart nor in your mouth.

—I have nothing to say, that's all.

The three children left the table without a word.

—You all leave me with a father who remains silent enough to cover this bad ambiance that appears to be heavy and unhealthy.

—What do you mean by that, my wife?

—Well, I feel abandoned by all of you, that's all.

A coldness of silence and indifference was established all over the household that evening. Héloïse gave the order to the children to get the dishes done before going out. Alexis went to bed early. He was now living with the family. As for the children, they murmured their displeasure while hurrying up to put the dishes away in the cupboard.

Héloïse walked in the street her hands in the pockets of her weekday coat. She had not thought of wearing her other coat, her light green Sunday coat. She thought of it but did not want to stop and turn back home and change coat. She was frustrated and totally absorbed in the fact that her husband had refused to utter a single word about her new job at the boutique on Main Street. She was joyous at at the same time distraught by this breaking in her life as wife and mother. Why did things go so bad for her since she thought she had done the right thing, she asked herself. Yet she thought she had been a good person with everyone in her life, she reassured herself. Why did Alexis act that way with her? Why did he not love her more? Why did he not show it more? Probably he had never really loved her? That's was the truth. She told herself that she did not care and that she would continue to forge ahead of the objections and the obstacles in her life today. She would show them that the beautiful Héloïse is not made of lace nor marshmallow, but she is made of iron when she wanted to and made of tender love when circumstances presented themselves. She went towards a small street that cut into Main Street and opened up on a line of bars and taverns. She hesitated to go into one of the taverns and turned around to the small street that invited her to spend some time to drink one beer. She walked slowly not determined enough to get away from this line of attractions if not seductions. She started to feel soft in her body and in her soul. She could no longer make decisions on her own. There was no one in which she could confide. What to do? A past where drunkenness raised its head and took away confidence in the self and the capacity of doing what was right for herself and her family. She looked up at the sky but there was no indication of some intercession on its part. Not even a suspicion of compassion. She really felt alone and neglected. She lowered her head and closed her eyes. There was nothing that could prevent her from drinking a glass of beer, she murmured, only one, only one glass of beer to raise her morale. Only one to spend the rest of the day a little more at ease. Her heart was being torn apart and her soul wanted to get out of that beastly and troubling stupor. All of a sudden she found her willpower to do what gave her pleasure and not what forbade her to have a little bit of pleasure, "There' so very little pleasure in life, in my own life," she told herself. The hell with the intoxicating words of *Monsieur le curé*, the hell with the convictions reintegrated in a life that had been submitted to alcohol in a past where demons of alcohol came to render her a head full of remorse and worries. "I had such a crazy head," she said to herself, "not only the head but the soul also. Dieu help me to safeguard a head free of confusion and hallucinations, she shouted loudly. A passerby had just come to look at her and to run away from her and her folly. He believed that she was truly mad, that woman there. "Go to hell" murmured Héloïse, *"Vas chier"* go shit yourself.

Héloïse went into a bar not so illuminated, dim and somber and not too welcoming. It was **Bar Helena.** There was only one person sitting on a barstool that seemed lost in a dream surrounded by her cigarette smoke. She looked at Héloïse somewhat cross-eyed continuing to drink her glass of beer by little jolts of sips. Not a word from her mouth. The barman came to meet Héloïse and asked her what she wanted to drink. She hesitated and she even thought if she should not leave the bar and avoid the temptation of drinking. The barman was pressuring her and she could see in his eyes a veiled impatience but perceptible to her. She hurried to order a glass of beer knowing quite well that the first one would lead to another. Her mouth and her tongue were dry. She really wanted to drink. The barman brought her a draft beer, brown and somber. She drank it in one gulp and ordered another one. After two it was three then four. The late afternoon had already gone by with the hours lost in the comfort of a numbness mixed with a wave of stupor. Nothing told her to go home where someone would be waiting for her assuredly. Nothing.

Héloïse went inside her house around eleven at night. She was inebriated. Her coat was askew and she was, as the say, "woozy." She did not know who had brought her home. All was calm in the house, the lights out except for a dim little lamp that gave a yellowish feeble light. No one in the family came to get her. She fell on the couch all dressed and felt herself falling into a stupor of sleep and nightmare. She dreamed that she was being followed by monstrous giants and she was afraid of them. A terribly stupefying fear. She was losing her head so fearful of these beasts as black as the stove. She was out of breath. No way of extirping herself from it so abominable was the pursuit. She woke up when her husband shook her by her right arm and shouted, wake up. She felt dejected and humiliated by her condition of a woman coming out of her drunkenness, the eyes blinking and the mouth arid like a desert. She saw herself totally dressed, a pocketbook open with nothing inside.

—Wake up, Héloïse, and go wash your face with cold water.

—Yes.

—Go right away.

—I'm going. Don't give me a hard time.

—Where do you come from?

—I don't know. From somewhere.

—From somewhere? You come from a bar or a tavern where you drank for two days. I thought you were lost.

—You didn't come to my rescue? Didn't you look for me? I was only in town.

—In town? Yes, I looked for you but I didn't find you. Someone told me that you were gone with a woman and you two went running around, you galavanting creatures.

—But, I don't remember. I'm telling you the truth.

—The holy truth is hidden in your rush to hide yourself in alcohol. You had promised me that you wouldn't touch this darn crazy drink anymore. You had promised me.

—Yes, I know but it was stronger than me. When we have no more love to receive and to give to preserve us from the fault of drinking, well then we fall and fall again in the night due to drunkenness. It's so somber and it's night in this cavern of malicious demons.

—You only have yourself to blame.

—Yes, I know.

—But why did you do this?

—You should know, my husband. You should know.

—No, I do not know.

—That's your problem.

—My problem?

—Yes, your problem. You don't realize that you are the cause of my fall.

—Me?

—Yes, you.

—How's that?

—It's because you don't love me anymore.

—Not true.

—Yes, it's true. I don't feel your love anymore because you don't share your feelings nor your expression of love anymore. You have become the coldness of an extinguished brazier filled with darkness. Nothing. There's nothing to be expected of you. You have become the robot not only of the mill but also of the Charbonneau house. We, Alexis, us.

—I'm not a robot, Héloïse,. I'm human and I have feelings.

—Liar.

—Don't accuse me of being a liar. It's you who tells me lies by your conduct of an unnoticed presence as a woman and by your absence from home when your children and me we implore you to remain sober.

—That's why you accuse me of being a phantom of a spouse and mother.

—Yes, Héloïse, a phantom that we no longer recognize. You've changed, my wife. You're not the same, I tell you.

—I'm the same Héloïse that you married and who gave you your three children. It's the same person.

—No, Héloïse, you're not the same. You are in quest for something that I cannot give you. I believe that you are on a quest for a Timiskamengo, a phantom of a past romance.

—You're nuts, Alexis, you're absolutely crazy.

—Not crazy but crazy for no longer having you in my life

—Yet, I'm always there.

—No, you're only there in the absence of a woman who is looking for something she cannot find.

Silence.

—Well, Héloïse it's time to unhook ourselves one from another.

—What do you mean with that?

—I mean that we should separate once and for all. One goes one way and the other another way.

—Where am I supposed to go?

—You go wherever you want. I don't care. Silence.

—I don't want that, Alexis. It's too much for me.

—What do you want?

—I want us to stay together as in the good old days.

—The good old days do not exist anymore. It's finished all of that. Finished the dreams of belonging to a heritage that no longer suffices.

—Don't separate yourself from our heritage and don't blame me for our family troubles.

—Our troubles in the family are from long ago, my dear. No one spoke of it in the past and no one speaks of it today. No one. We hide all of that. We cover that up with good sermons of *Monsieur le curé* and the semblance of a forced smile.

—You're bad, Alexis. You have a hard heart.

—And you, my wife. Isn't your heart hard?

—Sometimes, maybe but not always. I have a tender heart and often broken by a lack of love that has inserted itself in my life as a woman. How can you not understand me?

—I don't understand you anymore. I don't understand you at all. What troubles you so much that I do not understand you anymore?

—I told you but you don't listen to me. With your ears, yes, but not with your heart.

—Here we go again with your romance stories.

—There's a need for it in the life of a woman, Alexis.

—You've become a woman Don Quixote, that's all.

—Don Quixote?

—Yes, Don Quixote de la Mancha. He's a great dreamer disillusioned by his dreams of knights errant. You also are the female counterpart of this knight *manqué*, a Madame Bovary.

—Don Quixote and Madame Bovary. Where do these people come from? I know nothing of this, Alexis. I'm not as educated as you, you know. I'm ignorant and well, dumb, I suppose.

—Madame Bovary is a character in a novel. She read too many romances and she threw herself into the craziness of prohibited love. She's a prostitute who abandons her marriage vows. A true slut of the streets. You are getting to be like her, Héloïse.

—Don't say that, Alexis.

—You have a good head on your shoulders but you don't used it wisely. You float in the air of your dreams of success and enterprises damned by obstacles of a strike or those of a lack of love that you fabricate.

—As for the strike, it happened and it wasn't my fault. The lack of love, it's altogether true in my life.

—So you don't remember the love given voluntarily by your mother and your father and especially that of Célie who had a great love and saved you from being a sick being lingering with nothing to do as a bedridden child.

—Oh, yes, my dear Célie. I will never forget her and her benefits towards me. Dear Célie had a great love for Timiskamengo who lost it by the wastefulness of time.

—Here you go again lulling your spirit with a love story.

—Yes, Alexis, it's very important in my life this love found in a heart softened by feelings of love.

—Get out of your feelings of love and live life, true life. Life is not made up of dreams but of everything that is living and real.

Lucienne, the Simple-Minded

—You don't understand a heart impressed by love.

—Go wash and get dressed properly and clean. I don't even know if the Mademoiselles Maheu will want to greet you with redened eyes and the face bruised by alcohol. You should have thought about it, Héloïse.

—Oh, the Mademoiselles Maheu. It left my mind. I didn't think about them. I have to believe that I was off the track all day Monday.

—Not only Monday but Tuesday also. It's Wednesday today.

—Not true. Don't tell me that I lost two full days.

—Yes.

Héloïse went to freshen herself while her husband left for work. The children had prepard themselves either for school or for work. They left without Héloïse noticing their departure. She did not want to go to her work at the boutique of the Mademoiselles Maheu because she felt glum about it. She felt depressed and she did not want people to see her like that. She decided to take the rest that had been refused by her recent drunkeness phase. She knew that she risked the confidence and good will of the two Maheu sisters. She would ask them forgiveness for her absence and would insist on working without wages for two days for the lost time. She knew she needed to pay a certain retribution for her fault in neglecting her job, her duty and her self-esteem. She slept until her husband came in from his job at the mill. There was no long conversation that evening. Everything had been said before. Now silence reigned and the supper was eaten in total silence with very few words except for Héloïse who asked her husband where were the children. He answered that they were either with friends or with the neighbor Madame Laverrière whom Joseph-Arthur esteem greatly. Héloïse asked herself if she as a good mother or not for the children. She did not dare say it out loud for she was afraid of the reponse.

After some short conversations the following morning, Alexis decided that the time had come for the definitive separation of himself and his wife. That everything had been said about that and nothing could reconcile them if not tear them apart forever. Alexis told Héloïse that he would like to remain friends with her and that she would get money from him so that she would be able to survive this last alcoholic catastrophe. He told her that he was leaving her the house, that is to say the rent, and that he would pay it every week. It would be up to her to take care of it and feed herself the best she could. He reassured her that he would always be available to come to her assistance if she ever needed him. As for the children, Hermance had already decided to leave for California where she would seek a job in San Francisco and she was going to live with her friend, Suzanne Underwood. Joseph-Arthur did not want to leave his father and he had decided to live with him in an apartment next to the mills. He was hoping of attending high school in Newmarket. He would be the first of the Charbonneaus to go to a secondary school. He wanted to become an accountant. As for Lucienne, she had told her father that she would never leave her mother and that she would live with her as long as her mother would want her with her. Everything was decided before the definitive separation of the parents. Héloïse could not get over this. All was decided without her participation, she told herself. Everything was done without her consent, not even one word. Héloïse was at a point of tears of desperation. However, she accepted everything with the resignation of a religious who gives herself to the Lord with the expression of her solemn vows. Moreover, she had become a penitent for she wanted at all cost to to expiate her sins of alcohol. Penitence for a good québécoise Catholic like Héloïse was the only way to expiate and wash her sins against God and her family. It had to cause pain, said people, pain to the body and especially the soul. They established all kinds of penitence such as prayers kneeling down for hours, fast and abstinence, the hair shirt for some, the offer of one's own will to a severe but merciful God. Héloïse decided to follow the road of penance in order to put put herself in just order with God and her family that she had offended. She opted to suffer rather than avenge herself against the only beings that had merited her love. That is why she accepted everything without a word of regret and without pity in her heart.

However, she found nothing to erase the sorrows of a lost love. Timiskamengo appeared so very often in her memory and in her heart as a woman. This image could not be eradicated much like a sacrament or a solemn vow that has an indelible character for a soul solemnly vowed for life. What sacrifice could she not make in order to repair her faults and calm if not deaden the gnawing worm of remorse. What had she done wrong in her life? Héloïse asked herself. Nothing.

But had she done enough good for her daughter Lucienne, the simple-minded? That's what she asked herself, enough to have a mind full of worries. Poor Lucienne whose perverse fate has caused me so much sorrow, she murmured. Why her and not the others? Yet there are other retarded beings on this earth, but why her? Why? Why? My heart is sick and the soul is crushed. All these why's that I cannot stop pronouncing are yet the sign of my reasoning about the simple minded that's my poor Lucienne... I know that Alexis and even Lucienne herself used to tell me to stop asking why and to continue living fully my existence as a woman...but I could not do it.. It was stonger than me.

Alexis came once or twice a week to visit Héloïse and bring her fresh fruits and a few vegetables to make hot soup(she so loved vegetable soup) as well as some small pasteries or jams. He knew what she loved and he wanted to satisfy her cravings that she neglected buying something to satisfy them. Sometimes Joseph- Arthur accompanied his father but he did not stay long. It seems that natural attachment for his mother had been reduced by the difficulties and especially the abominable episodes of drunkeness on her part who fell, one day to another, fell from her identity crisis as a mother and a woman. She plunged herself into the straying that alcohol granted her. Joseph-Arthur was still young but he wasn't so young that he couldn't feel the faults of a mother taken with alcohol. With time, Joseph-Arthur stopped going to visit his mother in spite of his father's angry pleadings.

Lucienne did not abandon her mother in her distress in spite of not fully understanding the erring conduct and the vacillating depression of her mother. She tried to encourage her the best she could but too often Héloïse would pull back into her shell and refused to accept her daughter's encouragement. "I should be the one who encourages you, not you encouraging me." said Héloïse on a grave and humiliated tone. However, Lucienne did not stop telling her good words in regards to her way of seeing things. That things would fix themselves and that the future seemed to be rosy for her and her mother.

—You're too optimistic, my dear Lucienne. You don't see things the way I do. There was a time when I enjoyed the top of optimism but that has now disappeared, devastated by the reality of pessimistic situations that gnaw at the soul and the heart if not the head. Oh, youth gives itself easily to optimism without knowing the results of maturity. The world in which we live is not an earthly paradise but a hell where suffering and sorrows do not stop ravaging us. You'll see some day what I'm telling you is true.

—But 'man you don't have the courage you once had. You let yourself fall into a mournful depression and you don't want to get out of it, and that's why you go to bars to buy forgetfulness and comfort. This comfort is not permanent. It's a temporary comfort that leads to nothing.

—You're teaching me the lesson now?

—No, but I'm trying to bring you comfort my way, the best I know how. I'm not too well educated and I know I'm retarded. I'm simple-minded. You remember?

—Yes, but you have the talent with words and memory. That counts for something.

—Yes, for instances of clairvoyance, but not for a life where reason and math are cut off. I'm not like others, you know.

—Often better than others. You have a heart. You know how to heal and that's a gift.

—You know maman what I would like in life, it's to be able to appreciate music. Not only appeciate it but also play pieces of music with an instrument. But I don't have the capacity to do so. I'm too simple-minded. There's not much I can do except wash the dishes, scrub the floors and do the cleaning. Everybody can do that. I'm not only simple-minded but talent-simple. The *Bon Dieu* has shut the door when he was distributing talents to his creatures. I only have one, It's to scrub with my rag and scrub the dishes. I have no talent to go and seek a job that demands a level of intelligence over and above what I have. I know that I'm dumb and too simple-minded to learn a craft like others do.

—Don't denigrate yourself like that, my dear. You have what others don't have, the frankness of heart and soul. Only, it takes you an extraordinary effort to do what you want. However, you can do it once you put your head in gear and you struggle for results that are worth it. But it takes you an extraordinary effort while for others it's a lot easier. You must not get discouraged and lose the strength of both spirit and soul. Those forces are eminent in you. Believe me, you can heal.

One day, it will be your calling.

—Merci, maman, but I have a great difficulty in appreciating what you are telling me.. I'm simple-minded and that's all.

—Stop saying that. You are not so simple-minded as that. I'm going to do with you what I should have done a long time ago, but I did not do it.

—What?

—Instruct you slowly with all my strength and capacities that I received from *le Bon Dieu*. I must admit that I failed in that domain. *Le Bon Dieu* gave me three children and I did not do what was necessary for the simple-minded one. Yes, simple-mindedness does not mean a lack of spirit, but a certain lack of refined intelligence. Thus, I'm putting myself to work right away to assure you of my efforts for you and the instruction you deserve... The best I can, I tell you, the very best I can. That's all. As for the music, we're going to ask your father to pay for music lessons for you. He won't refuse you, I'm sure.

—Do you think that your plan will work for a simple-minded like me?

—Stop saying that. You are simple but not that complicated. Simple enough to teach you something that you like and you will retain in a well-animated future. Your destiny wills it, my dear. It's written in the stars.

—Yes, in Van Gogh's stars on a canvas in some museum.

—You know Van Gogh?

—Yes, of course. I know something about him and his paintings. "*La Nuit Étoilée*"/Starry Starry Night is one of my favorites.

—You never told me that you were studying art.

—Yes, I did it at the boarding school but they took me away from there, do you remember?

—Yes, one of my errors in your youthful life. I wanted so much for you to grow up in wisdom and in intelligence that I did not take in consideration the progress that you made over there. It's because I listened to the rumors that ran around this convent. Too bad.

—I could have learned better if they had let me stay there. The nuns taught me well and I learned fast with them. It was, if you remember, their methods and their *savoir-faire*, their therapeutic know-how for a retarded like me.

—It's my fault. Forgive me for my furtive action so impardonable. I didn't know that my action would be so harmful.

—It's not your fault maman. It's no one's fault. All that you wanted to do was centered on my benefit as far as a young retarded like me.

—Yes, but I should have known better.

—It's part of the past that darn affair. Let's put our two heads together and resolve the problem of my retardation.

—I know that I'll never be able to change things and solve this problem totally, but at least I will try to do my best to render your life less tangled and more promising. I will not put obstacles on the path of your success in your life, the one you will lead especially when I stop living. You'll be all alone without a compass in life. Not that I'm a good compass but something to offer you of all my experiences in my life. I'm not null, I'll have you know.

—I know maman. However don't worry about my future for I'll get along just fine. I'll learn to survive by educating myself to think more clearly and more reasonably. I can, you know.

—Yes, you can once you put your hand on the wheel. That's what people say.

So Héloïse began to undertake Lucienne's education with the fervor of a saintly woman who wants at all cost make herself not only useful but generous towards a beloved one. She showed Lucienne how

Lucienne, the Simple-Minded

to mend and darn, how to baste the hem of a dress, how to wash and iron one's clothes, how to light a gas stove, and how to take care of a house from top to bottom. Lucienne already knew how to clean but her mother told her that she did it fast and not too diligently. Then Héloïse spent long evening hours instructing her daughter so that she would deepen her knowledge of words and sentences. She spent more time and insisted on math since Lucienne had difficulty with numbers. Héloïse tried to put in her head methods of managing her property and put money aside for the future.

Unfortunately, Lucienne ignored the value and importance of money. She had never managed it by herself. She relied on her mother or her father. Progress could be seen in her little life with her mother but there were often some hitches. Her mother used to tell her not to get discouraged for with time, there would be well-earned progress.

As for Héloïse. she threw herself into volonteer work and got to be successful at it by her strength of willpower that merited some praises from those with whom she worked. Her health of mind and body got better. She ended up by conquering, it seemed, the demons of the past.

Once Héloïse passed in front of the boutique of the desmoiselles Maheu and she saw them standing up with their arms crossed waiting for the clientele to come assuredly to buy hats or some jewelry. Héloïse remembered the scene when she announced to them that she was leaving. It seemed to her that the demoiselles were not too disappointed for she could see in their faces a certain contempt if not the trace of disdain for their employee who had dared to do what she did.

They had supposed a conduct pushed by drunkeness that had spread not only in the neighborhood but all over town. Moreover, she had found them a bit snobbish, real angry old maids in the depth of their souls convinced that their sense of morality was ideal. They wore rigidly and coldly this morality pushed to an extreme and they wanted at all cost to impose it on one and all. Héloïse had felt repugnance for that kind of behavior. At first, Héloïse had found them delicate in their way of expressing themselves and sympathetic towards all the gentle ladies that frequented their boutique. But Héloïse learned afterward that they were filled with contempt for each and everyone of them by murmuring in a low voice to one another how they found the eye makeup of one, the red lipstick on another's lips, the way another one had put powder on her face, or the hairdo on yet another, never a good word for any of them. Héloïse found them hypocritical, petty and mean. These demoiselles with pinched noses made remarks on the posture of one while they did not like the skirt of another for it did not match with the blouse, too mismatched they said in a low voice. Héloïse did not regret for having escaped from them in spite of the fact that she regretted that the departure was done with a lack of sobriety on her part.

The volunteer work was going so well for Héloïse that she felt very good about it and she took advantage of her free time to help out Lucienne who found these moments beneficial. She devoured everything her mother gave her as far as precisions were concerned such as with words and sentences as well as math and especially with advice hinging on intellectual matters. She showed her how to ask questions, questions that are linked to other questions asked and the problem mentioned. Not that her advice was philosophical or greatly intellectual but of an integrity modeled on common sense. Héloïse had found a way of clarifying things so that her daughter could better understand them and so participate in a way valuable and sensible in discussions produced. Héloïse was proud of this.

If each day brings its sorrows then each day also brings the delights of feeling intimate with one's feelings and desires. This was the case for Héloïse these days. Her heart was filled with joy upon seeing that her daughter Lucienne was progressing from day to day in her struggles with retardation. Rather she asked herself if Lucienne was really retarded or if it was a question of intellectual retardation not as serious as being fully retarded. She started reading all kinds of manuals on intellectually retarded and the brain problems associated with it when it comes to mental faculties as well as cases of nevrosis and psychosis. She often confused the librarian with her questions and worries with her research.

The librarian could not always answer her questions often mixed with incertitude and confusion. Finally, Héloïse decided to abandon reading these manuals too advanced for her ordinary intelligence and not developed enough by a formal instruction. At least, she had tried to understand the problem with the retarded a far as her daughter goes.

Seeing her mother leaning over a pile of books each night after supper, Lucienne asked herself why maman spent so much time and energy on a problem that could not be solved with a pile of books. At least, Lucienne was grateful in her heart for all the efforts spent on her and her so-called problem. However, she did not want to interrupt the readings of manuals that her mother was seriously doing "At least, maman is occupied reading and that keeps her against the troubles and worries of alcohol," she murmured.

Héloïse and Lucienne saw less and less of Alexis and still less of Joseph-Arthur. The months were slipping by more and more with their daily activities. Then Héloïse adhered more firmly to volunteering. She sometimes begged Lucienne to join her and those who participated in the social and volunteer activities. She wanted her daughter to learn how to socialize better and with her heart in it.

However, Lucienne already had in herself the talent to meet people and to engage herself in any conversation. She had, people said, always a nice disposition and a nice smile. It was an ace in the hole for her which kept her simple-minded but open to every disposition of simplicity of heart and soul. Simplicity for Lucienne was not only an ace in the hole but a virtue that gleamed in her and manifested itself with words and actions. Héloïse recognized more and more that Lucienne was growing up with an opening of soul that she had not realized up to this point. She often told herself all the efforts towards her daughter, this simple-minded, was worth the effort and that she, the mother, was recompensed above and beyond. Certainly, there was at times some hitches in their humble lives together, but they disappeared the moment that Lucienne blossomed forth by her enthusiasm and her way of seeing things. Everything was a gift from God, she said to her mother, and everything must return to him by prayers and the little daily sacrifices. Héloïse believed her to be a growing mystic. Yet, the mother had not influenced the daughter in the domain of personal and individual spirituality. She even had avoided that domain in the education of her daughter for she herself remained almost indifferent to a spirituality strongly exercised.

One had to believe that this spiritual gesture on Lucienne's part came spontaneously from her. "I always learn something new from her, " Héloïse told herself.

One fine October day when he leaves started to change colors, they heard in town the sirens of the firemen. It was to signal that there was a fire somewhere. That place was the Cushnoc mill. It was a Monday morning like any other Monday mornings except there was tension in the air as if there was imminent danger that had been introduced in the environment. People said to one another that there was an enormous sword suspended over their heads. Their fate was affected by a morbid tension in the air. Hearing the sirens blasting, they became very fearful.

Their daily lives were in danger and the Cusnoc that employed so many employes was in danger of losing a good part of its employees. Not only their lives but their wages each week. Wages were important to them. They were the insurance against debt and misery. No wages no well-being for the families affected by this troublesome danger. It would be the torments dealing with the troubles and worries of having to find money to live on. Could these poor mill workers survive the catastrophe? Would the fire devastate not only the buildings and certain departments but tear from them their jobs once and for all? They were talking of transferring the mill down south where there was no union with its demands, said to be ridiculous. Sometimes Alexis used to talk about it to Héloïse. He used to say that if the company moved south, it would be a catastrophe for hundreds of workers who lived day to day to earn a low salary but reliable for their everyday needs. They had learned to live without spending for nothing. Those who did not have the bad luck of sickness or financial reversals, they could save modestly and put money aside for the days when they got old, they said. They counted on the wages of each and every week and especially the company who gave them their earned money. Without the mill, without the wages was the emptiness and the end of the road that led to either success or failure. Many of them thought of returning to Quebec, but the farms were already sold and many relatives had disappeared, death or whatever. The dream of returning to a time when they all helped one another and lived as a community in a village centered on the parish church and its *curé* was almost totally gone. Moreover, the farms and their lands produced nothing and they were worth nothing too. That was the reason why they had moved to the States to look for work that would fill the empty pockets of the emigrants. They had found it in the mills of New England such as the Cushnoc in Newmarket.

The fire was in the departments of the spinners and weavers. There was practically no male hands in these two departments except for the loom fixers such as Alexis Charbonneau. The fire had spread throughout both departments where the spinners and the weavers had hurried to flee this conflagration that threw a great fear in each and every worker including the loom fixers. There were loud shouts while the workers were going hurly-burly in every direction wherever they could find exits. Unfortunately, the exits were wrongly indicated and there were not enough of them to handle these hard-breathing women. Too few exits, they said. Too few exits for so many people in fearful flight. Not adequate enough, very dangerous, people said. All these workers were trying to find a way to flee fom this imminent menace that incited them to a riot.

Fortunately, the loom fixers arrived on the scene to guide these women filled with fear and panic to the two exits. There were some who shoved and pushed others very hard in order to gain an exit. Others afflicted with a nerve crisis, did not know where to go and they were directed towards the back rather than the front and their actions tumbled the entire movement. The black and gooey smoke rose above their heads then went downwards towards their bosoms and came to engulf them so much so that they could hardly breathe. Then came the desperate cries"Save us, merciful God, save us...save us Virgin Mary" and then there were others who shouted, "Guardian Angel come to my aide...anybody, save us...Lord, Lord we're perishing." Evidently there were very few fixers and a lot of weavers.

Not sufficient enough to lessen the fear and guide each one to a safe haven. There were some who had fallen down on their stomach on the floor and couldn't get up so that they could not join the fleeing mass of workers.

Alexis arrived. He knew how to direct these disoriented women. He wanted to make them go out of the large side doors that led to the hallway that, unfortunately, was very dimly lighted. Alexis was suffocating from the smoke and was coughing almost constantly. However, he did not abandon his mission of control. While directing an entire file of weavers outside the weavers' room, Alexis noticed that the place where the weavers worked was blocked on all sides with enormous chariots of bobbins. He hurried towards the chariots so as to get them out of the exit ways. He opened one of the large side doors in order to let those who were pushing the exit door with such monstrous fearing strength.

They were all tumbling and started to shout like wild beasts in the process of saving themselves in spite of the efforts of a calm and able man. They got out so fast and with such wild power that they flattened to the floor their poor savior, Alexis. He remained incapable of getting up and breathing normally. He felt the heat of the enormous fire and its thick smoke surrounding him like a black mortuary cloth. He lost consciousness and woke up later in a small clinic with a nurse at his side. She was trying to give him oxygen for his lack of respiration. She also examined him for his burns. Then she decided to send him right away to Mercy Hospital. The ambulance carried him away with the loud cry of the siren that pierced his ears but assured him that he was going to get good care once he arrived at the emergency room. Everything was hazy and loose in his head and he lost consciouness from time to time to wake up somewhat shaken by what had just happened at the mill that was called *le moulin*.

Once at the hospital and the burns on his face and arms were relieved, Alexis was released from the emergency room and transferred to the department of the respiratory therapy for he still had the problem of respiration. They advised him to stay in the hospital for a while until he regained his normal respiration. He asked the doctor who was taking care of him how much time and he answered him that he did not know. That his case was severe enough to send him to a hospice where they would treat asphyxiation cases and pulmonary ills. "It's that serious?" asked Alexis. "Yes, Monsieur Charbonneau, as serious as that."

So they transferred Alexis after four days in the hospital to the Newberry Hospice a bit outside of the center of town in Newmarket. They told him that he would be under the special care of a therapist specialized in respiratory insufficiency. He was called Doctor Lupinsky. He came from Poland and he had emigrated to the United-States when he was twelve years old with his parents and his two sisters. He had obtained his doctorate in medicine from Harvard University. He had a very good reputation. He spoke three languages, Polish, French and English.

—First of all, Monsieur Charbonneau, I assure you that we will do our best to reestalish you in good health in spite of your pulmonary difficulties. The're quite serious but I believe with time and the good care over here you will return home safe and sound without too many residues of a respiration damaged by the intense heat of the fire caused by the conflagration in the mill and especially the noxious smoke that damaged your lungs.

—What does all of that mean to a man who hasn't much education?

—It means very simply that you must submit to a therapy of restoration with the aide of a respirator.

—For how long, doctor?

—For quite some time. Six months, eight months or more, that depends on the pace of your rehabilitation.

—All that time?

—Well, they're pulmonary troubles that demand a particular care with a long duration.

—Will I get over this?

—Yes and no.

—Yes and no?

—I do not want to lie to you, Monsieur Charbonneau, in cases like yours there arise sometime dangers and upsetting feelings that are given rise by a hematosis affected *degrandis*.

—What?

—I will send you the therapist specialist and he will explain all of that to you in words that will not blur the intelligence of a worker like you.

—I know my intelligence is not strong but it's not blurred. The worker is not simple-minded. He knows things thay even those with a high diploma like you do not know. He knows how to live and follow common sense.

—We'll see, Monsieur Charbonneau, we'll see... With that he left and did not return to see him again.

Alexis remained for a long time in the Hospice Newberry therapeutic hall. For several months. This embarrassed him profoundly since he could no longer provide for the needs of his wife who stayed alone with Lucienne without work and without financial resources other than those that Alexis gave her. Now, he would not be able to do it. He was nailed to a bed and to a machine that helped him with his diminished respiratiion. "For a long time," he told himself, "for a very long time."

Héloïse came to visit him two, three times a week, after having visited him every day immediately following his entrance into the hospice. She went with Lucienne who tried at each visit to make her father smile by telling him little funny stories. Sometimes, Héloïse and Lucienne met Joseph-Arthur in the long gray corridor of the hospice who also came to visit Alexis. The three of them had short conversations and Joseph-Arthur told them that he was in his last year in high school and was planning to go to the university if the occasion and especially the money presented themselves. Héloïse tried to encourage him but she admitted to him that she could not help him with money. She depended on the financial help of her husband who was now out of work on account of the gasping circumstances of the Cushnoc fire. Joseph-Arthur told her that he did not count on her at all and understood her lack of money and that he would get along without too many difficulties. Héloïse could not find the words to tell him that she felt a profound pain in her heart not being able to help him out when he needed it so much. Joseph-Arthur added, "Don't worry 'man, I'm tough and I have plenty of resources at hand. I will make my future by myself." She answered him by saying, "Just don't forget your heritage and your religion."

—Once I'm on my own, I'll adapt very well to anything. I'll need to.

—That's alright but don't lose what you have, what formed you and gave you your identity.

—You know 'man the ideas of language, heritage and religion don't merit my attention and my efforts in order to succeed in life. Damn all of that cause it's not worth it. It's not worth shit.

—Don't you dare talk like that. That's not the way I raised you. Not the way your father raised you.

Joseph-Arthur lowered his head without another word. Héloïse then told him that he was going to lose his true identiy and would be assimilated into a public at large only to find that this public had no sensibility for ethnic values gained by so many people in the past and transmitted to their children and grandchildren and so on. Joseph-Arthur answered her, "Who cares, 'man?"

After five months of pulmonary therapy, Alexis insisted on going home so that he could eat a healthier and more appetizing nourishment. He was told he could not do that since he still needed several sessions of therapy and that he could not live alone by himself at home. Héloïse offered her own care and the care of the house as well as the offer of accepting Alexis in her own home even though they had separated for good. Alexis refused her offer since he did not want to become a burden as well as becoming totally dependent on her. She tried to tell him that she and Lucienne would be able to care for him conveniently once released from the hospice. However the discharge did not happen. Alexis fell again in his pulmonary troubles followed by unexpected complications. His case demanded much more care not planned but required. So the poor man fell into a depression and did not want anymore visits no nourishment and no more particular care.

They even had to tie him to his bed with leather straps in order to control his fits of depression at times lugubrious. He just did not want those straps that tied him down and forced on him against his will. He was a man of pride and strong will.

He did not like to be told that he was not capable to regulate his own life and do what he wanted to do in spite of his pulmonary incapacity. He simply could not accept the misery of being incapable of living without depending on whomever or whatever. Misery of having to do what one doesn't want to do and the misery of not knowing if one will get better with time, he told himself. "It's dark misery of living tied to a hospital bed with men and women who don't even know us," he told Héloïse one day when she was visiting him even though he did not want visits. Héloïse could not find anything to say or do to relieve Alexis' strong desire to subtract himself from this care that he did not want. She found nothing to give him back his courage that he had in the past and used it to give courage to his own. She herself began to lose courage and think often of a good stiff drink to relieve her of her own troubles. Fortunately, Lucienne always came to her aide telling her to pray and ask God and the Virgin Mary to give her courage. Lucienne had become a devout person of prayers and sacrifices in which she had great confidence. On her part, Héloïse was pulling through with the little money she earned here and there added to Lucienne'a minimal salary. This one now worked in a religious article shop. Life was thin, as Héloïse said, but it was a life where love and good understanding existed.

One Tuesday morning, Héloïse received a telephone call at her neighbor's house because she had no phone at her house, to hurry because her husband was dying and she should get to the hospice as soon as possible. The neighbor's husband, Monsieur Lévesque, gave her a ride in his car. Lucienne accompanied her mother and both of them went inside the hospice with trepidation and a great doubt that they would see Alexis alive one more time. The pulmonary therapist met them at the door. He led them to Alexis' room. Alexis was very pale and his face was quite thin. He hardly breathed, only with quick and hard breaths. His breath was feeble and trembling. His eyes were glazed over, his cheeks hollow and his nose pinched. He looked like a dying man suffering with the last breath of a dying man. Héloïse asked the therapist if there was anything that could be done so that his life could be spared. The response was negative and cold on the part of the therapist who had taken care of Alexis for a long time. Héloïse could not understand why the therapist had no more compassion than that for his patient, Alexis. Alexis opened his eyes and recognized his wife and his daughter for an instant. What came out of his trembling lips was a single word, "*Merci*" and then "I can't anymore." Alexis fell asleep in the peace of a man watching the sweetnees of eternity. Lucienne came close to his bed and kissed her father's forehead and murmured, "Go papa, go to your eternal rest where everything will be erased and rendered into grace."

—Your husband, Madame Charbonneau, gave us a hard time, you know. He did not want to cooperate any longer with us at the end. We had to restrain him with straps and prohibit him from fighting so much. He was a hardheaded man your husband. He was not docile at all, said the therapist on an exasperated tone of voice.

—You do not know my husband at all. He's gentle and sweet like a lamb and generous like a prince. He's not hardheaded. He's got *du casque* my husband but he's not obstinate with any hardness of heart. Not at all.

—*Du casque?*

—Yes *du casque*, audacity. Not full of wind but audacious in his deliberations and his actions. Not hardheaded either.

—It's true that I didn't know him well enough to sound his motivations and his desires to live a full healthy life. I gave him my best care.

—He had such a hard time breathing as you well know yourself that he couldn't go on. That's not being hardheaded but wanting to get back to good health and the dignity of a man who did not want to rely on the sad offerings of others. He knew how to fight for himself and for the others. You did not apparently recognize his tender qualities of a life full of hope and vim. He is not a man who abandons easily the game. No, he was a brave and courageous person, my Alexis. He knew how to love and wanted to be loved all of his life. It's going to be hard to live without him.

The therapist did not feel capable of answering her with compassionate and sincere words. He nodded his head and left without saying a word.

—Let's go. Let's get out of here, said Lucienne to her mother. I have had enough of this hospice as cold as ice in January.

Lucienne and Héloïse left arm in arm without saying any other word than, *"Merde."* shit. Poor Alexis, he had been Héloïse's knight in shining armor, armor of defense and compassion but not the knight errant of love and romance. That was true of Célie and Timiskamengo and Héloïse knew it.

The following day, Héloïse left with Lucienne to make funeral arrangements for her husband. She wanted a funeral worthy of her spouse and with the dignity of québécois values. Unfortunately, there were not enough finances to give Alexis a funeral worthy of a convinced patriot, as she called him. It was a very simple funeral and absolutely modest in the church of Sainte-Thérèse-de-l'Enfant-Jésus in Newmarket. The *curé* Pontbriand had known how to answer Lucienne's demand in granting the small family a low mass without chant and without grand ceremony. It was she who took the first word while her mother could not explain why her husband and her were separated but not divorced. That she wanted in no way or with no intention on her part of accepting a *libéra* rather than a mass. The *curé* had understood the situation and he had showed an attenuated condescendance towards her and her desire to give her husband a full funeral worthy of her Alexis.

—You know, Madame Charbonneau, that the Church does not allow full funerals in a case like yours and your husband's, but I understand better now your situation and I allow myself to grant you at least a low mass without grandiose ceremonies that ordinarily we grant fervent parishioners who remain faithful to their Catholic cult and to their Church who enjoins them to not abandon their faith.

—Alexis and I, we always kept our faith.

—That's good, Madame Charbonneau, and that's reason why I granted you a concession on my part as *curé*.

—Thank you *Monsieur le curé*.

—You have a very nice and gentle daughter. Lucienne is truly a good example of faith in action and conviction. She's a true devout one as I have seen.

—Yes, she is more devout than me.

Lucienne looked at her with piercing eyes. Héloïse knew at that very moment that she had said too much.

Alexis' funeral was very simple and modest as the *curé* had announced. A handful of neighbors and two or three friends were in assistance. Hermance was at the far end of the Continental United States and could not afford a plane ticket to New Hampshire. She sent a sympathy card to her mother in which she expressed her condolences. Joseph-Arthur refused to enter the church because he no longer set foot in a Catholic church, he had said to his mother. All that he allowed himself was to wait on the church steps and watch the casket go by. It was draped with a black cloth of some kind. He was no longer there when the small funeral file was exiting. Héloïse was disappointed and sad.

After the burial of Alexis in a small cemetery adjoining the parish cemetery for they did not bury officially non-parishioners in the parish cemetery but buried them in a cemetery, convenient but not blessed. Héloïse told Lucienne that she would have preferred burying Alexis in a cemetery in Quebec, but money was lacking. "If some day I fall into money enough to bury him over there, I will have him transferred as soon as I can" she told Lucienne.

The days of mourning went by slowly but peacefully while Lucienne went to the cemetery to place eah day some flowers that she picked in the garden of a neighbor called Alma Laverrière. They were tiger lilies followed by fire-engine red gladioli that wilted fast in the full July sun. After the neighbor's flowers had terminated their season of blossoms, Lucienne went to pray at the gravesite of her father without bringing flowers. The neighbors noticed that she was faithful to her daily visits. When the wind and the rain arrived in November, Lucienne cut short her visits to the cemetery and only went once a week and then every second Wednesdays. The winter months arrived early that year and Lucienne could not displace herself in the snow and the ice to go and pray at her father's gravesite. All the same, she prayed for the soul of her papa for she could not pay for masses for his eternal rest as people usually did, people who had the two dollars for a low mass.

Héloïse had found herself a job at the corner laundry and she worked six days a week which gave her a salary of eighteen dollars per week. It was enough to pay her rent, buy food provisions for her and for Lucienne as well as pay the small debts that she had incurred during the week. Lucienne worked part-time at Madame Lacombe's house where she did the house cleaning of each week for the little old lady. It wasn't the *grand ménage*, spring cleaning and fall cleaning. It was only dusting the furniture, wash the windows, scrub with soap and water the stains on the kitchen floor, and clean the black stove. Sometimes Madame Lacombe would ask her to put the kitchen utensils in order since they were spread here and there. She also wanted her to clean the slits and cracks of the cupboards. She did not like the dirt in those cracks, she told Lucienne. Madame Lacombe was vey particular about the managing and care of the household.

Lucienne arrived home late in the afternoon, happy to have pleased Madame and satisfied of her work that earned her a very modest recompense. Madame gave her ninety cents per week. Héloïse found that only minimal as a salary and she told her daughter that Madame was taking advantage of her and her hard work. Lucienne answered that she did not preoccupy herself with the sum of money earned but the fact of working for the money was worth it. She was fully satisfied with her work and especially the little conversations with the old widow that she considered intimate. The old lady lived alone and she wanted someone with whom she could open her heart and chat, she told Lucienne. Lucienne considered herself the carry-on joy-basket for people like Madame Lacombe. Moreover, she enjoyed so much the visits she did with the old people. These people did not even consider her retardation. They did not even recognize her handicap. Lucienne was not really retarded, said her mother to whoever asked her about her daughter.

Lucienne, the Simple-Minded

She told them that Lucienne was simple-minded which meant simple-hearted and simple of soul to her. Be it that she was slow in her talents for learning and calculating numbers and things that were too complicated to her, it was the fault of bad interconnections in her brain, insisted Héloïse. She insisted even though she hardly knew what that meant. However, this did not mean that she had a poor intelligence and an inadequate way of managing things and doing things right. Lucienne could manage and do things very well, said Héloïse, and she did it without too much difficulty. Slow was the word that came to mind. However, those who observed Lucienne in her attempts to do things and in her speech, said that she was not really slow but meditative...and that she had a darn good memory, *une mémoire de chien*. Lucienne could remember such and such a date that touched upon her lived experiences and of those who lived close by. She could also remember the names of those who had touched her life. For example, she remembered the names of cousins that she had met once during a short visit in Canada. The others did not remember but she could without great difficulty.

Sometimes even, she could enumerate an entire series of events at a certain point in her life as well as the lives of others without losing the date and the places as well as the names of persons that were part of a given event. "It's a marvel of a memory," said the old uncle, Armand Bergeron, who had married the sister of Marie-Louise Beaufort of Batiscan. Many people were dazzeld by the fact that Lucienne whom they had known a long time ago could remember the names and events little known or even remembered by a girl that was recognized as simple-minded. "Imagine you people, that this is a person who is gifted with a rare and incomprehensible talent to those who knew her, said the old Jean Vêtineaux of Arthabaska county who had known Lucienne when he worked at the Cushnoc mill. He and his wife returned to Canada after the death of his mother in Batiscan. They had without a doubt recognized clearly the great talent of a simple-minded and then marvelled at what they called a phenomenon of nature and of an incomparable destiny. Another couple who had known her in Newmarket, Monsieur et Madame Edgar Neault, said that such a talent of the memory was irreconcilable with retardation of a young girl like Lucienne. As for Lucienne, she did not care at all about these remarks made about her. She lived, breathed God's air and everything was going fine with her, a simple-minded gifted with a talent that was quite rare and remarkable for her age and her mitigated intellectual capabilities.

Héloïse noticed that Lucienne went to see, from time to time, a lady who was called Ange-Yvonne Desrochers. This lady lived on Ashley Street right next to Monroe Street where the president of the Association of the Inheritors of the Good Grace of Divine Counsel lived. The members got together once a month to discuss a pre-established agenda and distributed by mail five days before the monthly meeting. Lucienne rarely got mail, sometimes a letter from her cousin Alberta Simard of Oakland, Maine. She was a Charbonneau and she had married a man named William Arthur Simard. The couple had no children. Lucienne had met her at the wedding of Marie-Ange Desroberts in Woonsocket, Rhode Island when Héloïse was invited to the wedding in Sainte Famille church. The wedding reception was held in the grand hall of l'Union Saint-Jean-Baptiste. It was at this wedding that Lucienne met Ange-Yvone Desroberts. She was the bride's sister.

Lucienne and Ange-Yvonne became friends quite fast. Lucienne had an open character but a little bit too naive when it was a question of religious movements or spiritual causes such as l'Association des Héritères de la Bonne Grâce et du Divin Conseil. The two of them had discussed the objectives of the association which was to establish links between the associated ladies and the organizations that had vowed themselves to the service of those who proclaimed the word of the Gospel and had become oblates of the Communauté des Religieuses de la Sainte Face. These ladies resided in the areas of Massachusetts, New Hampshire, and Maine. Lucienne was so impressed with the association and convincing words of Ange-Yvonne that she easily fell into her hands. Thus, Lucienne wanted to recruit if not everyone for the cause and the objectives of the Association, at least as many as she could. She talked about it day and night to whomever wanted to hear her. Her mother told her that she was too imprudent in her recruitment to the Association and that she did not even know what these ladies and their Association did. She asked her daughter what did the Association des Héritières de la Bonne Grâce et du Divin Conseil mean. Lucienne could not explain the definition of the words and the meaning as well as the objectives of this organization said to be spiritual. Héloïse told her daughter to ask the president the next time Lucienne would go to one of their assemblies to define the objectives and to give it to her in writing all that touched upon their official aim.

—If you cannot explain all of that to me, then you too cannot absolutely understand anything about this association and you should stay far from it and the associates. I believe that these ladies want to brainwash you with Inheritors of what, I ask myself, of good grace? The grace from whom and from what? A gift from heaven? Then the divine counsel? Do these ladies have a direct line to *le Bon Dieu* who grants them good counsel so that they can beg for money from those who have none? Or are they ladies of leisure that dream of ideals and plan means of keeping themselves occupied because they are lonely all day long? That affair means nothing to me. It's all an affair of snobs. Snobs who want to be intellectuals and spiritual beings. Hypocrites on top of that.

—But maman it's a beautiful association that has a spiritual aim and a very holy character, Madame Desroberts told me.

—Yes, some *saint-nitouche*, hypocritically pious, I'm sure.

—It's not like that maman.

—It looks to me too shady this affair. They want to draw you in with all these beautiful words and their holy slogans and I'm sure they will ask you for money. Isn't it true?

—Ange-Yvonne mentioned dues that all the members pay in order to support the cause.

—Yes, the dear cause. Everyone speaks of causes when it's a matter of money. How much are the dues?

—She told me twenty dollars every six months.

—Twenty dollars?

—I told her that I didn't have any money. That we were poor.

—You didn't need to tell her all our affairs.

—She answered me by saying that there were grants for people like me and that I need not worry.

—Yes, grants, grants of lies.

—Maman don't you want me to join them?

—That's not what I said. I only told you to be careful. This affair can fall on your nose later.

— I'd like to join this association simply because the president told me that this would benefit me. Specifically my soul.

—You don't need associations for the benefit of your soul. You pray, you make sacrifices, and you do good to everybody, I know. I'm a witness to that.

—But I want to do more.

—Well, pray for your mother who needs so many prayers. I suffer in the soul, my dear daughter, I suffer in the soul.

—I did not know, maman. You have made sacrifices all your life, on the farm in Canada, here in Newmarket and the loss of your enterprise, not to mention the dagger of separation with papa. On top of it all having a retarded daughter. It's a huge sacrifice for parents.

—Not at all, Lucienne. You are a benefit from heaven for me. Your father thought as much.

—It would have been different if I had been normal.

—Don't say that. It's not true at all. We take what heaven gives us and we appreciate it as such. That's all.

—I would have liked to be able to help you and papa. I would have earned enough money to keep you in good health and in good circumstances of well-being.

Whatever you say or whatever people think, I'm not normal. I have the intelligence of a poor beast. I'm like the donkey, difficult to understand and hard to take control over. If only I could change brain with someone who thinks clearly and calculates precisely.

—If's are difficult things.

Both of them started to laugh.

Early in the mid-October morning when a hasty frost had already entered the undergrowth of the valleys and the other lower parts where the cold accumulated fast and without delay, Lucienne went out of the house furtively and left heading for the parish church Saint-Antoine that was not her parish. She wanted to attend the six thirty mass in order to participate in the prayers after mass to plead the cause of a stigmatized one who had just died in Woonsocket. It was 1936. Her name, Marie-Rose Ferron. Lucienne had walked one and a half miles to get there.

Marie-Rose Ferron was born in Saint-Germain-de-Grantham in Quebec in 1902. Her parents moved to the United-States when the little girl was but three years old. They arrived in the city of Fall River, Massachusetts and took possession of their rent with nine other children. The father, a former metal smith by trade found a convenient job. Later, the family moved to Woonsocket, Rhode Island. It was there that the little Rose was bedridden for more than eleven years having received the stigmata of the suffering Christ. Later on, she had acceeded to the demand of praying and suffering for the amicable resolve in a Christian way the Sentinelle Affair in which Monsignor Hickey, bishop of Providence was implicated. He had excommunicated fifty-six parishioners for their opposition to his decrees. The renown of the stigmatized one was fast spreading throughout New England. It was thus that Madame Desroberts recognizing the sensibility of Lucienne for extraordinary spiritual cases such as that of Marie-Rose Ferron, this lady shared with her devotion to the "*petite Rose*", as she was called. Lucienne marvelled at the story of the stigmatized one and decided to join those who avidly proposed a séance of prayers each week for the beatification and later on the canonization of "*la petite Rose.*" Already there was a propagation of images, books and even relics of the young girl with the stigmata. At her death, more than fifteen thousand people visited her body exposed in a casket. All these anecdotes about Marie-Rose Ferron hit Lucienne's imagination up until she became harassed by them.

Her mother told her often that it was time to get rid of all of that and live in the present, but Lucienne kept her spiritual impressions of the young stigmatized girl inside her and refused to get rid of them. Lucienne rocked silently the dream that one day she herself would get the stigmata and would suffer with Christ crucified.

It was a way of redeeming herself and compensating for the retardation that bothered her at times.

Héloïse found herself alone on a weekday at the beginning of the fall season. She found herself incapable of getting up from her rocking chair where she loved to rock herself and read some pamphlet or an ad for the promotion of sales. She loved thumbing through some of the pages of weekly sales. This kept her alert and interested in each sale for she did not like to spend for nothing, said she to Lucienne who went with her mother to the city center to shop and purchase provisions. Lucienne loved these sprees with her mother that she called her adventures of knowledge and math. Lucienne projected the betterment of her knowledge up to now attenuated. She told her mother to comfort her that one day she would be proud of her simple-minded daughter for she would see a palpable progress in her daughter. Héloïse told her that she only expected progress of the heart and soul, nothing else. This made Lucienne smile until she exploded into a joyous and sincere laughter. Héloïse had the right way of making her come out with bursts of laughter.

Héloïse remained nailed to her rocking chair for at least four hours until Lucienne found her like that when she got home around five o'clock. Héloïse had suffered from a terrible headache all day long worst than the others that she had had for weeks at a time but she had not mentioned it to Lucienne for she didn't want to bother her with her personal problems. Lucienne had been to Saint-Antoine church for a séance of prayers for the "*petite Rose.*"

—Where do you come from so late in the afternoon? Still running around to séances of prayers for the little Ferron? asked Héloïse.

—I'm not running around. I do simply what my heart and my soul tell me. That's not running around. It's doing propagation of faith here at home and not overseas.

—It's Madame Desroberts who told you that? She's teaching you nice things, the madame.

—What do you mean by that?

—I'm saying that she has you in her hand with her sharp nails and she will never let you go. A real she-devil.

—Don't say that, 'man. She's a good Christian and a good friend.

—Do what you want, my dear. Do what you want. I'm not getting involved any longer. I'm tired of this and I'm at the end of my rope. My health is diminishing as you can see. Help me to get up from this darn chair. It's back hurts me terribly and my arms are weak from having to try and displace myself one way or another.

Come, help me, my dear. Your mother needs you. Come and do your sacrifice of the day. You'll offer it up for the souls in purgatory which includes the *"petite Ferron."* I'm sure she did not go to heaven right away. She must have had some imperfections on her soul and on her conscience. She wasn't perfect like all humans are.

—Don't say that 'man. You don't even know her. A stigmatized person suffers a lot and Marie-Rose has accomplished what Jesus told her with a great devotion and an immense accomplishment of sacrifices and mortification. If she's not in heaven today no one is.

—Come on, Lucienne, Marie-Rose Ferron is not as saintly as that. They're all rumors of old spinsters. They're also rumors of the *mangeuses de balustres*, eaters of balustrades, such as Madame Desroberts.

—'Man you are so hard in your evaluation of these people. You know nothing about them and you launch yourself in prejudices not defined by facts. Frankly, you astound me and you make me sound foolish on that matter. Yes, foolish in my simple-mindedness. I don't understand you anymore.

Lucienne hastened to go to her room and shut the door with a brusque and frustrated clacking. Bang!

—Hey! shouted the mother...you leave me alone in my chair without helping me. You have become hard of heart and despicable of spirit. I'm telling you that this affair of a saint and the stigmata are making you more simple-minded than you were before.

There was along moment of silence...crushing and heavy. Héloïse then murmured out loud,

—My head is turning...everything is turning...oh, my God I'm getting to be crazy...my Jesus, mercy... Have pity on me... Have pity on crazy men and women like me... Holy Virgin Mary, my head is splitting... I can't anymore due to my head.... I'm having a hard time... no one knows how...pity, oh, pity, oh my God.. I can't anymore...yes, I do have a very hard time with this life of misery and worries... There's nothing I can do to change things around...my God, isn't it crazy to come to nothing like that... I can't anymore...my head is splitting in half... The head... The head... How crazy have I become for not having seen how Alexis loved me in his own way... The head, oh, the head is turning, turning it turns like a foolish top...yet I loved him and love, love.... The head, the head, I'm becoming crazy enough to die...Alexis, come to my aid... I need you so much... I need your help so much... I need God's mercy so much also... I failed in my life... I committed errors, stupid and hard to understand...my God, my God, I can't anymore...yet I'm not drunk, I'm clear in my spirit but my head keeps turning so that I feel drunk like a debauched woman who doesn't know how to stop drinking... The head, the head... The head is splitting in half...oh, oh, oh, oh...

Héloïse fixed herself so that she could get up from her rocking chair, after so much effort on her part that she managed to direct herself towards her room where she lay down on her bed flat on her stomach. We could hear her murmur something that ended up as a desperate sobbing. She remained there all evening as well as the night until the wee hours of the morning.

Lucienne got up early and did not make any sound so as not to wake her mother who without doubt slept a profound sleep. She heard no sound in her mother's bedroom, not even a coughing not even a breath. After more than an hour, Lucienne decided to go and see what was happening with her mother. Probably she was unconscious and could not get up from her bed. Perhaps worse than that. She hastened to open the bedroom door and enter into the room that had been her mother's room for a very long time. She discovered her mother spread flat on her stomach on her bed. She did not move at all. Nothing. Not even her head and not even her little finger. She was cold at the touch. Lucienne was filled with horror and acute trembling. She cried out so loudly that her neighbor ran out of her house and rushed to her aid. Lucienne showed her mother laying down and not moving at all, no longer breathing and having no sign of life. She sobbed so much and so loud that her shoulders were trembling without stopping one moment, not one second. The neighbor took her by the shoulders in order to calm her down. Lucienne lost consciousness and the neighbor lay her on down on the floor and hurried to get a glass of water to give her. Lucienne opened slowly her eyes and noticed that she was lying on the floor. She started to sob again although the trembling had left her.

—Yes, I know it…said the neighbor…she is dead.

—Madame Lupien, I am alone, absolutely alone now. Alone like a abandoned one and simple-minded at that. Absolutely alone like a dog.

—You are not alone. You have friends like me who will take care of you the best we can.

—O, *ciel de Dieu, Sainte Vierge Marie*, help me. I am alone and I cannot do anything without you.

Silence. Without any words. Without the testimony of sobs. Not a single sound. Nothing but the tic-tac of the clock. Héloïse was dead. Lucienne left the room and went with Madame Lupien into the kitchen where both of them sat at the table in order to contemplate what Lucienne should do now. She was still filled with doubts and fear that the future for her would be a series of sorrows and misery.

Madame Lupien tried to console her by telling her that she had to make plans for her mother's burial. Yes, Héloïse was dead. Héloïse who had so much "*casqué*", audacity, who could not confront death with effrontery and bravura. She had thus lost the *toupet*, the cheek, as well as the *culot*, the nerve, facing invincible and biting death. It was a careless and distressing death. A death without expectation on the part of the victim for Héloïse was not expecting to face such a biting death. She had seen hers, that is her family, leave. She was expecting it. As for Alexis, she had seen that it really was an unexpected death and hard to endure for her and for Alexis who died in an unbearable *ennui*. On top of that, he died in a foreign land in a hospital that was cold and without mercy with strangers who seemed not to care at all for him as far as compassion and human support are concerned. Death, the darn death had used its sickle on them both.

• THIRD PART •

The Story of Lucienne Charbonneau Rafferty daughter of Héloïse Lanouette Charbonneau formerly of Batiscan, Québec

Lucienne, the Simple-Minded

After her mother's burial, Lucienne left with Madame Lupien to go and visit the *curé* of Sainte-Thérèse-de-l'Enfant Jésus- parish in order to have a low mass for the dead in particular for her mother and her father. She had a firm belief in the mystery of the holy mass in helping the souls in purgatory to expunge their pains of sin. Lucienne believed in the mercy of a compassionate and pardoning God.

She would not have wanted that her father and her mother languish in the darkness of purgatory especially in the eternal flames of hell. No, they had been too good as parents and then they had suffered too much in life to be eternally punished. That, she believed very firmly. She probably was simple-minded but she was not crazy, she told herself at certain times. She was satisfied to do what her heart told her to do and moreover she was accomplishing what her head asked her to do. She felt in harmony with her heart and her head and everything was going well for her. At least, she often told herself that during the course if the day.

With help from the neighbor, Madame Lupien, Lucienne tried to contact her sister, Hermance and her brother, Joseph-Arthur, but after having looked everywhere in the house, she found nothing to indicate where they lived. There wasn't even one Christmas card with a return address. One would have believed that Hermance would have sent a Christmas card once a year to her mother. As for Joseph-Arthur, well, thought Lucienne, he doesn't have enough genius or familial sentiment to find a single moment to send his mother a simple wish be it a birthday or Christmas card. Both of them are gone from the bosom of the family and will never return, she told herself. It's not worth anything to try and touch base with them, she thought. They would not even come. Madame Lupien suggested to her to go to city hall where she could get information on her sister and her brother but Lucienne told her that she had done her best to find them and that it would be useless to try and do more.

—Both of them are gone and I will not see them again. They don't have a heart the both of them. They cut themselves off from the family that maman had established for them, for me and for papa. They were links to the heritage of Batiscan, as she called them.

—Poor you, you have at least this that lasts, your heritage and its values.

—I'm telling you, Madame Lupien, that I am alone in the world, no sisters, no brothers, no uncles, no aunts, maybe a cousin somewhere, but I'm absolutely alone.

—It's so sad not to have anyone in whom to trust. I'm close to tears right now.

—Don't be sad on my account, dear lady, don't lose any feeling for me. I will make my own links, friendships that will last and flourish. I guarantee it. I don't have much intelligence but I have a heart and a will that do not bend.

Later on, Madame Lupien brought Lucienne to her house for supper. That's when the lady asked Lucienne if her mother had left a will. Lucienne asked her what exactly was a will.

—You don't know what a will is?

—No, Madame Lupien. I have an empty head and I don't understand those things.

—Well, a will is a large piece of paper on which is written the desires and the legs of the dead person. The will indicates what will be shared among the members of the family be it money, a house, a farmland or even precious jewelry. I myself have received from my mother a beautiful gold watch that used to belong to my grandmother Lajoie.

—What does legs mean?

—Well it means the disposition of the goods of the dead person. It's to avoid the family quarrels. Like that, everything is done in writing and we have to follow the directives after the death of a person. The will is very important for everyone especially for us who come from a québécois heritage.

—Maman had nothing, absolutely nothing except some used and cracked dishes and a few pieces of furniture that came from the Vincent de Paul. Maman often told me never to mention to others that our belongings came from the hands of charity. No money either and no jewelry that is worth much of anything. My mother was poor. Poor like the devil, my father would say. *"Pauvre comme la galé"* Poor like scabs, my mother would say. You see that I have nothing to share with my brother and my sister. Like that, no quarreling. As for the will, I have no doubt that neither maman nor papa had one. If there was one, I've never seen it with my eyes and maman never told me about it.

—Like that, you are really poor.

—No, Madame Lupien. If I am poor in goods, I am rich in friends and in God's good graces. I don't want anything and I assume that nothing is better than being cut off from all worldly riches. That brings only worries and sometimes troubles. It's much better to live a simple life tempered by detachment. We attach ourselves too much to things today and then we always want more. We're never satisfied. I know of too many who live like that. They're not happier. If I want money, I'll earn it, that's all. As long as I can live without depending on others.

That's what troubles my mind as simple as it is.

—Don't worry, my dear. You'll live and you will enjoy your life. I have great confidence in you and your capacities as a woman.

Lucienne continued to go to the séances of prayers in Saint Antoine church every week. She wanted to pray for Marie-Rose Ferron to be more and more recognized for we had, it seems, lost her memory. Few people talked about her now and her cause was abandoned by Monseigneur Hickey. Lucienne did not know why. Yet the little Rose had not wilted. She continued to open according to Madame Desroberts who always tried to enthuse Lucienne in the pursuit of this spiritual cause. There were hardly any ladies who went to pray at Saint Antoine church, only a handful. Lucienne thought that things would fix themselves since she was by nature an optimist. However, things hardly got better. Lucienne was disappointed. She thought of leaving the séances and no longer think about the cause of Marie-Rose Ferron but she could not help it.

The weeks fell into months and Lucienne's thoughts were directed towards her new job at the mill. Lucienne had found herself a job at the Cushnoc by virtue of the fact that they took pity on her but especially because her father had worked there and he had gained a good reputation. She worked in the spinning department. She took care of three spinning frames. She had learned fast. A demoiselle Vaillancourt had showed her how, all the necessary features to become a good spinner. She was good at it and adroit with her hands. The bobbins spun in her hands while she was placing the empty bobbins one by one in place on the frame. Then, she took off the ones that were full and threw them in a big wooden container. Lucienne learned very fast with her and in a short period of time she could imitate the speed and the adroit manner of Mademoiselle Vaillancourt. Lucienne repeated the operation of spinning many times during the workday. The second-hand, a Monsieur Theroux, was impressed by her dexterity and her drive. He often told her that she was doing a good job and that he admired her quality of work.

Moreover, Lucienne loved her boss a Mister McKinney, a first-hand, as well as Monsieur Theroux, the second-hand. Both of them gave her compliments for her handiwork that gave her joy and contentment in working like all other girls and ladies who were working full-time. Most of them were what they were called *"Canadiennes"*, by virtue of belonging to the québécois heritage. What was remarkable in the mill was the first-hands were most of the time Irish or Scottish with the English language. The majority of the second-hands were *"Canadiens"* speaking the French language. At the mills where the québécois immigrants worked, the order of the day was that the first-hands were people who spoke English and we called them "Yankees". They were not québécois immigrants while the second-hands selected for their talent as good workers and able negotiators for the small quarrels occasioned by misunderstandings and discontents. The fact that they spoke French and understood the québécois values of their compatriots was to their advantage in being selected second-hands. Consequently, these men became the intermediaries between the bosses, these higher-ups, and the employees. The higher-ups never spoke directly to the employees. And, the second-hands became quite often the scapegoats who carried on their backs the burden of the workers who were bent over by the hard labor required ny the constraints of the mills.

Many of the poor workers balked now and then at *"ce maudit moulin de coquerelles"*, this damn cockroach mill, an epithet created by those who felt like cockroaches, the dirty bugs that infested many a room. Cockroaches meant that the people working in the mill were reduced to the low status of little beasts chased by those who had no cares about the dignity of the human being. This monster, the mill, swallowed each day the manpower like the prey that is being swallowed up and doubts nothing. These mill laborers knew that they were taken advantage of with their capacity for producing. Although, they did get fully involved come hell and high water for they needed to nourish themselves and nourish a family that relied on the wages every week. So they went forth without complaining, without being sad about having to work in a damn mill.

As for Lucienne, she loved her work at the mill and she earned a salary that was good enough to make ends meet and earn her daily bread. She was always jolly and in good humor and she made the other spinners laugh with her little anodine stories. Moreover, she made some friends that she considered her work sisters. She came to know the names of all the girls and the women of her department.

There was one that she considered her favorite since she got attached to her on the very first day. Her name was Gaétane Lafrenière and that young girl always had a nice smile on her lips even when things did not always go well with the frames that she was taking care of. Quite often she would bring Lucienne a surprise be it chicken sandwich, two cookies with blond raisins, a ripened fruit, a small bag of popcorn, or some saltines with peanut butter. However, what gave her the most pleasure was the chocolate fudge with slivers of almonds. Gaétane always brought her four pieces wrapped in wax paper. Lucienne ate two pieces and brought the other two pieces home for dessert after supper. Both girls had a sweet tooth for desserts and they ate whatever pleased their palates.

Lucienne and Gaétane went for walks in the municipal park on Sunday afternoon and on yearly holidays in the summer months and in the fall. such as July fourth and Labor Day in September. However, before going for a walk on Sundays Lucienne pressured Gaétane and even tormented her into accompanying her to Sunday mass at Sainte-Thérèse-de-l'Enfant-Jésus church. Gaétane was Catholic by baptism but she was not a practicing faithful. One could say that she was *une catholique à gros grain*, as people in Batiscan used to say. It was evident that she went to church *de reculons as they say*, backwards. She only had a minimal level of faith. However, Lucienne insisted that she went with a good heart, in good faith.

After six or seven masses, Gaétane started to recognize that for her dear friend, mass was the culminating point of the week. After the very hard work at the mill for an entire week, Lucienne needed a respite. She realized that she needed a rest in order to go back to work Monday morning. She adored the Sunday promenades with Gaétane. Both girls were integating themselves in a nature that responded to their appeal if not their great need to regenerate their strengths not only physical but spiritual. Lucienne saw the Sunday mass being the first step of the day towards the aggrandizement of her heart and her soul. Her mother had often repeated to her that she had a good heart and a soul that was frank and open at the exploitation of the Creator, the grand love that never vacillates and would fill her with this love in order to clean her soul and her heart from the faults of retardation. She would discover some day the sealed marks of a faith in the deepest part of her soul as the attestation of this great privilege that God gave her. Yes, her mother had told her everything and remarked that a retarded child is a privilege for the parents and for the retarded one. Yes, she had told her everything she had learned from a seer she had met at a retreat. Who was the seer? She did not remember. Lucienne had asked her mother to explain everything but Héloïse could not do it right way. So Lucienne had kept in her heart up until now the sweet promising words of her mother.

Gaétane was so impressed with what Lucienne had told her about her mother that she started asking her own mother to give her catechism lessons so that she would be able to make her first communion. She was seventeen years old and she had not yet made her first communion. Although the mother was baptized Catholic and she had insisted on having her children baptized Catholic, the father was

Protestant non-practicing did not want his children to go to Catholic schools run by nuns that he did not tolerate well. So the mother and the children became non-practicing, fault of good example and convictions. Gaétane's mother refused to give her catechism lessons from which she had strayed and did not remember the responses that she had learned by heart. So, Lucienne declared herself catechism teacher in spite of her lack of intelligence. However, Lucienne was so well versed in catechism lessons that she did not hesitate to be of service to her dear friend. Anyways, her "dog" memory would serve her extremely well, she told herself.

The catechism lessons began the first Saturday after Lucienne finally found her old catechism with responses with dog-eared pages that she had stored away in an old trunk where her mother had the habit of keeping her quilts given to her by her own mother. She had brought the trunk with her in the States. It was part of her heritage, she said. "We sleep so well in our old rags and our old quilts," she assured her daughter when they were doing the *grand ménage*, the spring cleaning, and when she put her hand on her trunk in the attic. There were also several knick-knacks and some old handkerchiefs with fancy lace. Among all of that, Lucienne found her old catechism and took it out of its hiding place where it was sleeping in the attic.

It was a bit strange for Lucienne to launch herself into teaching although it was limited to the catechism. All the responses came to her clearly in her head. She remembered that she had spent a lot of time with her mother in order to put in her memory these responses to many questions in the book. There were many subjects and a pile of words that she asked her mother to define and explain so that she could understand in depth what the catechism was saying. Sometimes, Lucienne was not too happy with her mother's answers for she found them vague and disconcerting. Her mother tried to explain the best she could certain details in such and such response, but she did not always succeed in clarifying an idea, a sentence or a single word that bumped against Lucienne's thought process and her intelligence. So both teacher and pupil put the hitches aside and started praying to obtain the wisdom of the interpretation of the matter in question.

With time and patience the teacher made herself understood and the pupil assimilated the learned content. The mother was happy to have succeeded and the pupil relieved to have learned her catechism.

Gaétane found the catechism responses easy to learn but sometimes a bit too difficult to digest when it was a question of certain subjects such as the mysteries of faith: the Holy Trinity, the Incarnation and the Redemption. Lucienne tried to explain to her that they were mysteries and mysteries of the faith are inexplicable.

Either we believe or we do not believe. That was a question of faith, to believe or not believe.

—What's written in the margin here? asked Gaétane.

—It was maman who wrote that. Let me read. Ah, yes,"the mystery of faith is a truth inexplicable by reason." She wrote that so that I might remember this particular point on the mysteries. She copied it from a book she had.

—So the mysteries are contrary to the reason and the intelligence.

—I didn't say that. The mysteries surpass the limits. Do you understand?

—Not quite. My intelligence must have limits.

—If you do not understand fully, still less for me, me who's simple-minded.

—Don't say that, Lucienne. You're not simple-minded. You are simple of the heart not the mind.

—Maman used to tell me that all the time when I had doubts about my intelligence. I know my intelligence has limitations and its limitations are definitely great for me.

—You do not realize that you are in the process of teaching me catechism. That's not a lack of intelligence. It's a sign of an active intelligence.

—You flatter me, my friend.

—No, I don't say that to flatter you, but to tell you the truth as I see it.

— Listen Gaétane, I am not in the measure of explaining to you the catechism as it should be. So I'm going to ask Monsieur *le curé* Lacourse, we have a new pastor now, and he'll be able to explain better what we're studying together.

—But I don't know the *curé* Lacourse.

—Let me do this. I'll introduce you to him and everything will be fine.

Gaétane pursued her catechism studies with the *curé* and after three months of studies, he told her that she was ready to receive the Eucharist with the school children when they make their first communion in May. The day arrived and Gaétane was ready to receive the Eucharist with thirty-two students from the parochial school. She had on neither veil nor a little crown on her head, only a little white hat that went very well with her white cotton dress. Her mother was at church with Lucienne and both of them irradiated joy at the sight of Gaétane in her white costume. After the mass, the three women went to a restaurant called **Dupuis & Mackenzie** to have a quick lunch in order to celebrate Gaétane's first communion. Lucienne was proud of her efforts in bringing Gaétane back to her faith as a practicing communicant. She gave Gaétane a gift wrapped in bright white tissue paper with a white bow tied around it. It was a small missal with a little girl kneeling at the altar rail with her hands in prayer on the cover. The mother had tears in her eyes.

Lucienne worked every day at the mill and got into a flurry of ideas especially the one about the *grand ménage*, spring cleaning. It was spring and every woman who managed the house where she lived with her family felt forced to do the *grand ménage* when it was time. For most of of the québécois descendance it was the spring cleaning and the fall cleaning also. One must believe that it was inscribed in the heart of the good maman or the unwed woman vowed to tradition. In order to make a really good seasonal cleaning, one had to go in every corner of every room including the bathroom. There were some who washed not only the walls and the floors but also the ceilings. They climbed the step ladders in order to be able to reach up there and not only *"torcher"*, do a bad job, as the lady of the house in the good old days used to say. They had transmitted the *grand ménage* tradition to their daughters and to their granddaughters. Those who did not do the *grand ménage*, well, we made remarks about them and we designated them as *souillonnes*, dirty and messy ones. People who knew what cleanliness and dirtyness were, knew what the non-accomplished *grand ménage* was. It was like a mortal sin. Severely grave and almost unforgivable.

Lucienne had learned from her mother how to do the spring cleaning. The mother had learned it from her own mother and her mother had learned it from hers. The Lanouettes knew very well the spring cleanings as well as the fall cleanings when the household was turned upside down, perturbed, to say, even annoyed by the deception of a lack of habitual gestures. The habitual ones of the house felt also like being turned upside down so much so did they have to change certain daily habits such as the individual grooming and the absence of a shirt or a dress left in the large wicker basket which served as a collector for dirty clothes. It was the fault of not having done the laundry at the usual time established by the maman because the maman was busy with her spring cleaning.

Lucienne started her spring cleaning with devilish determination. First of all, she took out all the dishes in the cupboards and placed them on the tables, on the floor somewhere, and anywhere where there was room. She tripped, she hit an important dish with her arm, a dish that was left on the floor far from the other dishes that she wanted to protect from such an accident. Too bad, it was a wedding gift that belonged to her mother, a large punch bowl made of burnt- orange thick glass. It had two big handles, one on each side. She had broken one with her foot. Too bad, since it belonged to her mother, not a great accident because the bowl served as nothing special neither for her nor for her mother who had never used it. It had remained standing up on the last shelf of the cupboard for years. Every spring, the mother had washed it then dried it and put it back in its place. She did it in the fall also. Now it would be thrown in the garbage and good riddance! When Gaétane learned of the accident with the large punch bowl, she chided Lucienne for not having saved the bowl with just a little bit of strong glue. Lucienne told her that she did not know she could do that. She admitted that she knew nothing about kitchen things and fixing stuff.

End of May and the beginning of June, Lucienne started to think about the marvelous days she had spent in Quebec and then at Sainte-Anne-de-Beaupré. She had truly enjoyed the three days spent in Quebec and she had loved the cathedral there. She had visited the tomb of Monseigneur de Laval, one of the great founders of that city. The reputation of Monseigneur de Laval had crossed the Canadian border of Canada-New Hampshire. He was well known by everyone who knew the university named after him and his valiant work among the québécois settlers.

Then she went to visit with the other fellow travelers the basilica of Sainte-Anne- de-Beaupré. She had joined a bus tour along with thirty-two members of her local community. She had decided to go because she knew several travellers such as Madame Mondor, Madame Plessis, Madame Lantagne and Mademoiselle Doromère and others. The latter guaranteed Lucienne the safety that she claimed because she did not want to travel alone. She felt limited in her activities due to her doubts and her shilly-shallying dealing with her retardation although folks to whom she confided tried to reassure her that her case was not so severe as she thought. Lucienne started to be confident in herself and she dared more and more to hazard herself in activities before if not neglected at least avoided.

Later on, Gaétane invited Lucienne to a picnic proposed by the mill for its employees. It was the beginning of June the following year. Her response was an hesitating no but after her friend's insistence, she ceded to Gaétane's plea for the simple reason that everyone was going to be there. Lucienne did not want to see herself all alone, abandoned because she did not want o take a chance of joining so many people that she did not know.

—Get out of your shell, your fear of meeting people even though you don't know them. Don't be the *"savagesse"*, the wild one, Gaétane told her.

—But I never participated in such an activity and that scares me.

—Afraid of what?

—You know, the fear of showing my crazy side in front of all these people.

—Crazy side? What do you mean by that?

—Well show my crazy side because I don't know how to behave well with people who are strangers to me. You don't know how I feel when I find myself among so many people. It seems strange to me and who, without a doubt, judge me if I am normal or not. I'm afraid that people will laugh at me. That's my great fear.

—No one judges you. You make up things about yourself. Ideas that are stupid. Stop thinking that everyone judges you. The only person that judges you is you, my dear. You make up all sorts of imaginative things and you become so fearful that it shows. For nothing, my dear. For nothing. Did I ever laugh at you?

—No. It's because I'm not always sure that people will accept me as I am.

Anyways, Lucienne did not want to meet a young man to whom Gaétane wanted to present. She felt too doubtful of her condition of retardation to hazard in the domain of *"cavaliers"*, boyfriends, these pretenders of hazard.

—You are what you are. Not the worst one in the world. Not the best one either, but in the middle. As for the *"cavaliers"*, you will have the chance one day to meet one according to your taste.

Lucienne started to laugh.

—Listen, Lucienne, you will not change things. You can't. Everything is planned by heaven in our universe of normal people and those who are not even those who are not on track. I mean to say those who do not follow the movement or the pace of the simple or ordinary person like you. These persons are off track as my mother used to say. So, there some of all kinds. You're part of the *"potée,* group of people who exist and who have doubts and fears.

—The *"potée"?* You make me laugh with that. I've never heard someone say this expression.

—It means band, troup of people. My mother said it often." '*Garde c'ta potée de crève-faims ou 'garde la potée de chien-culottes*"Look at this band of starving people or look at the band of mangy skinny men,. She had an entire series of sayings and expressions that came from old Quebec.

—My mother had some also.

—Mine used to tell me often enough that the turn-up-nose vocabulary that we learn on the nuns's school benches was not the everyday vocabulary of the *"habitant"* like our ancestors in Quebec. "Our vocabulary" she said, "is the vocabulary of the little people like me and like hundreds of people emigrated to the States. Our true identity is in that, right to the core." My mother was from Sainte-Anne-de-la-Pocatière.

—My mother used to talk to me often about the farmland of the settlers in Batiscan. The land of the Lanouettes. I'd like to go there some day and visit the land of my ancestors. It would do my heart some good. Over there I would find my heritage and my identity of a woman descendant of settlers and *habitants* of ancient lands.

—Well, we'll go some day.

—You say that for real?

—Of course.

Lucienne worked each day thinking of the possibility of visiting those who still lived in Batiscan. Those who were part of her heritage and who were not reaped by lady Death. Yes, the great and terrible sickle that sweeps us up with her trenchant blade and brings all of us, small and large, towards an uncertain eternity, thought Lucienne. She was afraid of death, death that had carried away her family, father, mother and probably her sister and her brother from whom she never received mail. The silence on the part of one's own hurts the heart, she told herself.

In July, a summer month of heat and sweat, Gaétane came to talk to Lucienne about the great possibility of going to Batiscan shortly. She asked her if she had a baptism certificate for she would need it to *passer aux lignes*,cross the lines, that is to say, the border between Canada and the United-States. Lucienne answered that she didn't know where her baptismal certificate was but that she assuredly had one. "Look for it," ordered Gaétane.

Both friends left for Batiscan in Quebec with Gaétane's aunt and uncle. Gaétane had convinced them to follow the steps of a widened pilgrimage. The uncle and the aunt wanted to go to Notre-Dame-du-Cap. They could go to Notre-Dame-du- Cap and pass by Batiscan and leave their niece and her friend at the indicated village. Then, they would come back and pick up the two girls in Batiscan and then go home in the States. The uncle and the aunt acquiesced to their demand. The uncle's name was Omer Lantagne and the aunt was called, Obéline. The uncle had a Ford that had never gone very far. It was in very good condition enough to go to Canada, said aunt Obéline. Gaétane was happy to hear that she and Lucienne would be able to visit the old village of the Lanouettes and most probably a few of Lucienne's relatives. Lucienne did not even know her cousins from up north, as her mother used to say, but she retained on paper two names, Laurette Perspican and Anne-Laure Lanouette, a note that had been given to her by her mother in case Lucienne would find herself in Batiscan one day. One was the granddaughter of the grandfather Marjolain and of the grandmother Énevrine Lanouette, and the other was the wife of Gérard Lanouette, grandson of the same grandparents.

There was no address except that Héloïse had told her that her little cousins lived on *Rang #12*. This said absolutely nothing to Lucienne. However, she would find them one way or another if they were alive, as Gaétane had told her.

Having arrived in Batiscan, the two friends found themselves on *la rue principale*, main street, asking themselves where to begin to search for the lost cousins. The village had changed since several years since none of the Lanouette descendants in the United-States had visited their heritage village for years. It would be like looking for a needle in a haystack, said Gaétane to Lucienne. Lucienne responded, "I'm probably retarded but I know what the exact expression means. I'm not looking for a needle."

—You are getting tame, my dear, you are taming yourself from your retardation and you're becoming more and more normal like all the others. However, I always thought you were.

—Was what?

—Normal like all others.

—Not normal but a bit abnormal.

—Don't say that, *ma chouette*, my sweet owl. Don't say that..

They started to search here and there but they arrived at nothing. There was no one on the street to whom they could inquire. It was like an abandoned village if not a dead village where there are not even ghosts.

—It's a ghost town, declared all of a sudden Gaétane.

—Let's go and visit the cemetery. We could find the name Lanouette and discover the dates of births and deaths.

—What's that going to give us?

—It's a beginning. Then we'll go to see the *curé* at the rectory,

—Is he going to know things?

—Yes, for he will be able to consult the archives of births and deaths of his parishioners, living or dead. It's a start.

So Lucienne and Gaétane went to the parish cemetery that was located near Sainte-Geneviève-de-Batiscan church.

—It's like this that the village of yesteryear was named as well as the parish church, declared Lucienne.

—You're not afraid of the dead, are you, Lucienne?

—Not at all since they're dead for good.

—*Moi*, I always had a fear of the dead and that's the reason why I do not go to cemeteries when they bury the dead. It gives me chills only when I talk about it.

—Come on. It's not as bad as that.

—*Toi*, you don't know how much I shake inside me. It's as if they had thrown icicles in my belly.

—Take courage, my dear, one day you will go where you do not want to go, in a casket and then to the cemetery like all mortals.

—Stop talking about that. You frighten me.

—*Moi*, who thought that nothing frightened you, Gaétane.

They got to the cemetery while keeping a low voice so as not to scare the dead, said Lucienne to her friend. However, both started to burst into laughter.

—Shhhhhut, said Lucienne. We don't want to waken the dead. Another burst of laughter.

—I hope that nobody is going to see us snoot like that, said Lucienne.

—There's nobody in the surroundings. They're probably in bed by now. For the old people, it's time for their siesta. *Prendre un somme*, taking a nap, as the old people used to say. It was the order of the day, resting so you could replenish your strength and return to your tasks of the day when one has gotten up very early in the morning.

—It smells the old here, Lucienne. It smells *le cani, le chanci*, musty, as well- educated mouths would say.

—After all, we're in a cemetery, a very old cemetery that goes back to the settlers, I am sure.

They found a few familiar names such as Marjolain Lanouette and his spouse, Énevrine Bellevance Lanouette, deceased 1914. Lucienne recognized these names for it was from the family, her grandfather and her grandmother, her mother's parents. A little further, she found the burial plot of her great grandparents, the settlers Lanouette as well as the great-great grandparents, Edouard and Livine Lanouette.

All of a sudden, there came a *monsieur*, well-dressed with a felt hat on his head, He introduced himself as Monsieur LaFrance, the *bedeau*, caretaker, of the parish. He was sent by the *curé* since there were two strangers in the cemetery right next to the rectory and he was asking himself who could these two women be that he could not recognize. Two *vauriennes*, good-for-nothings from somewhere without a doubt. Yes, bums perhaps. So the *curé* sent his man to investigate what was happening in his cemetery.

Lucienne, the Simple-Minded

—Pardon ladies, what are you doing here in the cemetery?

—We are from the United-States and Lucienne came to get some information on her relatives who are buried here in the Batiscan cemetery. They're the Lanouettes.

—Ah, the Lanouettes. Everyone here knows the Lanouettes. Have you found them?

—Yes, monsieur. They're over there next to the Calvary.

—Do you have any questions about other former parishioners?

—Yes and no, monsieur, answered Gaétane.

—Maybe you should meet our *curé*, le Père Denoncourt. He's been here eighteen years.

—Oh, I would love to but we would not want to bother him with our little searches, replied Lucienne.

—It's not a bother for him. He's genteel, our *curé* and he would be pleased to meet you. Come with me.

They walked behind the *bedeau* and went towards the rectory, a whitewashed building with black shutters. The *curé* was waiting for them at the door.

—So where are you from?

—We are from the United-States, father, said Gaétane.

—The United-States?

—Yes.

—Are there many who speak French in the United-States?

—Yes, back home in New England.

—We have lost many members of our community who left for he United-States. Unfortunately, there were not enough jobs here to satisfy the needs of people who did not want to starve on a farm.

—Yes, I know the situation very well.

—And your friend doesn't talk too much.

—She's a bit shy.

—I'm not shy. I'm listening to you, that's all, answered Lucienne.

—Well, what are you looking for here in Sainte-Geneviève-de-Batiscan?

—My ancestors, added Lucienne. They're the Lanouettes.

—Oh, the settlers. There were many of these Lanouettes but they have all disappeared.

—There are no more Lanouettes here now?

—Not one except in the cemetery. A soft smile was on the pastor's lips.

—Would there be some people here who knew the Lanouettes?

—Maybe a few. There's an old lady that you should meet. Her name is Églantine Laverrière. She's one hundred two years old, imagine that. I believe that it would be a great pleasure for her to meet you. She loves to talk and she has no one with whom to hold a conversation except her daughter with whom she lives. Her daughter is eighty-two years old.

—One hundred two years old? Does she have all her wits about her this old lady? asked Gaétane.

—Yes, certainly. Moreover, she has a very good memory. She could give you information about the Lanouettes and many things that went on here in Sainte- Geneviève-de-Batiscan a long time ago.

—Oh, yes we would love to meet her this old lady.

—Listen. It's getting a little late and you do not have a place where to sleep tonight, I'm sure. I'm going to call a lady who could give you lodging for one night. Her name is Edwina Labrecque. She's a very lovely woman and very sympathetic with everyone. But before leaving, I'm going to tell my *ménagère*, house woman, to prepare three places for supper. You will eat with me tonight.

—Merci, Monsieur le curé, said the two friends with one voice.

Thus Lucienne and Gaétane slept at Madame Labrecque's home in a feather bed. The following morning, they got up early and took their breakfast that the lady had prepared for them. Then, they asked

Madame Labrecque to direct them towards the old lady's house, Églantine Laverrière.

—But yes. She lives not too far from here. You leave here and then you turn left then facing you, there's the Rang Lanouette. It used to be Rang #4 before. She lives on that road.

—The Rang Lanouette? That's a stroke of luck, declared Lucienne.

—How's that?

—The Lanouettes are my ancestors.

—I would like to alert her but she doesn't have a telephone. She still lives in the good old days, this lady. Nothing has changed with her. I'm sure that she will receive you well with open arms.

Lucienne and Gaétane went towards the house of the old lady and they arrived there somewhat out of breath for they hurried to get there. They knocked on the door and a lady whose face was full of wrinkles opened the door and looked very surprised if not frightened.

—What do you want? said she in a kind of washed out voice but firm.

—We want to see Madame Laverrière.

—She is not here at the moment.

Suddenly a weak but a clear and gripping voice was heard.

—Marguerite, who's there?

—Two young strangers, maman. I've never seen them in my life.

—Well, have them come in. We don't leave strangers at the door like that.

The old lady with hair as white as milk, thin and fine like silk threads, limped towards the door and greeted Lucienne and Gaétane with warm and good cheer.

—Come and enter. I beg you. Do not stay there like strangers. There are no strangers here in this house.

The two friends went inside the house and started to look at everything around them. The interior of the home was filled with knick-knacks and picture frames on the walls.

Marguerite looked at the two strangers with suspicion and miscontent. It appeared on her face, a face that was congealed with a certain disdain.

Once seated in the old and used plush armchairs, the two friends started to hold a conversation with the old lady.

—We are here because Monsieur le *curé* advised us to come and pay you a visit.

—For what reason?

—Explain it to her, Lucienne.

—Well, my ancestors were the Lanouettes and the Lanouettes were the settlers of this place, the Batiscan. I came with my friend, Gaétane, so that we could probe this place where my ancestors lived and died. Many are buried here in your cemetery. My mother is not buried here, she is buried home in the United-States.

—So you're from the States?

—Yes, Madame.

—What was your mother's name, my dear?

—Her name was Héloïse Lanouette, the little handicapped one, the daughter of Marjolain and Énevrine Lanouette. Célie Lanouette took care of her for months if not years.

—That's right.

—But you're not telling me that Héloïse is dead is she?

—Unfortunately, yes, Madame Laverrière. She died last year.

—Like that, you are her daughter, Lucienne the simple-minded?

—How do you know that?

—News travel fast, They cross even the country lines. It's Louise Dudenant who told me. She often went to Newmarket to visit her sister and her brother-in-law. She knew your mother, Héloïse. Like that, you're in good health enough to displace yourself to Canada.

—It's Gaétane's uncle and aunt who brought us here with them. They left for a pilgrimage to Notre-Dame-du-Cap.

—Ah, yes, I made that pilgrimage myself a long time ago. I remember. I am probably old and have gone beyond my strength and my capacity, but I am still living. The *Bon Dieu* has not yet come to get me. I have to believe that he doesn't want me or that he finds me too naughty for him.

—I do not believe that, Madame, said Gaétane.

—So, what do you do, my Gaétane?

—Me, I work at the mill and I'm training to be a nurse.

—I didn't know that, replied Lucienne all surprised of the fact that her friend had not told her before.

—Well, come and have a hot tea with me. It warms up the "*Canadienne*" as we say here at home.

While drinking their tea, Lucienne asked the old lady what she had done during her long life.

—Moi, I had three living children, and five who died. We were able to save them with great difficulty then. Yes, I have three, Marguerite who lives with me, and two others, one in the United-States and the other one in Montreal. The three are still living. I'm probably going to surpass them in years. One never knows. I must tell you that it's hard to lose a child. My husband died thirty-three years ago. I'm the one who finished raising the three children. Moreover, I got involved with natural medicine, the herbs and the native Indian medicine. I got to know well the Algonquin sorcerer, the medicine man, the Grand Chief Manotoskigoo. He was a truly good sorcerer and he's the one who taught me all of his tricks in natural medicine. Actually they were not tricks but ways and matter of medicine. I call it natural medicine because it comes from nature and the healing is natural and not pills and devices of all kinds. Here in the neighborhood, they recognize me for being a healer. I take care of people and heal them like the sick, the lame, those whose lungs are attacked by maladies, those whose kidneys are in a bad state or in crisis, as well as unknown sicknesses, not well-known by the Whites but truly well taken care of by the Indians. These people have the magic of healing with the care and healing taken from nature and transmitted from generation to generation. The Indian medecine has never known derangement nor disappearance. It has survived from the ancient times and even the times before the times known by the Whites. It's more than old. It's eternal like Manotoskigoo told me. He trusted me because he knew that I would grow old like a sorceress, ripe and the head and the heart filled with knowledge depended by medicine that comes from the Great Manitou, the Great Spirit that lives on the sacred mountain.

—You learned all of that?

—Yes, my dear. I did it through experience. Several of my neighbors and even relatives had no confidence in me and in my capacities as a healer. They truly believed that I was a witch, a debauched creature of nature. They imagined me sitting on a broom and flying in the air like an old demon ready to launch herself into demonic rituals. I scared them but I also healed them.

—Did you know Timiskamengo, the Algonquin? asked Lucienne.

—Yes, I knew him. He and his lover, Célie. Everyone talked about it in my time. It was like thunder. A veritable explosion of rumors, I'm telling you.

—Poor Célie. My mother often told me about her. She was her best friend.

—Well, I will tell you a secret later. Now, I have to rest.

She went to take a nap on the soft cranberry-colored couch in the ante-chamber of her salon. Lucienne and Gaétane returned to the cemetery to explore the names of the deceased buried there. They amused themselves by pronouncing these names that were not too familiar such as Giguère, Plamondon, Parafinère, Grandmaison, and Néaploton. The giggles took over them and they could not stop themselves from laughing. After a short period of time, they went back to the old lady's house. She was seated in her armchair meditating on a prayer that she said each day. It was an Indian prayer addressed to the Grand Manitou. She told the two friends that even the Indians had their own prayers and they recited them while singing and at times dancing.

—You are going to stay for supper tonight and I will declare to you my secret after supper. The meal is very simple, some pea soup, homemade bread and jam that Madame Cormeau made. My God, how she makes good jam that one! When are you leaving?

—We leave the day after Wednesday. Today is Tuesday so we will leave Thursday. My uncle and my aunt will pick us up after their trip to the Cap.

—So you still have time to yourselves. You have a room at Madame Labrecque? She's a good person, Madame Labrecque. She has a good heart.

—Yes, replied Gaétane.

—She's always asking if we are cold and if we want more blankets. Yet, it's not so cold outside. She keeps her house very warm, added Lucienne.

Supper had just ended when the old lady started her story and her secret. She told them that this story was hers and that she had preserved it in her heart during many years. She did not like to tell it to anybody, said she.

—I'm telling it to you because you, Lucienne, you are of the Lanouette descendants and this story and my secret concern you. Gaétane can stay. She will learn something that's hidden but worthy of the Lanouette memory.

—Go ahead, Madame Laverrière. Lucienne and I, we are listening.

—Well, here's my story. In the time when Célie was living alone after Héloïse had left from her house on the 4th rang, we still talked about her Algonquin lover, Timiskamengo, and how he had been abused at the boarding school. He had run away into the forest where no one could find him. The Algonquins protected him and his story. As for Célie, she remained alone and penitent for having offended

God and her lover. She found herself guilty of his case and his flight, Timiskamengo, and even his abuses. Yet, she had done nothing wrong. All she had done was to love an Indian, a Redskin.

—Everyone knew that?

—Yes, everyone for we were a very small community and we still are. The big tongues did not stop ever to tell what they did not even know. They said that Célie had left her religion and had gotten involved with this Indian, this savage not even Christian.

—But he was baptized. He was a Christian by conversion, said Lucienne.

—Yes, but not a practicing one.

—What's that got to do with Célie?

—By mixing in with him, Célie was becoming a traitor to her religion and to her heritage. She was thus cut off from her community like being excommunicated by all the parish. At that time the *curé* approved this punishment for a disobeying soul. Poor Célie, poor her, she no longer had anyone of her race and of her family to bring her aid and comfort. No one. You call that being Christian, people like that? As for me, they're lacking or lost Christians. I said it loud and clear on the steps of the church. He did not reply, the *curé*, with the hard heart, hard as stone.

—Why were people so villainous and so detestable towards Célie?

—Because she had dared to go contrary to the values of her own people. She had committed the worst sin in our community of Quebec Catholics. She had dared to fall in love with a savage. Then, she had pursued him for months and months until she realized that she would never have him. Some even dared to say that she was pregnant with his child. A bastard and an Indian besides that.

—It wasn't true, that ugly rumor.

—Yes, I know.

—But what happened to him? asked Gaétane.

—That's my secret that I want to confide to you because you are wise and good girls, and you, Lucienne, are of the generation line of Lanouettes. Moreover, your mother knew her very well. What I'm going to tell you please do not repeat it to anyone. Especially not to Monsieur le *curé*. My secret is that Célie and Timiskamengo are buried in the Algonquin cemetery. It's a hidden cemetery. A sacred cemetery for the Algonquins They do not want people especially the Whites to dishonor and desacrelize (it's word I made up... It means to undo the sacred character of something) their cemetery where repose their ancestors. It's part of their sacred duty that has been given to them as a shared trust according to the traditions of their tribe. The Algonquins confided to me their secret because they had confidence in me and that I had Indian blood in my veins. It's the Grand Sorcerer of the tribe who has confided everyrhing to me in giving me the details.

—How's that? asked Gaétane.

—Well, by the intermediary of a *coureur de bois*, runner of the woods and trapper. It's part of my genealogy. The son of a great grandson who became a *coureur de bois* had linked himself to an Indian woman, the daughter of one of the Algonquin chiefs. They had one child and that child is one of my descendants. That happened often then. The *coureurs de bois* ran everywhere. They were snooters and hunters. They brought back furs to sell at the grand open market.

Unfortunately, it was them who introduced alcohol to the Indian. Alcohol opens many mouths and pocketbooks. Well, since I was considered like an Indian descendant, they told me this secret. It's truly a secret since it is part of their sacred heritage. Yes, Célie is buried with her lover.

—But I did see her grave in the parish cemetery. How is it that she is buried with the Algonquins and the tombstone with her name on it is in your Catholic cemetery? asked Lucienne.

—It's because we stole, I should say appropriated, her body in secret under the cover of night her body from the entrepreneur's shop. Then we transferred her body to the Algonquin cemetery. Without the Whites knowing it, you understand?

—How did they do that?

—One of the Algonquins knew well the undertaker's aide who was very poor. They offered him fox furs so that he might open the casket. They replaced Célie's corpse with a scarecrow wrapped with a sheet. Then, the two Indians who came to get Célie's body left without the undertaker knowing it. The casket was closed because there were no plans to verify the deceased. All that was granted her was a **libera**. Imagine that, a **libera** without a corpse. A casket with a scarecrow on top of that. Then they buried the scarecrow without anyone knowing about it. What a blow of an intrigue! If only Monsieur le *curé* had known about it. Oh, my God!

—But I thought that permission had not been granted to bury Célie in the Catholic cemetery.

—By exemption, my dear, by exemption and by respect for the Lanouette descendance. Everyone knew that Célie Lafortune was married to that lamebrain. The chatterbox Lanouette. When he died in the logging camp, well Célie found herself alone. She only had the memory of her lover Timiskamengo. You know the story, my dear Lucienne, since she took care of your maman a long time. Certainly, your maman told you this story, the story of a White-skin who loved a Redskin enough to become crazy in love. Yes, she died alone, *toute seule* and abandoned by all that was dear to her. The wooden plaque is there in the Algonquin cemetery with her initials. The initials CLL are on the wooden plaque that was placed on the tomb of the two lovers. Célie Lafortune Lanouette. I saw them myself. I respect their doing this, these Algonquins, concerning Célie and Timiskamengo. It's truly a thing of the heart for the two lovers. Célie doesn't belong next to the lamebrain Lanouette, she belongs with Timiskamengo, her lover and the only one who could have loved her as she deserved it. Imagine that, a scarecrow in the hole of the Lanouettes in the Batiscan cemetery. It's enough to turn the deceased in their tombs upside down.

—Your story is very interesting. You really are an integral part of the history of Quebec.

—That;s why I am old, to tell stories and to render testimony to the truth of acquired things. Things like the knowledge of a past sewn with stories and legends.

—You know so many stories and legends.

—If you have the time, enough time at your disposition, my dear Gaétane, I would tell you some for hours if not days on top of that.

—Oh, I would love that.

—Listen you two, tomorrow I will make arrangements so that you will be able to go and visit the Algonquin cemetery. I know enough Algonquins to render me the privilege of going into their reserve. They do it quite often for me. If I ask them to allow you to pass through and go to their cemetery, they will give you permission to do it. I'm sure. They will know, you Lucienne, that you are a Lanouette by relative relationship in a way associated with Célie and Timiskamengo. You will see they do honor their memory, a White woman and a Redskin.

Once the table was cleaned and the dishes were washed, dried and put away by he two young girls, the old lady went to bed. Marguerite grabbed a book and started reading a Medieval romance,"Yvain, Chevalier au lion"/Knight of the Lion. She did not pay attention to them. She was a woman with a sanguine temperament but hardened by years of isolation and inner frustrations. She had had an intimate relationship with a young man who adored her but they separated when World War I occured and the young man left for France. He was killed in the trenches where asphyxiating gaz floated constantly in the air.

Marguerite never recovered from this defeat of unforgotten love with a non- willed separation. She became bitter, intolerant, fierce and hardhearted. Her bitter irascibility had hardened the heart and had given her stomach pains like burns as well as a pernicious malaise. Her mother called her *"marabout"*, ill-tempered. Marguerite was at a certain point in life when one feels separated from everything, cornered and deprived of everything that renders one happy. Marguerite was Marguerite, that's all, said her mother, the old lady who had surpassed the years and had filled them with stoic stands and lyrical healing. *Elle avait rempli sans vie avec un lyrisme de guérison et de bon conseil algonquin/*

she had filled her life with lyrical healing and good Algonquin counsel. Furthermore, she had kept her sense of humor.

The following morning, the two friends arrived early at the old lady's house. She offered them coffee but they refused because they had already had their breakfast at Madame Labrecque's house. They were in a hurry to leave for the Indian cemetery. The two friends were led to the cemetery by a young Algonquin who entertained them with the story of the cemetery and its heritage. Apparently, he had been well instructed on this subject. He gave them many details of the cemetery such as it had been founded by his illustrious grandfather, the Grand Father Bafoutesko. He was the ancestor of Timiskamengo and the ancestor of several illustrious Algonquins who had fought for their freedom and their independence from the Whites. However, they had lost this independence at the battle of Fontauville right next to Batiscan. The Canadian government had taken away their independence and their territory. They were placed on a reserve that they did not like at all. The land was rocky and they could neither harrow nor cultivate the soil as it was traditionally their habit. So the harvests were meager and disastrous. Many died of a lack of food. His grandparents had told him the story of that particular time. It was the Grand-Father Bafoutesko who had consecrated a cemetery worthy of the Algonquin heroes, the brave ones of the tribe. Then, they had added more land for the women and children. It's a sacred land, the young Algonquin told them, proud of his heritage and his history.

The young man also told them that he had received a mandate from his own father to go and get two white women and bring them to the cemetery because the old white sorceress wanted them to be witnesses to this sacred land.

Specifically, witnesses to the gravesite of Timiskamengo. The young Algonquin following the dictates of his father, took Lucienne and Gaétane to the entrance of the cemetery. He cautioned them to observe silence once inside the sacred place. Yes, it was a sacred place for the simple reason that the deceased who were buried there had by their spiritual presence, made the soil of the cemetery sacred especially where they were buried. However, the presence of a White person would compromise the intrinsic value of this sacred ground. "That's why," he told them, "I'm going to bless you with smoke from our heritage before penetrating this Algonquin sanctuary."

The young man lit a tress of sacred aromatic grass with a match and blew on these herbs in order to obtain smoke. Then, he put the smoking tress in a terracotta vessel and washed himself with the smoke in order to clean himself of all impurities, what the autochtones/the natives call "smudge." Then he passed the smoke over the heads of both friends singing a few Indian refrains. Once the little ceremony had terminated, he brought them to the grave site of Timiskamengo on the corner of an alley reserved for special cases. The young man explained to them that they would receive a surprise once at the burial site. He told them nothing else. Standing in front of the designated burial spot, the two young friends began to read what was written on a plaque. It was in Algonquin but they believed reading the initials CLL right next to the name Timiskamengo.

They were really surprised for they had not expected, especially Lucienne, the presence of a White woman, Célie, in an Algonquin cemetery. It was precisely what the old lady had told them.

—My God, it's Célie next to her lover Timiskamengo. I cannot believe it with my eyes, shouted Lucienne. Two big tears fell on her cheeks.

—Yes, it's your Célie. Our tribe made an exception for Célie although exceptions are rare. Knowing well that Tmiskemengo loved Célie sincerely and Célie loved him with a depth of soul never known before here in Algonquin country, the tribe in concert with the other Algonquin tribes decided to grant both lovers a place in the sacred cemetery, which makes the presence of Célie now sacred as well as that of Timiskamengo. Their allied presences is worth a marriage in the eyes of our tribe.

Lucienne and Gaétane started to shed tears of joy and comfort.

—I cannot imagine these two lovers side by side in the same cemetery after so many dramatic adventures throughout which they traversed, said Lucienne.

—It's truly romantic, added Gaétane.

—Not romantic but heroic, I would say, added the young man.

—Oh, it's so very beautiful this act of compassion on the part of your tribe, said Lucienne to the young man.

—It's not only compassion but an act of justice that your people did not want to recognize.

—Your people?

—Yes, your people, the *curé*, the parishioners, and the Lanouette family.

—A real dishonor. Shameful! It's shameful, I say, shouted out loud Lucienne.

—The Algonquins knew much better how to act than the White skins, added Gaétane.

The young man bent down toward the soil and picked up a very small stone on the ground where the two lovers were buried and presented it to Lucienne.

—I should not do this, picking up any object of our cemetery, but I believe very much that such a souvenir will make you happy.

—I thought of picking it up myself, this stone, but I did not feel myself capable of doing it, not worthy enough. Thank you.

After a long moment of reverential silence the three of them went out of the cemetery slowly.

—Pardon me. I forgot to ask you your name, young man.

—My name is Jean Timiskamengo. Jean since my parents had me baptized in church and Timiskamengo because my mother suggested to my father to give me a name after a hero of all the beautiful tragic stories of the Algonquins known as the story of two lovers with crossed destinies.

—Ah, my God, what a beautiful gesture, said Lucienne. It's Timiskamengo returned to earth.

Lucienne and Gaétane thanked the young man and directed themselves towards the house of the old lady. When they entered the house, the old lady was waiting for them with a wide smile on her lips. She greeted them and told them to sit down. She had done her duty as healer and caregiver. Healing the ills of the heart and soul was her vocation, she told them. She had done so with perspicacity, both tender and sharpened, she assured them. Gaétane's aunt and uncle had made their pilgrimage at the Cap but she, Lucienne, had just done hers. It consisted of two sacred places, she said. Two places of predilection.

After having thanked the old sorceress of Batiscan, Lucienne and Gaétane were in the process of leaving the area. It was as if one says *adieu* to the Lanouettes of yesteryear. Lucienne felt the nostalgia linked to this old country of her ancestors. And, the uncle and the aunt would arrive in a short while, the old lady told Lucienne.

—Kiss me and hug me, my dear, and do remember that your retardation is not a retardation of heart and spirit for you.

—My mother already told me that.

—So, you must pick up your courage and fly towards the stars. Please don't remain in the mud with your two feet stuck. Fly, my dear, fly towards the stars and the dreams. Learn from Célie and Timiskamengo that life is made to love and share with the beings who are dear to you. Dare to love and find yourself a nice young man that will make you happy in life. Don't remain alone mooing at the stars like a cow.

The old lady murmured in Lucienne's ear, "One day you will discover that you have a gift, the gift of healing. You are going to perceive it by a sign in the heavens that you have it and that you must exercise this gift from heaven."

The uncle and the aunt arrived around the first hours of the afternoon. They picked up their two passengers that they had brought with them and kind of flew back to the United-States without too many words on the road. One must believe that the four pilgrims were tired if not drawn out. Lucienne and Gaétane closed their eyes and slept up to the border. They woke up when the agent asked them for their papers and they gave him each their baptismal record. Then he asked the uncle a few questions and then after having answered them, the uncle started the car and went on his way.

Having arrived home, Lucienne and Gaétane each went to their own house to put away the clothes they had brought with them, and Lucienne threw herself on her bed because she was so tired from her adventure-pilgrimage. She slept until eight o'clock that evening and then she washed her face, ate cereal with milk, drank a glass of cold water and went outside to fix her gaze on the sky. She looked at the crescent moon, glowing and welcoming, as well as the milky way in a firmament so deep and so intense that she thought of the depth of an insolvable mystery.

She had never realized that the milky way could draw you in and take hold of your vision.

She stayed there her eyes fixed on a firmament profoundly dark but shining with stars. And then she asked herself when she would get the sign promised to her by the old sorceress of Batiscan. Could the milky way furnished with millions of stars be the sign promised to her now that she was perceiving it as bright white shining with stars that she had never scrutinized before with her eyes. It was a miracle for her, she who had never seen such marvelous signs. So she thought. She felt as if numbed if not frozen by a precarious and fleeing feeling that came to her that night. Was it really a sign of her call to be a healer, she asked herself. Assuredly night would reveal her secret that the silent constellations in a firmament so deep and so intense that even the stars can penetrate the presence of the unimaginable. If the stars could talk, they would tell her that she had accomplished the ritual of her initiation as a healer by her intense and spiritually accomplished gaze upon the immensity of the heavens and its stars. It became truly a vision, somehow and somewhat a sacred sighting that transformed her limits or low capacities into enlightened ones. The light of the stars. She thought of *"La Nuit Étoilée*. The stars, the stars and the old sorceress! Lucienne had finally reached the level of intelligence of others who also struggle with doubts and fears. Know it or not, she had in a way absorbed their intensity and the power to heal just like the autochtones/natives who gathered to themselves the experiences of healing for centuries and centuries. It was the magic given to those who become part of lives outside of the daily tasks, even the souls said to be retarded like Lucienne. She felt as if she was in a new world that of the marvelous that she could not totally understand nor absorb as if it was the language of magic that was opening up and operating in her and was giving her a new language and a new vision. There's magic in a life somehow called abnormal. What is magic?

Well, it's charm, enchantment, spells and other wanted denominations that give a thrust to the human soul. Magic according to those who believe in it and exercise it is the trampoline between earth and the stars up in a firmament that talks but profoundly silent to those who do not know how to listen. It is incomprehensible and unexplainable. There are some who believe it to be malevolent and dangerous, but the simple souls and even the simple-minded know better. They enjoy its goodness and its predilection. And, magic or the marvelous become the trampoline for healing and the healer since healing means transformation and benefit for a being such as Lucienne who knows how to heal by way of a gift, a spell transmitted by the supernatural forces. Talk to Lucienne about it, she will explain it to you one day.

The weeks rolled by fully and each day found Lucienne and Gaétane at work with their trade in the mill. Lucienne as spinner and Gaétane as weaver. They saw themselves from time to time and took a coffee or a tea at the little restaurant kind of a quick-lunch place next to the mill. They exchanged the last news items and sometimes told amusing stories.

Mid-August, the Cushnoc mill announced that there would be a field day in early September in order to celebrate Labor Day, a holiday. Gaétane pressured Lucienne into joining her in this celebration that she anticipated with enthusiasm. Lucienne hesitated at first but Gaétane succeeded in convincing her to come in spite of her doubts and her "*je-ne-sais-pas-si-je-veux-y-aller*", I-do-bot-know-if-I- want-to-go reply.

The field day was an occasion to reunite the mill workers, their families and the bosses as well as one or two mill "highmuckamucks". There was a lot to eat, sandwiches, hot dogs, chips, sliced cucumbers and tomatoes, soda pop, and, of course, watermelon. To end the meal, there was dessert, small apple tarts, raisin pies and raspberry pies that the Mesdames Poulin, Sauvageau and Demers had baked. At the height of this feast there was a giant cake with a mouth-watering icing that children so desired to eat.

During the course of the day, Gaétane introduced a young man to Lucienne. He had reddish cheeks and he seemed jolly. His name was Roger "Rocky" Laliberté. She called him"Tit-Cric" because everyone called him that on account of his beautiful white teeth. He was a handsome young man and he showed an air of superiority as well as a nice sardonic smile that made the girls blush whenever they met him. Lucienne told Gaétane in a low voice standing behind her that she did not appreciate at all that she was forcing her to meet this young man that she did not even know. Gaétane answered her that a young girl has to meet a young man openly even if she does not know him.

—After all, you don't want to remain an old maid the rest of your life, Gaétane told her.

—I don't know. I'll live a consecrated life just like the religious but at home not in a convent or a boarding school.

—A boarding school?

—I'll talk about it later. Let's go take our snack.

The young man followed them up to the long table where the food offered for the holiday was spread out. Lucienne cast a look a bit shifty and disapproving on Tit- Cric while Gaétane was nice with him. Lucienne did not like having him on her heels. It's then that Gaétane showed silently to her friend her displeasure without openly telling her. After the looks and the movements of indifference on the part of Lucienne, Tit-Cric disappeared without the least trace of interest in her. He had not obtained from her any mark of genuine interest and especially not one sign of affection on the part of the young girl who had not a single nice word for him because he did not appear humble and generous with his words to her. Tit-Cric to Lucienne was not a Timiskamengo. There she goes again on the haunting thought of a lover that she believed to be ideal. She just could not banish him from her memory. Unfortunately, all future pretender of love would be placed at the irreplaceable level of a Timiskamengo. What to do?

Three or four days later, Lucienne came to Gaétane's home and asked pardon for having offended her with her moves of an old maid gone mad, said she.

—What do you mean by that?

—Well, it's the way that I treated you the other day at the Cushnoc feast day. And then the way I did not accept well meeting Roger, the Tit-Cric. I'm sorry and I blame myself.

—Listen, you are my best friend and I love you as you are with your qualities and you defects. But your greatest quality, it's the frankness of heart and soul. That's what breaks open the barriers of retardation, this simple-mindedness that people call. They often call you Lucienne the simple-minded one because they do not understand you. They think that you have a lack of intelligence and that you are retarded. That you are behind others and that you do not understand things as they should be understood. However, you are truly in advance of the others for you see things otherwise than others and you see with the clarity of the elect. The elect of the Creator. The one who gives special gifts to those who whom he loves especially like you, They are the elect. You are a healer as the old sorceress told you. I know, I know, I heard her say that. So, that you refuse certain things or not is not an injury. I understand your frank and well-advised movements.

—Wow! you've got me! I did not believe that you knew me that well and that you realized that I was other than the other persons and not by a certain retardation but by simple-mindedness outside the vocabulary of others, outside of their comprehension. I thank you.

—That's O.K. dear Lucienne.

—Listen very carefully to me for I have something important to tell you and I want to tell it to you right away before I change my mind.

—Is it as important as that?

—Yes, more important than all the things that I ever told you.

—It must be a mortal sin or a kind of severe or atrocious aberration.

—Don't laugh at me. Gaétane.

—O.K. I'm letting you talk.

—It's serious what I have to tell you.

—I'm listening.

—When I mentioned the boarding school and I told you that I would get back to you and talk about it later, well, it's time and the right hour to tell you about my boarding school story. I never told anyone about it. No one. Not even my mother. It's time that I unload my heart.

Lucienne let out a long sigh and began to talk about her story concerning the boarding school.

—My mother absolutely wanted to place me in a convent that was truly a boarding school for retarded children and the less intelligent. It was a convent of religious nuns. The nuns who ran this institution were of good heart and good intention, believe me. However, there were some who did not see things the same way than those who had a pure heart. They launched themselves into corporal and psychological abuses that gave me chills even today.

—As bad as that?

—Let me finish my story.

—I'm sorry.

—Well, you remember the Algonquin cemetery where Célie and Timiskamengo are buried?

—Yes.

—You remember that I told you standing there on their grave that the two lovers were enjoying a non-anticipated eternity, she the loving Québécoise and the Algonquin tarnished by the vicious abuses of a boarding school of yesteryear.

—Yes, I remember.

—It's not all. I also suffered abuses at the boarding school. I did not tell my mother nor my father until my father died. My father suspected something that was shifty over there but he never said it. I mentioned it to my mother only after years of keeping silence. I did not tell her the entire story. I was ashamed of it.

—Tell me what you want to tell me and I will listen.

—At the very start, the convent-boarding school appeared to me welcoming and promising for my progress in the domain of retardation. My mother wished that I would learn to act by myself and get out of my state of a lack of intelligence. Since I was not learning fast and my reactions to the questions asked of me were slow and vague, she believed, however, that things would get better once the good and fruitful therapies were applied with good care and good training of those who would take care of me and my failings. At least, that's what she believed, my mother. My father did not say anything ever pushed by the fear of offending my mother who was convinced of her cause in my favor. She had heard talk about this boarding school - convent in Saint-Hyacinthe that propagated a publicity of rehabilitation and Christian education by the intervention of the former clients as well as from mouth to mouth. My mother was convinced that it was a good remedy for me. So here we are on the road to Quebec. I was a bit fearful of going so far from home and be put in the care of a religious community that I did not know. I went with a heavy heart and a disoriented spirit.

Once we got there, we made the introductions and my parents left without too much pain in their eyes. They told me that they would be back in one week to verify if all was going well or not. They returned after only four days. Everything was going well. I had made friends and I loved the therapy and education program in which I was placed. My parents came back several times to visit me, especially my mother. No reproaches on my part for the boarding school,

However, one day when I had refused to participate in a ball game outside because I did not like that game and I had a hard time throwing the ball, they called me to the office of the superior and then they introduced me to a religious whose name was Soeur Bougraise-Marie. She seemed severe and hard to me.

They warned me that it was for my good if she who controlled my progress had charge of my discipline when an infraction of the rules that govern the establishment is committed. Soeur Bougraise-Marie would be the disciplinary agent in my case. I asked her what was the infraction of the rules in my case. She replied that I had been indocile in refusing to play outdoors with the others and that my indocility was a reflection of my lack of will bending to the demands of the established rules. I told her that my life was but docility and a will bending to all established rules. That I obeyed all demands from my superiors and that they had told me that I had the sweetness of soul like a lamb. No compassion nor interest in my cause that I pleaded. They placed me in a very small room so small that one would swear that the four walls would fall over my head. I got no food only a glass of water twice a day. I was famished and I begged for a bit of nourishment. They refused it to me. The tiny room was totally dark without windows and without any light. I wasn't scared of being punished. The lack of food confused me and made me ill at ease if not sick to my stomach. An empty stomach doesn't go well at all. What I feared the most was the absolute darkness and the beastly silence. Sometimes I cried when I asked God to console me and get me out of there. After four days, they released me saying that I had done my penance. The superior warned me of never telling my parents of this punishment for there would be more if ever I did not keep silent concerning this disciplinary affair. I answered her that my heart would keep the memory of it but that my lips would remain closed on this subject. Then they sent me to get a bit of nourishment in the refectory. It was good.

I knew how to hide and even interiorize profoundly this punishment fault of a lack of courage and reason well formed. I did not tell my mother right away because I did not want to displease her and maybe scandalize her with this abuse committed against me. Later on, I opened my heart out about the incident of the punishment, I should say abuse, and my mother told me that she had suspected it but that she did not want to accuse her daughter of fabricating such a story. That most probably, it was the fabrication of a simple-minded touching on ugly and morbid things that sometimes turn into rumors. I was suspect in maman's eyes.

Anyways, my mother did not want to revivify bad souvenirs that come to push back if not lower self-esteem in a young girl like me who suffers from retardation. It was in the past and it would not occur again since she told herself that she would watch over me so that nothing like that would ever happen to me again.

Later, my mother admitted to me that she had confessed to the *curé* and that she had told him that she would expiate her reticence about this affair of abuse and that the religious of the boarding school guilty and evil would expiate themselves their abuses, their faults, their sins in purgatory if the *Bon Dieu* was truly merciful. If not, they would burn in hell for eternity. Damned! The *curé* said to her that one must not judge others like that and that God's justice would find its fullness at the appropriate time only known by God. That's what my mother told me.

—My God, how terrible and insane is that story. I can't get over it, Lucienne.

Do you know why I told you and why I feel worthy of your compassion towards me? It's because I feel all riled up and sharpebed like a knife about the case of Timiskamengo who also suffered abuses worst than me, I'm sure. He ran away in the virgin forest never to return to his tribe in Batiscan. They found him dead in the virgin forest eaten alive, I believe. They buried him with remorse and regret. They blamed the Whites for the loss of a tribe member and for his death, especially the government and the Church. The abuse had totally decomposed his identity to which he held so strongly and with such pride. That's the reason why I feel so affiliated to him. Abuse solves nothing and only worsens things that come and tear the heart and soul apart. I'm telling you, Gaétane, abuse hurts and it stays stuck there inside....she pointed her finger to Gaétane's breast who remained immobile and numbed by the fear of this happening to her one day.

With time and work at the mill, Lucienne became more and more gay and open about her destiny of a woman facing the future with an enthusiasm unknown beforehand. She went to the market and saw some women with whom she chatted and held long conversations about all kinds of things that exploited more and more her knowledge and her ardor for living fully and with assurance. She had confidence in herself enough to give her a strong desire to explore the full possibility of becoming a healer as had declared the old sorceress of Batiscan. At the beginning, she did not know if she should venture herself into this domain or not. What did she know about medicinal herbs, brews, onguents, camphor oil, toning lotions, and therapeutic advice that she could give people who would ask for advice if not their healing. She felt being called to serve as healer for the people who were suffering and did not want a doctor or an apprentice. These people knew how to render them comfort and good care. She would be a caregiver and a healer, she told herself. After all, it was her vocation to heal the sick afflicted with certain maladies or malaise that too often even doctors could not heal. She, Lucienne, the simple-minded would have recourse to prayer in order to heal and comfort. She prayed to God for healing others and at times the saints to intercede for her and her sick people. People swore that prayer renders sacred the demands and the rites of healing like certain chosen Indians that she had known like Jean Timiskamengo. These people had recourse to the Grand Manitou and supernatural forces and then they had received the energy of efficacious healing granted to people gifted with the will of heaven. Without being too proud, Lucienne felt ready to develop her gift of healing that she had gotten by the inexplicable natural and supernatural forces of the cosmos created by the *Bon Dieu*. Without any formal education in the domain of natural and scientific healing. she felt the energy and the strength of medicinal knowledge went into her by some kind of osmosis. Of course, she knew nothing about osmosis but she perceived within her a kind of mysterious force that energized her. It acted as a foil against her retardation, she told herself. In spite of years of confusion concerning her call in life, Lucienne discovered her vocation and her assessment in a life sewn with errances and derailments. She would indeed become a healer. That was all. After all, it was written in the stars, she said to herself.

Lucienne had met on her path to the pursuit of care based on natural therapies, an old lady whose name was Georgette Simard. Everyone called her, "*mémère-la raconteuse-de-belles-guérisons*", grandma the teller of beautiful healings, perhaps due to her advanced age and perhaps she

Lucienne, the Simple-Minded

inspired a certain confidence in people. In any case, *mémère* knew how to heal. She had been a caregiver/healer for years and years. Everyone knew her for her particular care.

There was her *onguent sainte,* as people called it, for example. [*onguent* is masculine in gender but *mémère* and people made it feminine]. She put together a mixture of rosin, wax from blessed candles, holy oil, as well as other ingredients known only to her. She would put everything in an old pot and place it on her old black wood stove until it all came simmered for the time prescribed by the recipe that she had kept for years. In the meantime, she knelt before the stove and said certain prayers that she knew by heart with an intense ardor that only old people wizened by sincere devotions and sacred trust can do. Once the ritual completed, she removed the confection from the stove and let it cool. Afterwards, she put what she called the onguent into small white glass jars. The great benefit of this onguent was that it could heal all septic sores by *en tirant le méchant,* drawing the bad stuff, said the people who had witnessed such healings be it caused by a splinter, grains of sand hidden under the skin or other matter such as small splinters of broken glass. Everyone came to her house to get this onguent called miraculous. By dint of supplicating *mémère* for her recipe, Lucienne received from her an oral recipe for the grandma did not want to put it on paper. Lucienne was going to use this onguent for she knew that one day the *mémère* was going to disappear from the neighborhood. She already was ninety-five years old.

Mémère had learned the making of this onguent from her own maternal grandmother. So, it was of a long time ago this onguent of the healer.

Later, Lucienne heard of other healers such as Senora Lampantiene of Mexican origin who was established in New England with one of her daughters married to a Franco-American named Laurent Desjardins whose relatives came from Quebec. He worked at the mill just like most of the emigrés. Lucienne had met the senora at the parochial bazaar and they became fast friends without too many words and without delay. The senora recognized in Lucienne that she was a healer also. She talked to her about *curanderismo,* an indigenous therapy in Mexico where this lady came from. She was a *curandera*, a healer of natural elements and faith which was of the Hispanophone tradition. Lucienne knew nothing about that and was stupefied at the knowledge of this old lady. She had learned it from her own grandmother who had learned it from an old aunt, named Estella Festival. The senora taught Lucienne some therapies that she could readily use in her healing sessions and Lucienne, the so-called simple-minded at one time, added them to her list of caregiving/healing therapies. What was a bit strange was the fact that the senora spoke in Spanish most of the time since she only knew a few phrases in French because her son-law-law had taught them to her. However, Lucienne and her got along well and sort of understood one another without too much effort. Some would say that it was the language of the stars and healing that got into their conversation. Most Hispanophones believe in the stars and their mysterious presence and the way they influence the healing of people and their destiny. Lucienne was indeed in good company. It's like this that Lucienne came to learn some Spanish. She said that it strongly resembled French. The simple- minded was not so *gnochonne*, stupid, and so *niaise*, naive as that.

Lucienne talked about it to Gaétane who was surprised but not shaken by her declaration of devoting herself entirely to the vocation of caregiver/healer.

—I knew that you would find your niche in life someday. The more you row the more you will go far.

—I'm not a rowboat neither am I a fisherman of eels nor a sailor.

—No, but you can row without oars.

Both of them started to laugh. It did not take much for them to laugh. Just a little pun or funny story.

—Listen, Lucienne, when are you going to meet the man of your life? When you're dead?

—Don't ask me that if you yourself remain single.

—It's because I want it this way.

—You want to stay alone by yourself until you die?

—If I want to. However, there's a young man who pleases me. He's so handsome and straight as a picket from a fence that he could easily make any movie star jealous.

—What's his name?

—His name is Jean-Paul Lacoursière from Weymouth. He's a door-to-door salesman. I see him sometimes knocking at the door of future subscribers. He sells books and magazines. I met him in town where he was buying candy at the boutique **Calvados-en-Rien**. They sell all kinds of candy and drinks there. We met once or twice at the cinéma **Globe**. I find him nice and goodhearted but a little too proud in the way he dresses and somewhat of a braggart and show-off I might say. He tried to kiss me one time only. I immediately shoved him away for he smelled of a man's cologne strong enough to make you pinch your nose, so strong and disgusting was it. He would be a good companion for you, my *chouette*.

—Not if you don't want him.

—I could have you meet him one of these days.

—No.

—No?

—No. I said no. I'm going to meet a man, I tell you, a man who pleases me and knows how to please with kindness and compassion. But he won't be a man of your choice. I can choose one by myself. Your choices are almost always null and void for me.

—What do you mean by that?

—It's that you do not know how to choose. You always have the capricious taste of choosing beings difficult to determine whether they are intelligent enough or if they have holes in their socks.

—What do you mean by holes in their socks?

—Holes in their socks, you know. If they have any it's because no one takes care of them or else they are not proud enough to keep themselves presentable. They do not walk with hidden holes only but with holes in their brains.

—You are bad, Lucienne, really vicious.

—Do what you want and think as you want. As for me, I do not want any part of those creatures. I'll find myself one somewhere sometimes.

—If you wait too long you'll find yourself with empty hands and an empty heart.

—My heart will never be empty because I keep good memories of people who loved me and I loved them. Love is a healing factor you know. It heals everything from soup to nuts.

—You're crazy.

—But I must say, just like your mother, Célie and Alexis used to say and do, and I must not forget Timiskamengo, even though you never met him.

—What do you mean by say and do?

—I mean follow their love magic. They knew how.

—Yes and there are others too but I can't enumerate all of them. like the old lady of Batiscan.

Yes, the old sorceress, the healer and caregiver *hors paire*.

Lucienne continued her research on the different modalities of healing and caregiving with natural therapies. Her research was not essentially based on scientific methodology but on what she had learned from other healers that she had met on her road to impressionistic but intelligent therapies. She called it mysteriously supernatural. They were people that had received one way or another the gift of healing. How can one define the gift of healing was altogether a challenge for her. It wasn't a question of definition but a question of accepting what was given freely. A gift was a gift, Period.

After months of apprenticeship, Lucienne still pursued her research either by her reading of texts in the library either by meetings and conferences with interesting people who knew their trade of healing, either by getting together with caregivers/healers, or by her own experiences with people who came to her door to ask her to heal them. She had accumulated a whole stack of knowledge concerning natural healing. She had to sift through all of that and gather the essence of know-how. In the process of apprenticeship she realized that she had the gift of healing by virtue of her capacities for extracting certain facts and measures of the art of healing. Yes, it was an art and someone did not need to convince her of it. Art was an appreciation of the human quality of being creative. Creativity was indeed a gift. She had learned that along with her research that explored so many facets of knowledge. All of this came to her naturally casting aside her stamp of simple-mindedness that others had offered her or even endowed her critically. She could now do the tangible experience of healing. The doubts and the lack of self-confidence had evaporated with time and patience.

Now it was a *fait accompli* to heal without the fear of failure. Lucienne had spent long hours praying and meditating so she would be able to depend on her inner talents and her spiritual capacities. She told Gaétane that prayer was the glue or adhesive that bonded with strength and power to hold everything together. And Gaétane replied that she was so right in spite of her new-found intelligence that made her apparently superior to people like her. Lucienne simply smiled and lifted her nose in the air like a monkey.

Lucienne had not neglected her dear friend of many years. Gaétane was her reinforcement, her inevitable support, said she. And then, Lucienne no longer ranked herself with those of limited intelligence but on the side of a remarkable know-how. Not that she had become a brilliant person, an extraordinary person gifted with remarkable knowledge and skills but she had acquired a sense of balance in her life, balancing both talents with the wisdom of a ripe person in order to come to the help of all those who solicited her to heal them be it medications that did not work or something less effective. Lucienne the simple- minded had become the simple-knower of healing.

Without abandoning her work at the mill for she still needed to earn her daily bread and money to pay her bills, Lucienne started to practice her art, that of healing. She purchased provisions such as camphor oil, lotions, preparations for natural brews and curative infusions, three ointments and other things that she thought useful in her trade. Then she consulted a Monsieur Ruel that we called *arrangeur* and sometimes "*amancheur*", a fixer and manipulator of bones and muscles, recognized for his natural therapies and especially for his "green oil" that everyone proclaimed as a good rubbing oil. This oil once applied to contusions and body members had a certain virtue of relief and softening of pain. This Monsieur Ruel, natural healer offered the patient a new life without extreme suffering, so said those who frequented his home-practice. His fame went from mouth to mouth throughout the neighborhood and even farther places. Some called him a quack unfortunately.

Then Lucienne went to see an old lady healer also, a Madame Leclair who told her about the seventh boy-child gift known by many who were interested in supernatural elements. She told her that if there is a seventh child born in a family and he is the seventh son in a row without interruption of a girl-child, then this boy is definitely a gift from God. He can heal and do other gifted things such as healing and certain things that are considered miraculous by some. People talked about the gift of "*le septième*" and believed fervently in his powers to affect change and healing. Then she gave her precisions on the power to stop bleeding when bleeding too much was an issue. Another factor of healing was the stopping of burns and their sensation of pain whenever someone burned himself. Burns can be extremely painful, the old lady said. These powers of healing were acquired by means of transmission from woman to man or man to woman, she told Lucienne. There were always prayers attached to these efforts of healing. She was told. Lucienne said that prayers were always in her practice of healing.

In her free time, Lucienne learned from day to day, week to week, and from month to month the means and methods of healing in the most natural way. Madame Leclair told her that she was not the one who healed but the Good Lord with the help of fervent prayers and sacrifices on her part. Monsieur Ruel told Lucienne that he was not the one who healed but that the person who sought healing had the power in him and her to affect natural healing. He was simply an agent of healing, he told her. With all of these methods of healing and advice from people she met who were healers, Lucienne developed a fervent and determined practice of healing that she recognized as a gift. She also recognized that a doctor or practitioner can cure people but the patient is the one who heals.

The old sorceress of Batiscan had told her that. There were some who called her a charlatan or some kind of derogatory appellation. Nothing hurt her nor rubbed her the wrong way. She continued practicing her skills as a healer in spite of the insults, the name-calling, the effrontery of certain people who still considered her simple-minded or even lamebrain. Lucienne still continued to do good to whoever went to see her and asked for help no matter what. She was often considered a comforter of broken dreams and broken desires by some. She had had those herself and she had overcome them through patience and hope that some day she would be healed herself. Her mother, Héloïse and her father, Alexis, had thought the same.

One day, Lucienne was called to the bedside of this woman who was advanced in age but young in spirit, she was told. She lived with her adopted son and she suffered from pains in her legs as well as back pain that her doctor could not sufficiently diagnose. He had given her prescriptions for medication but nothing seemed to relieve her of her pain. So Lucienne was called to the house and took a look at the bedridden woman to see if she could give her the necessary care she needed. The son was called William Henry Rafferty, son of the second husband of the old lady. She had adopted him as her son but she had retained the name of Vaillancourt, the name of her first husband, for she did not want to change her name and have an Irish name instead. She often used both last names, Vaillancourt Rafferty. The adopted son was thirty-six years old and single and taking care of his adoptive mother and doing everything to bring her comfort and affection. Lucienne knocked at the door of the house where the lady Vaillantcourt lived, the one who was constantly in pain. Pain especially back pain was definitely a challenge for any healer, thought Lucienne. The door opened slowly leaving a gap through which the profile of a man could be seen. He opened the door wider and Lucienne saw a young man with a thin body, an air that was docile and frank and the stance straight and clean. At first glance, Lucienne was surprised and impressed by this young and mature man she saw. He was handsome, charming and he appeared polite and genteel with his mother. She found him according to her taste.

The young man brought Lucienne to the parlor where the old lady was sitting in very soft armchair resting. Her two legs were perched up on a stool. She greeted Lucienne warmly and told her to sit next to her while the young man stood standing right next to his mother. The lady introduced herself as Madame Vaillancourt Rafferty. " *Je suis la belle-mère de Bill,*" she said. Bill corrected her by saying, "William, William is my name."

—What can I do for you, Madame?

—Well, Lucienne, your name is Lucienne, isn't it?

—Yes, Madame.

—My name is Églantine. You may call me Églantine. I hurt everywhere, my back, my legs, my feet, and I do not have an appetite for anything. It's terrible, my dear. I was bedridden for days.

—That's too bad. That's a lot. Let's begin with the back. I'm going to rub it with green oil then I'm going to apply a poultice. That should give you some relief.

Then I'm going to rub your legs and both feet with a toning lotion to alleviate the pain. Then we shall see for the appetite.

Lucienne started to get fully involved with the proposed therapy. She was fully devoted to her skills as a therapist/healer and it showed. The old lady and William Henry looked at her intently knowing full well that she was indeed a professional healer. She rubbed the back with agile and vigorous hands well enough to invigorate the nerve endings as well as the muscles. Then she went to look into her large canvas bag to find the preparatory items for the poultice. Then she asked the lady to loosen her nightgown in the back so that she could probe the back to see where the pain was and then rub it with warm oil and then apply the poultice there. Finally once the poultice was applied gently and firmly with professional skill and talent, the patient was told to breathe easily and with little or no stress and wait for the time to unwind and release the tension that caused the pain. Then Lucienne asked the young man to bring her some hot water for her special brew. He came back after a short while with a small kettle of hot almost boiling water. Luciennne thanked him and began preparing the brew. She put some special medicinal herbs in a large bowl, added some spices and let the whole concoction sit still until she sincerely thought that the infusion was ready to be served to the old lady in pain. She gave it to Églantine very slowly and let it slide down her throat carefully until it was successfully swallowed without too much heat in her mouth and throat to burn tender tissues. After a few long moments, she asked the lady,

—Are you feeling a little better now? Do you have the same level of discomfort you had before?

—Yes, my dear, much better, thank you. It's also the effect of your presence next to me that makes me feel better. The pain is still there bur oh so softer. Thank God!

—Yes, we have to thank him for his merciful help.

—Do you want to pray with me? asked the lady.

—Yes, Madame, we must, because the healing depends on the fervent prayers that are said.

The young man rejoined his mother and Lucienne and all three of them recited a short prayer that the old lady had on a piece of paper in the pocket of her apron. She had worn her apron over her nightgown in order to protect the cleanliness of good and often expensive clothes so much appreciated by older women her age. It was a prayer to the Virgin Mary, Our Lady of the Seven Sorrows.

The seance of therapy concluded and Lucienne prepared herself to leave. She gave instructions to the young man for the continuation of the therapy she had started with Madame Vaillancourt. She told him that she would be back the following day and verify if the therapy was successful enough to proceed further. The young man wanted to give her some money but she refused saying that she did this voluntarily and that it was free. The young man thanked her and she left feeling in her heart the accomplishment she had done. Well done, she murmured to herself.

The following day, Lucienne returned to Madame Vaillancourt Rafferty's house, she remembered that the old lady had two last names, and she discovered that the old lady was walking with a cane and did it without too much pain. She told Lucienne that the pain in her back had abated and that she had taken her first breakfast since the week before when she started feeling so much pain. She was happy and so was her son William Henry. Lucienne felt proud of the success of her work and happy at the same time. The young man had a wide smile on his face and kept looking at Lucienne with contentment and admiration. She felt like blushing inside of her. She did not want to show it in her face. She chatted with the old lady before leaving. As she was preparing to leave, the young man asked her if she wouldn't like to have lunch with him in a small restaurant that he frequented for their delightful food. The restaurant was not far from his house, he said, and that he would go and get her if she accepted. It was the right thing to do, he said. Lucienne was somewhat stunned for she had not expected that but she admired his politeness and sense of generosity. Curiously on her part and without too much hesitation, Lucienne accepted the offer which apparently was somewhat of a revelation to her, the once simple-minded girl grown to womanhood. It was somehow a revelation since she did not really know that she could be that spontaneous and that accepting an offer from a young man she had just met was new to her. It was truly a surprise for her. Her mother would have been proud, she thought.

 The following day was a Saturday and Lucienne did not work in the mill on weekends. So Lucienne got dressed, a dress that she did not usually wear during the week but since this was a special day for her, she decided to wear one of her Sunday dresses, the bright floral one she loved. She was going to try and impress this young man that she admired and had the beginning of some affection for him. She was surprised at herself and the way affection begins without wanting it to happen so interestingly and almost suddenly. She felt happy and free of those doubts that had pursued her for so long before. She felt liberated and glad.

 Lucienne walked to the restaurant for she told the young man that she could do it and not bother him to come and get her. She was still the independent girl/woman she had been. She did not want to separate herself from her independence too soon. It was somewhat part of her talents, she said. So she walked to the small restaurant called **Chez Lucien** designated by the young man and saw that William Henry was waiting for her at the door as he had told her. It was around one thirty on a bright September afternoon and the air was fresh as new mown grass.

—Oh, this reminds me of the little restaurant my mother started and it was called **Chez Héloïse**, if I remember. My father helped her and it became a local hangout for so many people that it turned out to be a genuine success. However, with time and strikes at the mill, the clientele became very thin and desolate due to a lack of money on the part of the millworker who had such a hard time making ends meet. So the restaurant had to close. I was too young then to remember things but my mother told me all about it.

The two of them entered the restaurant and were greeted by a petite lady dessed in black. She looked very demure and was well groomed.

—Hello, William Henry, how are you and how is your dear mother, she said to him. Welcome to your restaurant of choice.

William Henry smiled at her with a dignified and joyous smile. He then told Lucienne that this was a part owner of the restaurant and that her name was Gilberte.

—Hello and welcome Mademoiselle.

—Mademoiselle Charbonneau, said Lucienne.

—What a lovely French Canadian name.

—Oui, answered Lucienne upon hearing the family name that she bore. It was her parents' name, Héloïse and Alexis Charbonneau, she said.

—Now I know your full name, Lucienne Charbonneau, said the young man.

—Oui, Lucienne Charbonneau. My mother's maiden name was Lanouette de Batiscan.

—That's settlers country, replied Gilberte.

—Yes, it is, Mademoiselle.

—It's Mademoiselle Paradis formerly of Sherbrooke. Come follow me. I've prepared a table for you two. It's right next to the bay window. You can see the lovely roses still in bloom. They're waiting for you.

Gilberte led the two to the table reserved for them. Everything looked fresh and clean. It was the French-Canadian way of doing things, *la propreté avant tout et après la nourriture,* cleanliness first then the food.

—Merci, Gilberte, said William Henry. And how is your mother?

—She is fine, thank you. She hardly steps out of the house, however. She has problems with her back and she keeps dragging her feet. She complains that she is in constant pain. She walks with a walker which she hates.

—Too bad. Perhaps Lucienne could help her. She's a fine therapist. She helped my mother. She's a good healer.

Lucienne looked at him with somewhat of a blushed face. She did not want to discuss her work with people and their illnesses.

—Ah, ma mère, said Gilbert in a somewaht exasperated voice, my mother would be horrified at the mere mention of a healer, *une guérisseuse* as they are called. She calls them charlatans and false practitioners of medicine.

Lucienne winced at that statement by Gilberte. William Henry could see Lucienne's reaction to this and tried to change the subject but could not stop from saying,

—Yet Lucienne is neither one nor the other. She is truly gifted with a rare talent of healing. She did it with my mother.

—Let's talk about something else for Gilberte certainly does not want to hear about a *guérisseuse* like me.

—But, of course, Mademoiselle Lucienne. This interests me a lot.

—I am a humble *guérisseuse,* I assure you, and I'm not one who brags about it. I do not like to shout it from rooftops. I simply help people.

—Of course, Mademoiselle, Lucienne. I'm sure you have special gifts for healing if William Henry dares to say so. I believe him. However, I'll let you two order your meal and we'll talk about that afterwards. Yes?

The two new found friends ordered a hot soup and half a ham sandwich on homemade bread with a little bit of mustard. While chatting, William Henry asked Lucienne if she loved to read. She told him, yes, and she gave him the titles of some books she had borrowed from the municipal library: *The New Age of Healing*, *La Guérison naturelle*, *The Curative Power of Prayers*, *The Curanderas and Their Heritage*, *Healing and the Medicines of the Ages* and others.

—But all these titles are concerning natural, folk or ethnic healing. You do read a lot of books, I might say but nothing to stir your imagination or prod your sense of culture and history.

—Yes, because the subject matters to me and it excites my curiosity about healing. After all, this is my trade. However, I did not always understand fully what I was reading. I never had a good formal education, you know. They declared me simple-minded and there were some who stamped me retarded. I always was confused about that.

—Yet, you are not retarded. You have a very good measure of intelligence and especially talent for getting along with people. And I saw very well in my mother's case that you have an extraordinary gift for healing and caregiving.

—Thank you. I recognize after many years my capacity to take care of the sick and people who suffer one way or another is very good. Not necessarily extraordinary but good. I have been able to recognize the possibility of being useful in life. I never thouhgt I could be. So now I'm at work in my trade of healing and I love it.

—The gift of healing is a remarkable gift, I must say.

—Yes, I must thank the good Lord. I cannot get over the fact that I am blessed by him.

—You are a charming young woman and frank in your feelings and I admire that in people like you.

—You're making me blush with your compliments.

—Listen, you always call me William Henry. It's Bill, that's it All my friends call me Bill. You know you are my friend, don't you?

—Yes, agreed. Why do you call the old lady my mother when she's not really your mother?

—Good question. She is my adopted mother by marriage with my father. My true mother died when I was but two years old. My father remarried with Madame Vaillancourt who was a widow without children. So, she has like adopted me and I call her mother. Besides, I do not like the name of adopted mother. I prefer mother instead. She did not adopt me rather she took me in like a loving mother. I love her as a mother.

Lucienne and William Henry ate their meal mostly in silence because they had said everything they wanted to say before. They had a hot herbal tea afterwards and they discussed he case of Madame Vaillancourt and that of Gilberte's mother, Madame Héloïse Paradis. William Henry invited Gilberte to his table so they could discuss her mother's case.

After the three of them had discussed the two cases and that Lucienne promised to look into Madame Paradis' case and give it her best attention, the two friends continued their conversation and Gilberte went to wait on two other people she knew. Gilberte was very good at friendly conversation.

—Lucienne do you like reading, I mean literature, French literature?

—I love to read and I read what I can put my hands on. However, I do not know much about French literature, any literature. I was never initiated in it. My parents were not readers, certainly not of literature. I was told that Célie was.

—Who is Célie?

—A very good friend of my mother and her caregiver. I'll tell you her story some day. Hers and her lover Timiskamengo.

—Timiskamengo? Sounds very exotic.

—He was an Algonquin Indian, the son of a well-known Indian chief.

—Oh.

William Henry followed up on his conversation about literature.

—Well, I love the literay works of Gustave Flaubert and I will introduce you to some of his books. The first one *Un coeur simple*, The Simple Heart is the story of Félicité the simple-hearted and her parrot, Loulou. You're going to love this tale. I will bring you a copy of it next week when we will meet again.

—Why, yes, we must.

Lucienne met Bill two days later at the same little restaurant where Bill offered her the small book of *Les Trois Contes de Flaubert*. She put it in her handbag and thanked him for his offering of a book that he liked very much. She promised him that she would read it and discuss it with him when he had time. They had their lunch, said goodbye to Gilberte and left. It was Sunday and Bill had to get back home to give some food to his mother. She had a good enough appetite now. She felt much better now but still had some pain in her back. Prior to this, Lucienne went to visit Gilberte's mother at home. She found her pale and thin. She complained of back pain and stomach pains. Gilberte told her that her mother hardly ate, only a few bites of toast in the morning and refused to take anything else before her afternoon nap. Lucienne tried to take the beat of the heart of old Héloïse and to palp her here and there, specifically where the old lady complained of pain in certain particular spots. The old mother Héloïse had complained all night long and in early morning hours too. Gilberte's mother was driving her crazy with her pains and her long-drawn complaints. She did not want to see the *guérisseuse* for she did not trust a caregiver like that. A charlatan, she said. Nor did she desire to se the family physician, *le docteur Perreault*, for she did not trust him. To her, he was nothing but a quack. Gilberte did not know what to do with her mother. She was simply desperate, *rendu au désespoir*, as the people in Quebec and those who had emigrated from Quebec to New England's mill towns said. That was it, Madame Paradis was simply an old cranky Québécoise who had never lost her dissatifaction with professional people especially caregivers and much more *les guérisseuses* like that Charbonneau girl that she had met because Gilberte's friend had tricked her into it, she claimed.

Well, Lucienne tried everything she could to get the old lady Paradis calmed down and be docile with the therapy Lucienne was attempting to give her. Gilberte tried to tell her mother that Lucienne was trying to do the best she could to relieve her of her back pain. Madame Paradis told her daughter, "What does she know aboutt pain? She never had any children. I don't trust her. *Pantoute*, not at all. She did not need therapy, she said, especially from a charlatan. Besides, she said, that young woman was a stranger, *un pur étranger*, she insisted. She also insisted that she got along very well without her. Gilberte tried to convince her mother not to be so *déplaisante avec d'la visite*, disagreeable with visitors. The mother wanted to let Lucienne go so she would win, just like a child who wants to have her own way, thought Gilberte."*Vous gagnerez pas 'man. J'veux qu'elle reste et vous donner les soins nécessaires pour votre mal. C'est toute.*" You will not win, 'man. I want her to stay and give you the necessary care for your pain. That's all. Madame Paradis started to cry and Lucienne went to her and tried to console her and she succeeded. She knew how. She had learned over the years how to soften the blow, she had said once to her friend, Gaétane.

So, Lucienne looked at Gilberte in the eyes and told her that she could not do anything for her mother without the willingness of the patient to participate in any therapy because it was precisely this that guaranteed at least a beginning of a good rehabilitation. Luciennne left the house of Héloïse Paradis without having the chance to give testimony to her healing capacities. "What do you want," she said to Gilberte, "When you put barriers in front of the promise of healing, then we leave and pray for the poor abandoned one."

Bill met Lucienne almost every Thursday and either they went to the small restaurant for lunch or they took a walk in the municipal park. Lucienne loved the park especially in late spring or the beginning of summer when the lilacs and the rhododendruns were out and the air smelled of lilacs and the delicious smell of blossoms in bloom. She loved flowers and so did William Henry whom she now called Bill.

They had grown close and the relationship blossomed forth along with the flowers. There was happiness in Lucienne's heart. After two months of frequentations, or some people called it dating or simply getting together, Bill told Lucienne that she should no longer work at the mill because she showed signs of exhaustion from work as a spinner. He could definitely see it in her face and in her slower gait due to the stress of the day. Walking and running showed the results of getting tired easily as if she had rocks in her shoes. Her healing practice was increasing due to her reputation among her peers and her following as a healer.

She realized herself that she could no longer continue this way. Gaétane told her repeatedly that she should give up something or else she would have a breakdown or something. She thought about it but continued all of her obligations as a millworker and healer. Besides, she had to work at the mill because she needed the money to live on as well as pay her bills. She was frugal and did not spend for nothing but still she needed the money. She continued to work at Cushnoc.

One day William Henry offered a proposition.

—I'm going to give you money each week so that you will be able to liberate yourself from the crazy labor at the mill. It's a place of exploitation and preys on poor people like you. I want to help you.

—I need to work, Bill, and that is that. I will not accept charity.

—This is not charity. It's a friendly offer. I want to do it. I love you, Lucienne, and I truly want to do this. This way you will be able to devote all your time to your work as healer and caregiver. You really need help and I know it. My father left me a substantial sum of money. My father was a rich man. He founded an insurance company that thrived and he was an ingenious man who knew how to do business while not spending his money foolishly. When my mother died, he was left alone with me and he was a lonely man. When he married my step-mother, you know I call her mother. I was happy for him. My father accumulated funds that even he did not know what he really had. He never considered himself a rich man and he gave money away to the poor and homeless. He was a charitable man, my father. He passed on to me, his only son, the merit of giving. I loved my father and I know he left enough for my other mother to be able to live comfortably. She need not worry about her daily bread. So, my dear Lucienne, put your pride aside and please, please accept my offer to you. I'm inviting you to share in my father's benevolent gift to me, my mother and now to you.

—I can't, Bill. I just cannot accept charity. I was not brought up that way.

—I know that your mother and father raised you well. I also know that you are the product of hard labor in the mill just like so many French-Canadians who came to work in the States. Your parents took very good care of you and they and followed you and your progress in your struggle with retardation. However, that was not your case. You know now that you are not retarded.

—But I was low in intelligence.

—You mended that by your constant efforts to educate yourself. Besides your calling is to be a healer and you are very good at it. Can't you see what I'm offering you is not charity but love.

Lucienne was suddenly surprised at his declaration of love. She had not expected that. She loved William Henry and she realized that it was a love that had grown with leaps of getting to know him, his lovely mother but not his money. She did not want any part of it. She was not poor; she was simply lacking resources to make ends meet. She did not know what to do. It was a difficult decision to make.

—Bill can't we just keep doing things the way we have been?

—Now you are forcing my hand. If you do not want my money then please listen to what I'm going to tell you. There is another way to offer it to you without pride and without the fear of charity. That is marriage.

Silence. A silence profound enough to shut off the cawing of crows.

—I don't know what to say.

—Say yes or no. That's all.

—Please don't rush me.

Lucienne, the Simple-Minded

She hesitated, wrenched her hands. She blushed a bit because she did not know what to tell him. After a long moment of silence, she murmured, yes.

—It's not that I want to jump into marriage or put you in the embarrassment of a refusal on my part, but I must admit that I am in love with you. I was from the very first moment I met you. Isn't that strange?

—So, it's yes.

—I've never received an invitation like that...a proposal of marriage. Think of it boys ans girls! I thought of it often I never found someone I could rely on and give him my love. I never knew how to love a man except my father. I repeat, I fell in love with you the moment I set eyes on you. Isn't that foolish. This love affair is so strange for me and at the same time crazy. I cannot make heads or tails out of it but I know that I love you, William Henry Rafferty. I know though that it comes from above this love and this proposal. I never never expected it *Bon Dieu, vous êtes généreux*, you are generous. Ah, I feel so dizzy. I feel so much like my whole inside is trembling like the leaves on branches that feel the gusts of the wind except for me it's your love. It's crazy, I tell you, it's crazy.

—It's not crazy. It's the thrust of the heart that spurs you on to say yes to love, to me, dear Lucienne. That's how I see it. I love you, Lucienne. That's all I can tell you.

—I love you also. I love you...*je t'aime à la folie*, as people say, yes it's foolishness. My heart beats so fast that I can't take it. I must sit down and catch my breath.

Love takes my breath away, Bill.

Bill kissed her and she looked into his eyes and saw love, generous, kind, and secure love.

—Don't you go crazy over this. This is not a misunderstanding, it's real, it's true. I love you and I want you happy and rid of th stress of working hard in the mill. I want us to be happy. Together, Lucienne, not separated like we have been. You will come and live with me and my mother. I just hope you will be able to live with me. I'm hard-headed and stubborn at times but I'm not mean. I trust you do not have any worries about living with us.

—Oh, no, not at all. Your mother is so nice, such a gentle person. I will take care of her and be her healer.

—That's not the only reason I want to marry you but because I do love you.

—I know, I know. Does your mother know about this?

—She will know when I tell her. She will not be totally surprised for she knows that I love you and that I want us to live together as husband and wife.

—Ah, mon Dieu!

William Henry gave her a big kiss and hugged her until she cried out, "You're hurting me." She held on to him for a long time. It was a tender moment of love for her, tangible and real. All of a sudden she started to tremble. Her hands and shoulders did not stop trembling. She was embarrassed and felt like a child who is not able to master her reaction to joy and happiness. She then stepped away because she wanted to glance deeply in his blue eyes, so deep and so ocean blue. Her glance was so ardent and filled with fire, it seemed. She wanted to appreciate him, his masculine beauty, his gentle look and his aquiline nose. She had never really stared at a man's face before not even her father's, Yet, her father had a very handsome face. William Henry was truly handsome. He was tall, had a thin and shining face and it shone each time he smiled, a wide smile revealing bright white teeth. He had that soft gentle look and bright if not glowing eyes that movie stars have on screen. Besides, he was endowed with a keen intelligence without the feature of the sense of pride turned to haughtiness that so many men have.

Lucienne also noticed his perspicacity and his sharpness of observation. Most of all, it was his tenderness that she liked and would have liked to make it her own if that had been possible, she said to herself. Everything ran through her head like a dream in the process of creating all kinds of images, all nice and dreamy right now. She thought very silently that there are not too many men who have the

Lucienne, the Simple-Minded

tenderness of the heart and soul like Bill. She murmured "I love you, William Henry Rafferty even though you are not "canuck" like me.

Lucienne hurried to share her good news with Gaétane. Her dear friend was working in her garden. She was preparing the soil for the planting and putting seeds in the ground that would later come up as vegetables. Gaétane had a green thumb and she used it wisely and productively.

—What are you doing with your hands in dirt, the waist bent over and the face dirty with something not too clean?

—Oh, I'm preparing the soil as I always do in the spring.

—Leave that and come with me. We will take a break. I have some exciting news to tell you.

—What? You're changing jobs, right?

—Yes and no.

—Yes and no. Is there something else?

—Yes. I'm getting married soon.

—With whom? This young man that you met at Madame Vaillancourt? I knew all along that things would work out for you this alliance of love and a man of quality. I thought that I had discovered something, a young talented and handsome man in love with Lucienne the caregiver/healer. Am I right or not? I knew it. Magic, yes magic! Wow! A redheaded man with reddish cheeks who looks great. It's him, isn't it?

—Yes, it's him. None other than him.

—So, you really like him?

—I adore him. I'm crazy about him, Gaétane. I'm going to explode.

—Not now, my dear, not before you get married. By the way, when is it?

—I don't know if we will have a wedding celebration or not. A church wedding, yes, but maybe *pas de noces*.

—No wedding celebration! Come on, such a wedding requires a celebration, a huge one. *Pas de noces, pas de mariage à la canadienne, tu sais,* No wedding celebration, no marriage French-Canadian style, you know.

—I'm not sure Bill and I want that kind of celebration since he's not French but Irish. Can you imagine a Franco-American girl, *une canayenne* marrying an Irish laddy? In the good old days, there would have been some kind of revolt. But, this is part of my mother's heritage, the Lanouette heritage and this is not Batiscan.

—No, but it's also your heritage, don't you forget.

The wedding was a simple one. The marriage vows were exchanged at a convent chapel. There were few people there since William Henry had no relatives, no aunts, no uncles, no cousins, just his mother and some close friends. As for Lucienne, she could not contact her sister nor her brother. She did not have any contacts for relatives in Canada. Batiscan was almost an unknown to her. Gaétane, Gilberte were there.

The locale was the chapel of the contemplative sisters of the Sacred Heart of Jesus. It was by exception and with the bishop's permission. William Henry knew him very well. The whole ceremony was done specifically with the approbation of Mother Superior once she heard from the bishop's office. Her name was Mère Marie de la Sainte Face and she had consented to the wedding in spite of her reservations because she was not too happy with something that was profane in her contemplative chapel. However, she too knew William Henry. He was the nephew of Mother Superior's sister. It wasn't an easy maneuver since one must admit that it was out of the ordinary. However, out of respect for the high authority as well as the efficient contacts and the personal influences went very well. It was all of William Henry's request for privacy and solemn diplomacy of special endeavors on his part that such a ceremony was approved. He wanted it this way and he had the respected influence of what is often called the "grey eminence." Lucienne went along with whatever William Henry desired and planned. It must be said that William Henry Rafferty was one of the big donors to the bishop's fund and that of the contemplative sisters of the Sacred-Heart. They never refused a generous gift from a remarkable benefactor such as William Henry Rafferty. He was indeed known for his generosity and gentle touch in private diplomacy.

The wedding took place a Saturday at seven o'clock in the morning. It was a bright if not glorious morning when the sun seems to conspire with nature and grant its rays of splendor for special occasions like the wedding of Bill and Lucienne.

Everyone in the chapel was smiling gratuitously. There was an atmosphere of peaceful contemplative splendor that existed there in the lovely but stark chapel. Flowers were allowed and a muted silence with whispers was not denied.

Everyone was anxious to see the bride walk down the aisle with one of William Henry's best friends since there was no Alexis available as father of the bride. Lucienne did think about his missing presence. She wore a simple sky blue dress since she had no desire to wear the traditional virgin white dress even though she was a virgin. She had told Gaétane that she was too old to wear white like the young women who have the hope and desire of displaying their sign of virginal purity. White was traditional in any case. Lucienne had chosen blue since blue was her favorite color and that it was deemed the Virgin Mary's color. Besides, The Virgin Mary who was pure and simple of heart, thought Lucienne, would watch over her a simple soul like her. She was not the simple-minded one but she did acknowledge that she had retained her simplicity as a humble soul.

Lucienne had white gloves and a small blue hat with a veil that was short but decent, she thought. It just covered her forehead. She held in her hands a small bouquet of lilies of the valley, her favorites. Nothing was out of her sense of modesty and reserve for she had been raised not to cross over modesty with airs of immodest costumes. She was calm although she was trembling a bit. William Henry was looking at her from the corner of his eye and murmured how lovely she looked.

Madame Rafferty who once was Madame Villaincourt was sitting in a front pew and looked radiant. She wore a tender pink dress and a hat that matched this soft color of her *crêpe georgette* dress. She had a corsage of pale pink orchids on her left shoulder. She looked proud and filled with joy as her benign smile indicated. Gilberte and Gaétane were seated behind her while the two neighbors of Lucienne shared another pew right next to the two friends. There was no one else in the small chapel except Mother Superior who was assiduously watching behind the cloister screen.

The priest greeted both Lucienne and William Henry with the deference and kindness of a disciple of Saint Francis. He was a retired Franciscan who served as chaplain for the cloistered nuns. The ceremony went smoothly and with the dignity a monk can bring to it. There was an ambiance of a monastic *recueillement,* and calm that hung over the participants. Lucienne especially who truly enjoyed this atmosphere that relieved her of her little fears that little things would go wrong in an unexpected manner no matter what and that she would be the one who would spoil the nuptial ceremony. Lucienne had never lost her hesitations and her worries facing a formal and imposing occasion like this one. William Henry often told her not to preoccupy herself with things that one could not change or modify. She just could not control the cares and worries that she had known how to temper but not fully dispel them.

Once the vows exchanged, the prayers from the missal said and the Eucharist shared, it was the *Ite, missa est* and the mass was done with the nuptial blessing of Father Lagacé o.f.m. The newlyweds and their invited guests went out the chapel quietly and with the reverence required by the cloister. The old lady had her left arm in William Henry's crook of his right arm while Lucienne held her by her right hand, hand in hand. They all went to the little restaurant **Chez Lucien** under the charming obligation to do so of Gilberte. They all there celebrating the couple, drinking a toast and wishing Lucienne and William Henry good cheer and a happy life together. The food arrived and everyone enjoyed it and became fully satisfied with each mouthful. It was delicious, said the guests and Gilberte thanked everyone. Then the wedding cake came. It had two layers and the frosting was simply creamy and delightful. On top was a small porcelain couple with the bride having a blue dress which surprised Lucienne. Gilberte had it done specially for her friend. Lucienne could not help herself crying out oh's and ah's that lent simplicity of heart to the celebration. Her husband looked at her and smiled tenderly. It was a nice and very pleasant *noces*, said Gilberte to Gaétane. The old Madame Villaincourt Rafferty did not stop smiling and taking bites on her piece of cake. One could see that she was pleased with everything that day, especially pleased that her back was much better and her appetite regained, thanks to Lucienne the healer. The celebration ended around three in the afternoon. They all had a very good time and Lucienne thanked all of them one by one while William Henry stood there smiling and glad he had done what he had done. He told himself that he had brought joy to several people and especially to his wife, Lucienne. A few of them were a bit inebriated but not necessarily drunk. They were celebrating, that was all. Gaétane was singing in French and invited Lucienne to join her which she surprisingly accepted. They were standing on the sidewalk and people in the street were staring at them wondering what was happening.

William Henry and Lucienne left the following morning in the black Buick that the groom had. They were headed for the White Mountains in New Hampshire. They found a chalet on the banks of Lake Winipisauki where they stayed three nights and then headed directly for the mounains afterwards. William Henry wanted to show his wife one of the most famous touristic attractions, "Old Man of the Mountain" formed naturally in effigy with the head and beard, so it seemed, of an old man in stone. He was way up there as many people stopped down below to gape at him with open mouths on some of them especially children and, of course, Lucienne. She kept telling her husband how happy that they had come to the mountains. It was as if it was all a dream or a fairy tale for her. She had hardly traveled before except to go to Quebec at the boarding school but that was not a dream nor a fairy tale, she said. It was rather an episode of a terrible time in her young life. It was an episode of a simple-minded girl searching for her identity while her parents were all so confused and dissatisfied with the whole process of finding a cure. She put it out of her mind. She did not wish to even consider it.

This was, after all, her honeymoon.

The couple found an inn where they settled down for four or five days where both of them could relax and enjoy good company if they met good people, good conversation but also a good time wandering around nature walks. Both of them enjoyed the valley next to the inn. It was filled with wild flowers and it had an exquisite aroma of freshly opened blossoms that just filled one's nose and one's skin, so they said. What struck Lucienne the most was the fragrance of the aromatic herbs and grasses. It reminded her of the aromatic brews she concocted for her therapies as a healer. The fragrance entered her every pore and she exclaimed that this was magic for her, the magic of healing self and others through the wonders of nature so open and so admirable to a simple-minded turned simply full-hearted and content to be who she really was. She was now Mrs. Lucienne Rafferty of Hadley, Massachusetts.

The first evening at dinnertime, both of them met a couple from Maryland. The man worked as a librarian in a small university while the wife volunteered as a caregiver to the poor and homeless. She did not do healing-related work but simply helping out where and when she could. They had both gotten a diploma from well-known graduate schools, the husband from Brown University in Rhode Island and the wife from Tulane University in New Orleans, Louisiana. When Lucienne heard these news she apparently became somewhat ill at ease for her lack of formal higher education. Why, she had no diploma, no high school nor university diplomas. None except for her certificates of training in the caregiving and healing therapies. She had barely squeezed by in grammar school. She called herself non-educated and she feared running into people such as the Maryland couple. She knew that this was not a problem for William Henry Rafferty since he was well-educated and well-read. On top of it all, she was for a long time designated as simple-minded. However, she reminded herself that this was but an error on people's part, people who did not know anything about retardation and its miscalculations by some. She had tried so hard to remedy this situation by ignoring it and realizing that she had special talents for healing. Besides her intelligence was not marginal but had to be developed further with education and reading. She asked herself when would things turn for the best in her simple- mindedness. Bill tried so very hard to convince her that her intelligence was not affected by some theories of certain people who tried to compartmentalize her condition and make her feel inferior. That she had great talents that other people do not have and that compensated for the slowness of her intelligence. She could not accept all the ideas and reasons that were given to her not even those of Bill, his mother, Gaétane sometimes and certainly not her parents, Héloïse in particular. How could she, she told herself. Lucienne had to convince herself that she was not inferior to other people, especially the educated lot. Bill tried to tell her that education was a formation and not an accumulation of knowledge of facts and figures. That one is educated if he or she knows how to think and deliberate. That's what the humanities had taught him, he said. Then he sat down with her and tried to explain what he had just said. Did she take it all in? Who knows, but Bill tried to tell her that she had talent, brains and particular skills at her disposition. That she was not stupid. He tried not to use this word but it slipped out. She often told him that she was born *petit pain*, little bread, and that she was going to remain *petit pain*. He used to reply, *petit pain va loin*, it goes far and she simply smiled at him. William Henry nodded his head and murmured "She doesn't understand. She'll never understand."

While at table during dinner one evening, the couple who had sat at Lucienne's and Bill's table because Bill had insisted on inviting them, John, the husband of the other couple began a conversation concerning books that both John and his wife Agatha had read. Both of them spoke very little French. All they knew were a couple of phrases such as *"Comment allez-vous?* and *"Pas du tout, merci."* They had taken a basic French course but did not remember much. They had very little interest in the language as many college Freshmen have. This was another hitch of bashfulness for Lucienne who felt ill at ease with English that was not her maternal language nor that of her parents and grandparents. Lucienne was silent during most of the meal. One could sense a coolness in the air. In spite of Bill's and John's invitation to join in the conversation. Agatha too tried to gain her attention to relax and talk with them. But Lucienne felt very uncomfortable with those people including her husband. She only uttered a few words with complete hesitation. That seemed to hurt her husband, Bill. He would have wanted his wife to be her complete self and come out of her bashful self that was hampering her open ability with words. Bill found it a powerlessness to socialize with people she did not know but that she could if only she wanted. He told himself that she had capacities to do it but not the willpower. It was a case of pushed back if not hidden intelligence and dynamism, murmured William Henry so often.

Having reached their room for the night, Lucienne got undressed promptly and went to bed without saying a single word. Bill asked her why the dead silence on her part. Why this pouting that he could not understand nor accept. She did not answer. That night there were no expressions of love not even a kiss. Silence and inertia. An inert mask where the smile had disappeared, said one author. That was Lucienne's face that night.

The following morning Lucienne regained her composure and her good humor. Bill was teasing her for having left him the previous evening. She excused herself and wanted to give him a big kiss as a propitiatory offering. He accepted it with tenderness and he told her that he understood her being bashful and her reluctance to accept someone and something that was not well known to her. She promised him that she would educate herself better and would try to read more often books that were considered top readings and would thus sensitize her to literary classics. He told her that it wasn't necessary to do that for him but to do it for herself and her desire to blossom forth by experience and determination and succeed in a universe of so much knowledge and possibilities. She kissed him on the cheek and returned to her task of doing the packing since they were leaving the following afternoon to visit the fine arts museum in Boston.

William Henry had often spoken about the fine arts to Lucienne and how much he appreciated the many paintings of various artists that he had studied in college.

He told her that he loved literature and fine arts enough to make of it a calling of the informed amateur. He tried to explain to her the various styles of the artists he knew as well as the colors they used in order to realize a painting specifically unique for the artist in question. Surrounded by masterpieces of what he considered splendid art, Bill took the occasion at hand to show Lucienne the magnificent paintings that the Boston museum took pride in. He pointed to Jean-Léon Gérôme in particular and his magificent classical painting large enough to cover an entire wall, he told her, **L'Éminence Grise**. He named another one, Claude Monet and his painting what was called the *la japonaiserie*, Japanese style and content. He told her that such a style was in vogue during Monet's time. This particular one was, **Madame Monet dans un kimono japonais**. The color red so vivid here that William Henry could not get over the brilliance and the audacity of this color used by the artist. Bill mentioned yet another one, John Singer Sargent, whose painting, **Fishing for Oysters at Cancale** makes one think of the beaches in New England, he said. Still another, Winslow Homer with his watercolors, **Blue Boat** that reminds one of the tranquility of the woods and ponds, he told Lucienne. She tried to absorb everything that he was telling her, she with an air of vagueness and indolence. Nothing he told her seemed to register in her head. It was too much for her. And, she was tired, very fatigued in mind and body. They left the museum late afternoon to return to Hadley and go home. Lucienne let go a long sigh of relief. The old lady was at the door waiting for them. She was with her guardian. She was happy that her two children were back home. Lucienne was very happy, happier being home than living in a chalet or an inn somewhere in the woods or the mountains. She was also glad to be away from the museum in the large city of Boston althougfh she liked the fact that her husband had a splendid time appreciating famous works of art. She realized that he was fully in his element. As for William Henry, he enjoyed telling his mother about everything that he and Lucienne had seen and experienced in food and works of art. He did not tire of telling her the details of the honeymoon tour in the mountains to the glorious city of Boston and the museum where he had taken his bride. The old woman asked Lucienne if she had loved the musum and she answered a very simple, yes.

    Lucienne wanted to go back to work in the mill but Bill prohibited her from ever going back there since she no longer needed to work especially millwork that pulls the sweat out of poor women like her.

"It's a man's duty to support his wife," he told her affirmatively with a certain dominance in his voice.

—But what am I to do with all this free time that I'll have?

—Volunteer work as usual, my dear.

—But that doesn't pay.

—You don't need to earn a wage. I'll give you money as much as you need.

—But I told you, I don't want to depend on you. I'm not used to it. My parents taught me to be independent and not depend on anybody. We are of Québécois blood and we are solidly independent-minded.

—Be as independent as you want but I'm the man of the house and I will take care of you as I take care of my mother.

—I don't know.

—Lucienne, it's your duty to depend on your husband and I'm going to see to it that you do so. I'm not going to be a millworker's husband and see his wife in a sweatshop like the mill.

—I do not understand an arrangement like that. Remember that I am simple- minded.

—That's an excuse not to think intelligently about something.

—Please don't accuse me of not having enough intelligence to take care of myself.

—That's not what I'm telling you, Lucienne. It's that you do not always understand certain facts in life, in your life.

—That's what simplicity of mind is. I cannot understand everything especially understand like others do and they do it with a facility that I don't have.

—Let's leave everything now and talk about something else, please.

—If you want. As for me I'm not done talking about it. It's my destiny and I need to talk about it to someone who is willing to listen.

—So talk about it to Gaétane.

Lucienne, the Simple-Minded

The days flew by with the rapidity of an eagle with the full span of his enormous wings. It was now seven months since the wedding and Lucienne woke up a bright Monday morning and discovered that menstrual cycle had changed. She was afraid that things had changed in her and that she did not, nor could not understand.

She started to get worried about it. What is happening, she asked herself. It was not usual that her *règles* her woman's cycle of menstruation were no longer working as they used to. Her mother had never explained that to her when she reached the age of talking about woman's stuff, she told herself. What was happening to her and why? She needed explanations but who would give them to her? It was a very private matter, she thought, severely sad if something was happening and she could not decipher it by herself. It would be another case of simple-mindedness, she told herself. Another dumb thing, she thought. Not understanding what was going on would be a lack of intelligence on her part, she thought. But what is actually happening? She muttered.

Lucienne took her courage with her two hands and decided to go and talk to the old lady, Madame Vaillancourt Rafferty. She would have preferred to talk about it to the old sorceress but she lived up north in Batiscan. She would have assured Lucienne about such things as a woman's situation at certain times as she was experiencing now. She felt alone and even somewhat alienated. She decided at last to go and talk to the old lady of the house. For sure, she will be able to explain these things to me, she told herself.

—Madame Églantine, I have something to ask you. In times of stress and worry, Lucienne called the old lady by her first name. It felt more intimate and familiar to her, and the old lady was pleased with it. I have a problem, said Lucienne.

—A problem?

—Yes, not so much a problem as a question I want to ask you

—Go ahead, my dear, I'm listening.

—It's a question of my menstruation.

—Your menstruation?

—Yes, my periods as they say.

—Yes, I know. Your mother never talked to you about it?

—Not much.

—Well, what's the problem?

—It's not normal, you see. It's off, not like it used to be. I'm so confused. I don't know what to make of it, Madame Églantine.

—You know what it is? It's most probably that you are pregnant.

—Pregnant?

—Yes, my dear. You are going to have a baby.

—A baby? Mon Dieu!

—You need to talk to a doctor and you must inform your husband, William Henry.

—That is terrible. It's almost shameful. I'm so confused.

—There is no need of shame with your husband. He'll understand and he'll be happy.

—I do not know how to do it. I've never conceived before. May God help me, Madame Églantine.

—*Le Bon Dieu est avec toi, ma chère,* God is with you, my dear.

—Oh, oui.

Lucienne went to talk to her husband who was sitting in the den reading a novel. She told him what Madame had told her to say. He jumped for joy and told her that he was truly happy.

—That's good news, very good news. Now you must consult a doctor. Our family doctor is Doctor Lévesque. I'll make arrangements for you

—Will you come with me?

—Yes, yes, I will.

Lucienne tried to remain calm but inside there were butterflies, so many of them but eventually they went away with the comfort of knowing that she was going to have a baby.

Lucienne, the Simple-Minded

—Oh, Bill, what am I going to do with a baby? I don't know how to take care of a baby. I know how to take care of grown people when they are sick but a baby.

—Don't worry, the doctor will help you.

So William Henry and Lucienne went to see Doctor Lévesque on a Wednesday afternoon. She liked him and followed his recommendations. The doctor told her that she was two months pregnant and that he would take good care of her. She felt relieved and told William Henry that she liked the doctor.

The affair of having a baby was a long one for Lucienne. She had not expected that. However, Lucienne was a patient woman and she waited for the delivery with the hope that the child would be a healthy one and not simple-minded like her.

The delivery was simple and without too much pain and displeasure for Lucienne. She was pleased with the way things went but displeased with all the bother she was causing. The doctor told her that having a baby should not cause displeasure for the mother and for everyone associated with the birth of a child. Lucienne thought that Doctor Lévesque was so understanding and kind in his way of caregiving and soothing the patient under the stress of delivery or having some kind of pain or simply being ill. Lucienne thought to herself that Docttor Lévesque was a very good model for her in her caregiving and healing efforts. She would endeavor to follow his practice of kindness, compassion and strength of intellect.

A little girl was born weighing six and a quarter pounds. She had reddish blond hair, pink cheeks and blue eyes like her father. Lucienne told Gaétane that the baby did not resemble at all any of her relatives, not her mother, not her father not even her and that she was not *une Canayenne*. But that was alright though for the baby was born healthy and strong like her mother. Lucienne thanked the Virgin Mary for her watchful eye since she had confided whatever baby she was going to have, boy or girl to Mary the mother of God. She herself felt comfort and strength with the Virgin Mary in being at her side. She thought of Héloïse her own mother and how happy she would be.

The baby was baptized Marie Célie for Lucienne had insisted on that particular name and William Henry complied with her wishes. She wanted that name since it was the name of a very good friend of her mother, Héloïse Lanouette Charbonneau, and Lucienne had marveled at the heroine of her mother's story of Célie and Timiskamengo. Of course, she admired the Indian lover but she put Célie on a pedestal as a woman of love, kindness and fidelity. That's why she wanted to name her daughter after her, Célie Rafferty. Of course, in her mind she thought of the baby as being alive with the Lanouette tradition, so the baby was really called in Lucienne's heart, Célie Lanouette Charbonneau Rafferty. She was proud of that full name hidden in her heart for it was a good name, a name that would live forevermore. The Lanouette heritage had not been broken, Lucienne told herself. Of course, one day she would tell her daughter the entire story of the Lanouettes and the tale of Célie and Timiskamengo.

Célie Rafferty grew up with the best care that one could get. She had developed a particular love and attachment to the old Églantine who adored the child. She spoiled her with her kisses and her hugs and at times with candy hidden in her pocket. The father did not want the child to have candy but the old lady kept giving her some once in a while. She also told Célie stories and tales that enthralled the little girl even though she did not altogether understand what was being told to her. But children have their own special understanding of what is being communicated to them. They live in the land of dreams and magic. Their imagination is their key to making bright images of things in their minds. Célie was very good at making images. She would draw pictures of things such as flowers or boats or even people that she had never known but well captured by her imagination. Her mother always wondered where the child got her imaginative powers. The old woman certainly had prompted it through her stories and tales but most of all through her lovely smiles and her joy-filled laughter that made Célie smile and laugh. It was also love that made sharing a blessing and a gift that children need to grow full of life and creativity.

When Marie Célie celebrated her first birthday, and her mother was pregnant for her second child, death came to assail the Rafferty household. Églantine Vaillancourt Rafferty died without too much pain or the misery of a long illness. They found her dead in her bed one Wednesday morning when Lucienne was getting ready to go out and give voluntary care to one of her neighborhood clients, a Mrs. Dumais who was suffering with breast cancer. She was on her last cancer stage, stage four and Lucienne found it hard not be of help. The lady wanted to die at home not in a hospital nor in a nursing home. Home was home to her and Lucienne respected that. The old lady, Églantine was ninety-seven years old. She had had a full life filled with joy and favorable accomplishments. She had been a musician in the parish(she played the piano and the organ), and the director of several organizations, and an active member of the community volunteers called "The Club Celsius 50." Her first husband was deceased. She remarried with John William Rafferty, an accomplished engineer who had invested his money in several productive companies such as Polaroid and Zerox. He and his first wife had only one child, William Henry Rafferrty who became the inheritor of his estate, the Rafferty fortune. The child grew up and became a solid citizen with many investments that worked well for him and gained him millions of dollars, although he did not like being called a millionaire. William Henry received a scholarship to Brown University and majored in the humanities. Later, he attended Harvard and took courses in civil engineering just because his father had majored in this discipline. People asked him why he had done both humanities and engineering. He told them that he was not getting an education for a job but to form his mind to cultural challenges and the fine arts and at the same time a knowledge of civil engineering to help form his character. That was the mix he wanted, he said, cultural studies and rational studies to form his mind and his soul, he said. He did not need to work as such, he told them. He respected those who worked hard all their lives and those who climbed the social and industrial ladders to attain a better stance in life. He did what was pleasing to him and succeeded in attaining his own level of education by reading and traveling around the world. He and his adoptive mother lived comfortably and she encouraged him in his own pursuits of the humanities which included traveling for personal development. Madame Vaillancourt received her undergraduate diploma from

Wesleyan. She traveled to France, Belgium, Spain, and Japan. She spoke three languages with French being her maternal language. French was her language of communication with Lucienne. English was for her a business language and a communication vehicle if and when she needed it. Lucienne did not like this language because it twisted her tongue. She did not like that. Who likes tongue twisters. The old lady was buried in Mount Calvary cemetery after a funeral mass held in Sainte-Thérèse-de-l'Enfant-Jésus church. Everything was in black, the sacerdotal vestments, the banderoles, as well as the funeral drape on the casket. They sang the latin psalm, *De profundis*, on a very lugubrous tone with the Gregorian mass. It was all so very dignified and respectful, thought Lucienne. This is what she would have liked for Héloïse and Alexis but the Church had not allowed it for reasons of Church laws. Lucienne wept the loss of her dear friend/confidente, dear, dear Églantine. Young Célie was caught sobbing in the old lady's room once or twice. She told her mother that she missed *mémère* and that she wanted to go to heaven to go and meet her there. Lucienne answered her, "*Plus tard, ma fille, plus tard. Il faut que tu vives avant.*", later, you have to live first.

William Henry took the death of his step-mother hard but he realized that her time had come and she had to go to her just reward. Old age does not wait for death to come, it just comes when it's time. He devoted much of his time reading and buried himself in the old soft armchair that was his favorite when he wanted to truly relax and enjoy the moment. The family spirit seemed to have been cut in pieces and the three persons involved were somehow torn apart for now. It was not the same, said Lucienne. She hoped it was temporary and not forever. No, it couldn't be. William Henry's distancing from his wife and daughter was deeply felt by Lucienne and Célie. Lucienne even wondered if it wasn't her fault. She asked her husband about it. William Henry replied "No. It's not your fault at all.

Mine most probably, I don't know." He told her that all he wanted to do was read and take a walk in the municipal park. Sometimes he took little Célie with him and they went to the park, just to breathe easier, he told his wife. The little girl came back with her dad singing

"*La Petite Poule d'Or*", the little golden hen. That softened and did good to Lucienne's heart.

After a couple months of waiting, the new baby came in what seemed in a hurry. The delivery was fast and somewhat easy for the mother. This time a mid-wife was called in since Lucienne wanted it that way. William Henry did not want to argue with her, after all, she was the caregiver and the mother. Lucienne had thrown herself into the reading and instructions on home care and the birth of the baby with a mid-wife in charge. Totally natural, the book said. She was convinced that this was the best and natural way of birthing. Besides, she wanted Bill around and not in a waiting room somewhere.

The mid-wife whose name was Edwina Compagna arrived on time at the Rafferty house and did everything she had to do to guarantee a safe and healthy delivery with Lucienne's cooperation, of course. Not bad for an illiterate woman, said Bill to his wife afterwards. Lucienne replied, "This good woman has a head on her shoulders and the hands of a good caregiver." She had learned it from her grandmother Beauchesne. Luciennne was so proud of having given birth to a boy, a boy with blue eyes, a tiny pink nose and curly reddish-blond hair. William Henry was overjoyed with having a boy in the family, a boy, a son, he shouted. Lucienne wanted to name him, Timiskamengo. Bill would have none of it.

—After all he's my son too. He's not Indian and he's white. He's of Irish stock. No, Lucienne, no.

—Why not?

—Why not? You will not win this time. It's going to be Thomas Eldridge Rafferty. That's all.

—An British name. No, absolutely not.

—Yes. He's my son and I do not want the name that is strange if not alien. Certainly not the name of a Redskin even though he's a romantic hero of the Algonquins.

—By virtue of a concession, the baby was named Thomas Marjolain and his maman was content to have won part of the argument. So the baby was baptized Joseph Thomas Marjolain since all Catholic babies in Quebec and even in New England had a "Joseph" before their given name while the girls had Marie/Mary in front of it. An old custom.

Things had gotten better since the birth of Thomas Marjolain. There reigned a bit more harmony in the household and Célie as well as Thomas Marjolain had brought a certain calm and tenderness that had existed before. Oftentimes, Lucienne told herself that it wasn't her fault if things had deteriorated and that destiny had jealously taken over her well-being. She kept thinking of the old sorceress. Yet she could not tap the true cause of a lack of joy and hope in a future guaranteed with marriage. She did not know if she should run away from it all or try to take the lead. Wouldn't it be better to separate, William Henry and her. But what about the children, she thought. It would be a separation of misery, she thought, *une misère noire* that ruins everything she had hoped for. It would be one who is lost in a world inaccessible to the beauty and goodness of harmony accorded to those who do God's will, she thought. God wishes and creates harmony and not discord, she shouted loud and clear. And I a simple-minded creature like me do I want or not the harmony of the Lord? He's the one who comes and assuages the doubts, the fears, and the misunderstandings and especially the awkward steps as well as the decisions taken in the void of miscontents, said she in an exasperated voice. Then she let out, *Bonté divine, que c'est fou de se rendre ici-bas tellement égaré de la bonté du Seigneur pour en devenir triste et déconfit. Tout ça pour une chicane d'une heure ou d'une journée. C'est fou!*/how foolish it is to run away from the goodness of the Lord only to become sad and downcast/crestfallen. All of that for an argument of an hour, a day. It's crazy!

With the slowed down pace of life in effect, William Henry began spending more time with his two children and this liberated Lucienne in a way that she was able to get back to her caregiving/healing practice. The two spouses had talked it over at various times and realized that what they called a misunderstanding in their lives was a difference in their education and affinities that had put them to rout. William Henry loved the fine arts, reading the classics and, if possible, travel.

However, he had not been able to grant himself the anticipated travel left undone on account of the decisions taken thinking that leaving the children with a guardian was not a good idea. Besides, Lucienne would not have decided to join him. She did not like traveling and going away from home especially leaving the children behind. She much preferred her calling as healer rather than the voyages to the ends of the earth that her husband proposed, she said.

Lucienne did not like the fine arts so much. She found it "highmuckamuck" as it is said by some disadvantaged people who, like Lucienne, think that certain things, and certain behaviors are above their status as human beings and the high social keepers of rules and regulations remain way above the little people. Those of the "little bread" remain *petit pain*. That's what Lucienne believed. However, Églantine had willed her a painting by Edward Potthast. "Starry Night" and she had found it lovely, as she said, It was a repesentation of a night sky illumined by millions of stars. We know quite well that she could not compare it to Van Gogh's painting, "Starry Starry Night" for she did not know how to compare paintings of two different artists. To her, it was simply a bunch of swirling stars in the night.

When she was told how much it sold for, she yelled, "W-h-a-t !, another "highmuckymuck" thing." Although she found Potthast's work real and natural with its representation of the stars and nighttime not mysteriously unreal.

Lucienne did not simply like artists who, it seems, threw colors on a piece of canvas out of which came *des simagrés*, "monkeydos" or unimaginable caricatures. However, she liked the watercolors that raised in her a sense of beauty and the mystery of soft flowing colors. She did not know why. William Henry did not know why his wife preferred watercolors to oils, but he had to admit that watercolors were considered art and he was glad that Lucienne was getting into art.

In spite of the differences in aesthetic taste, the Raffertys enjoyed each other's company and their excursions in nature, picnics next to a pond where pond lilies floated as if in dream, walks along a brook, or simply a gaze at a sunset filled with the magic of a sun basking in its fascinating glow of softer light and dreamlike colors. Sitting under an apple tree in bloom eating delicious ham and cheese sandwiches and a freshly picked red MacIntosh apple was a treat for the Raffertys. The children went wild over it. And then there was the picnic promenade when the four of them went for a long walk in the memorial park, the land given to the city by William Henry's father as a gift to the people who lived there. It was a lovely place to have a picnic, play games, read books or simply relax. It was a great place for mill workers who had worked so hard all week long and needed some rest from the exhausting time of labor and sweat. It was a delightful time for the weary ones. Laborers, housewives, street cleaners, teachers, artist and scholars were all invited to spend time there on a Sunday afternoon when scheduled work was suspended.

William Henry had brought with him a very large book illustrating several paintings in color. He wanted to show his wife two paintings of the American Impressionist artist, Edward Potthast: **At the Beach** and **A Holiday.** The first one shows women with their children on the beach while the second one reveals children playing on the beach in puddles of water. Both of the paintings were a pure delight to William Henry for they reveal the aesthetic values of fine arts in New England near the sea. Beaches offer such delight to whomever loved the sea and its margins of sand. Children play there, dogs scramble there with their tongues sticking out, and young people chat and chat while old people, arm in arm, walk the seashore with warm sand under their feet. Following this excursion, Lucienne showed her husband a growing interest in Potthast's paintings for she had discovered an immense pleasure in the sea and the beaches. As a young girl, she had never been to one of them in Quebec. When the family moved to the States, her parents never took the children to the beach. They were land lovers, the home especially, and party-goers, *les veillées*. William Henry told his wife that the family would not be able to go and visit the beach in Potthast's paintings for Brighton beach in New York was very far from where they lived. However, they could visit one of the beaches in Massachusetts. Lucienne acquiesced to his suggestion.

On a Friday evening, a very warm evening after a hot day of sunshine and humidity, the family was preparing to go to the beach. It was a lovely excursion, said Célie to her mother. Thomas played with friends at the edge of the water. William Henry read while Lucienne kept an eye on the children. The following day, a Saturday morning after breakfast and the dishes done, Célie ran to her mother with tears in her eyes. She had in her hands an old catechism, a very large book with huge images that she had found in her mother's trunk in the attic. Célie had gone where she was not allowed to go for her mother had forbidden her to open the trunk full of old souvenirs and personal items. What had troubled the little one was the huge drawing of a demon with a kind of pitchfork. It was the menacing look at the devil sitting there that scared Célie. Enough to put fear in the hearts of little children. Lucienne grabbed the catechism from her daughter's hands and told her not to be afraid for it was all a matter of a fable in order to teach children of her time. It wasn't real she told her daughter. Célie stopped whimpering and left empty-handed. However, Lucienne could not help thinking that the dark image of Satan with his huge fork of death and punishment was a stern warning of an imminent fatality that she dared not accept as fact. All of this gnawed at her stomach and her sad and troubled soul. She hurried to banish this terrible thought from her imagination. It just kept haunting her. Was it sorcery? she thought. Where was the old sorceress, the healer. Where was she when Lucienne needed her for healing of the soul. Surely, morning would bring consolation and calm to her soul, she told herself.

—The following day, a Sunday in July when he sun was beating down hot deadening heat and people's thoughts were on the anticipation of the beach and its cool refreshing comfort, the Rafferty family could be found at Revere beach where people rushed in like honeybees in swarms. It had been a nice ride from home in Hadley to Revere in Massachusetts. William Henry had promised his children a nice ride that they would enjoy. Lucienne on her part promised Célie and Thomas Marjolain a ride on the merry-go-round. William Henry wasn't sure if it was safe enough for them to go on the fast swirling merry-go-round. He was afraid for their safety. The children looked at their mother with disappointment in their eyes hoping for intercession on her part. Lucienne tried to put back some joy in the two children by singing some songs that she recollected from her youth.

They were all in French but that was one way of teaching them her maternal language, she said. Things quieted down. Then the two children began telling stories they had heard in the neighborhood. Thomas Marjolain at certain times kept asking how much further the beach was and how long would it take to get there, and his father to reply, "Not much further, just half an hour" However, they had a tire blow-out and that meant an added hour for repair. The children grew itchy and restless, tired of waiting and so did the mother.

Once they got to the beach, they spread the blanket they had brought on some limited space they were fortunate to get. The beach was crowded. Lucienne hurried to take the clothes off the children since they wanted to get in the water. The father forbade them to go by themselves. He wanted to accompany them because he had heard of huge menacing waves at Revere beach and he wanted to protect his children from danger. The mother did not want to go in the water since she was expecting her third child and did not want to hazard herself in the very cold water of the sea. However, she encouraged the children and their father to go ahead and enjoy themselves in the salt water of the sea since this was a time of family summer celebration.

There were large signs stuck in the sand and in plain view next to the dunes that read "Please use caution when swimming. Beware of dangerous currents. Be safe. Stay safe." Some people used caution while others did not. They were not careless; they were passively oblivious to the warning. William Henry hesitated to bring the children even close to the water but he allowed them to wade in the incoming surf waters that kept rolling in. There was no depth there but one had to beware of running into the higher waters, so inviting, so alluring, so cool in the sun. He watched over his children making sure they did not disobey him. Célie and Thomas Marjolain like most of the other children there were running and shouting and having fun. William Henry was watching them like a hawk or as some say, like a mother hen and her chicks. Hardly had he turned his back and looked at Lucienne to see what she was doing when he heard the stinging cry of a child shouting for help. It was Célie's voice panicky and full of anguish. He looked everywhere to see where his children were. They were not at the water's edge.

Where were they, he said to himself. He saw that Thomas Marjolain was no longer with his sister who was crying and appeared to be numbed with fear and regret. William Henry jumped as fast as he could into the cold and numbing waters like a father attempting to rescue his child. The lifeguard ran with long paces to follow the man who was swimming towards a young boy caught in the cross current. He had a life preserver in his grasp. Célie panic striken ran towards her mother. Lucienne took her in her arms to console her but at the same time felt the same panic as her daughter. Was Thomas Marjolain in dreadful danger, she asked her. Lucienne not only feared for her son's life but for her husband's also.

She could not help feeling this way for when loved ones are in danger one cannot simply ignore it. Fear is so strong an emotion that it can spread and catch you by the throat and freeze you there like a sudden pang of the nerves, said some people sitting next to Lucienne.

A crowd of curious and fear-filled people started to gather around the area where they could see what was going on. Many were saying that the sea and its currents can be not only terrible but extremely dangerous for the swimmer's life.

Children's cries here and there could be heard followed by the howling of a man. The lifeguard reached Thomas Marjolain and was able to take him with his strong and powerful right arm and hurried to take him away from the threatening current that was swirling and swirling. The lifeguard saw the father of the child struggling in the midst of the menacing current that could take his life. The lifeguard did not know what to do since he could not let go of the child and save the poor man. He threw the life preserver close to him hoping that could help him but William Henry could not reach it and the swirling current of very cold water would not let go of its prey and William Henry sank into the morbid and furious waters yelling, help. The waters had no compassion nor any regrets, this raging and troubling fit of nature and the sea. The sea had one more time overcome the struggles of its bathing victim. William Henry disappeared into the deadly cold and stinging waters of the sea. Everyone stood there as if frozen. They were watching someone drown.

A shrilling voice could be heard, a woman on the beach whose voice could be heard as far as the distant echo was carrying the sound of a pitiful cry. It was the voice of Lucienne. The cry revealed a woman filled with dreadful fear and a panic totally haunting. The two children next to her held on to her and Lucienne knew too well that her husband was gone through a pernicious drowning that took his life. The sea would forever be the site of and regret for poor Lucienne. The lifeguard tried to console her and her two children but nothing helped them. The lifeguard was totally helpless in his efforts to console the sobbing woman.

There were only tears and wailing that remained. The three of them were left there inconsolable while some people went to them attempting to calm the poor woman and help her the best they could. Lucienne could not be consoled. She kept crying out, "My husband, my William Henry, my poor Bill, why oh why *mon Dieu*. The municipal safety squad came to recover the body of the victim while the police addressed the young widow asking her where they should bring the body of William Henry. She did not know what to say at a moment filled with pain and sorrow. She told them to do as they best thought. It was a senseless thing this drowning, a terrible thing, a horrible thing that took her loving husband away, thought Lucienne standing there with her two children all three numbed with confusion and pain.

The body of William Henry was taken to the county morgue for further inspection and legal requirements. He was then placed in an ambulance and brought to Hadley at the Samson and Dallaire funeral home where it was thought to be convenient for the family and friends. Lucienne and the children were transported to Hadley by a municipal vehicle while someone drove the family car to the Rafferty home. A great pall covered the entire neighborhood like a dark cloud.

When she got home Lucienne threw herself on the floor and on her knees and began to pray with a voice that was trembling. She asked the good Lord and the Virgin Mary why, why this terrible accident and death. The death of William Henry was a horrible loss for her. She now lacked not only a husband but a father to her children with one on the way. A great veil of sorrow and dirge now covered the Rafferty home and its inhabitants. The widow Lucienne wore black and so did the children. It was customary, she told the children. It was part of the Lanouette tradition and heritage as she tried to explain this custom to her children. No music, no piano, no radio, no singing and talking with a loud voice, everything low and soulful. There was a certain monastic ambiance at the Rafferty home. All that was allowed according to Lucienne the one whose heart was filled with saintly devotions, was prayer and meditation. Lucienne spent hours praying in her room. Gaétane came to see her and tried to tell her that she had a life to live and that her children needed her to be active and open to more joyful things in their lives.

Lucienne insisted on praying and meditating whenever she found time. The children asked her why she was praying all the time and she answered them that it was because she was praying for their father to be released from purgatory.

They asked her what purgatory was and she replied with amazement, "My God, they don't know their catechism."

William Henry's funeral was at the Irish church, Saint Thomas Aquinas, since he had said in his will that is what he wanted. He desired a church that had an alliance with his own heritage, the Raffery heritage. Lucienne did not exactly like this straying from their parish church but she acquiesced to her husband's last wishes. The church seemed somewhat strange to her but she followed the prayers since they were in latin the same as in her parish church even though it was a French-speaking church. It was after all the universal language of the Church. William Henry was buried in the Mount Calvary cemetery where his adoptive mother, Madame Vaillancourt Rafferty was buried. They could not bury him with his father since the cemetery was miles away and Lucienne preferred Mount Calvary to a distant if not strange place to her. Besides, William Henry had not designated any particular cemetery in which to be buried. It was the widow's choice, they told her.

Lucienne buried herself in her cocoon of grieving and Gaétane took care of the children while her friend stayed placid and inactive for quite some time. Finally Lucienne came out of her apparent isolation and came back to the reality of the living. It was no longer night for her. It was day with the sun shining and the trees swaying in the breeze. Lucienne had been through a night of mercy and muted pain but now she was refreshed and ready to be herself again. A balm had slowly slipped into her soul and healed the pain that the return of simplemindedness had brought back. Yes, she had fallen back into it, the strain of lassitude and fearful doubts due to the awful strain of the death of William Henry. But it was short-lived. She now was in full possession of her strength and volition. She now had the control of things and not the other way round. She was determined to leave behind this damned so-called retardation and fly over the nets of equivocation that threatened her determination to survive this ordeal. She vowed to return for good to her calling of caregiver/healer. She even bought herself a female parrot that she named Loulou after Félicité's parrot in Flaubert's tale, William Henry's favorite author. The parrot was not some exotic bird from some exotic isle with audacious colors but a bird with tamer colors but somewhat bright. She loved her Loulou. The bird made her sing with the heart. The children loved Loulou. They sang to her when they went by her cage.

Yes, Félicité with the simple heart. The same sentiment of the heart that Lucienne possessed. Lucienne talked often to her parrot telling it that her husband had died and was now with the angels in heaven for she had prayed hard for her husband to leave purgatory and go to his eternal rest *avec le Bon Dieu*. She claimed that she had received a sign from heaven that she alone knew about it. She said this in a moment of mystical fervor. Yes, Lucienne had become the simple-minded again that flew in the face of common sense, it seemed. She had received as a gift from the Holy Spirit the word and the thought surpassing the intelligence and issued from a certain mysticism. It wasn't the mysticism of the saints such as Saint-John-of-the-Cross or Saint-Theresa-of-Avila but a mysticism that came to compensate her deficient intellectual attributes. And, Lucienne poured this gift into the vessel of caregiving/healing, her contribution to those who were afflicted with illnesses that even doctors could not heal.

Four months later, Lucienne gave birth to a little girl. She had her baptized Félicité. The little one had joy in the heart, so much so that she smiled all the time. That's what her godmother Gaétane said. Gaétane had just married an older man who gave her all that she desired in life, especially love and kindness. She told Lucienne that she did not want much, just a house and a little dog. Moreover, she was going to have a house full of children, she told her friend. Lucienne started to laugh upon hearing that Gaétane would have so many children. Not that Lucienne wanted to mock her friend and laugh at her but she had pity on her. Children are given to us by the good Lord who dares to confide them to those who take their task seriously and have the patience and fortitude necessary to raise them properly, said Lucienne to her friend. She knew that Gaétane had neither the patience nor the fortitude to raise kids. She knew that Gaétane did not have the talent to be a good mother in spite of the fact that she had taken very good care of Célie and Thomas Marjolain. She had spoiled them with love and, of course, candy of every kind but she had left them to their mother as soon as she could.

She thought that the task of taking care of children was very demanding and not satisfying the least bit. She who loved her freedom of spirit and her independence in all matters. So the large portion, the *potée*, became the absence of sons and daughters she would never have. A little dog came to fill the void. They named him Charlie.

Lucienne devoted herself almost totally to prayers, to small renouncements and sometimes to sacrifices that are not heroic but relieve the soul for having at least attempted to make the effort to satisfy her mystical tendencies. Not that she was a sainte-ni-touche, do not touch-me type, not even an overly devotion to God and the saints but she wanted to uplift her spiritual penchant in order to obtain calm in her soul that was promised to her by the power of prayers and devotions. Certain people habitually suspicious believed her to be hypocritical and sometimes strange in her manners of doing and speaking. Her words were too mellow like sweet-tasting honey for them. These people found that Lucienne had changed and reflected a soft and sweet temperament. Without doubt, Lucienne was trying to fill the emptiness left by her husband's death and especially the death of a father. She played with her children, did promenades with them, sometimes brought them to the cinema, and even at times to the municipal museum. She had taken a liking to certain museums that displayed works of art that she liked such as Van Gogh's *LA NUIT ÉTOILÉE* and Sargent's LADY AGNEW OF LOCHNAW. She loved the soft feminine pastel colors of the lady's dress. The children preferred THE SMOKE OF AMBERGRIS. The mother asked them why and they answered, "The large hat, mom, and the smoking of something of whale fat." Lucienne did not quite understand but respected their taste in subject matter.

Lucienne tried to show the children what the father meant by education, to form minds and hearts with the tools of the humanities and the fine arts, he had said to her. She always tried to remember that.

Lucienne's mother had given her neither the taste nor the lived experience of the fine arts. That was all surplus and non-necessary for Héloïse. Besides we thought her to be simple-minded and not capable to learn and appreciate much of anything especially what was called the *beaux arts*. Her home-schooled education was very basic and did not include things that did not prove to be factual, tangible and practical. The fine arts were not according to Héloïse's good taste in choices. That was the reason why Lucienne's level of education was not the same as William Henry's. That was quite evident to all who dealt with her. Her husband often said that Lucienne was not stupid. What she lacked was exposure to several things like the fine arts and literature. Well, when she realized that she did have talents and the intellectual capacities to learn on a broader scale, she took advantage of it and thanks to William Henry, she tried very hard to learn what her husband had told her about a good education. She had learned a lot about healing and caregiving but that wasn't enough, she needed to polish her growing education. Her children's education depended on it, she said.

Lucienne had learned to value herself as others did through the bias of her healing/caregiving which meant that she had to be real and transparent. The people who thought her to be hypocritical and a false devout woman realized that Lucienne Charbonneau Rafferty was not superficial but real and sincere in her words and her activities. Specifically, she convinced people that her healing was based on what was called holistic which meant both body and the spiritual facets of being human. She had learned and practiced the "art" of healing and that meant based on the holistic aspect of the person. She affirmed that all human beings were created in an indivisible totality, corporal, sensual, psychological, and spiritual. She admitted to not fully understand every facet of this totality but she practiced her trade or rather the art of healing with the conviction and tenacity of a good caregiver/healer. That was why people who needed genuine holistic care flocked to her and were satisfied that she was a good provider of natural holistic healing. It was surely a gift from God that she had and that gift did flouish in her ability to heal. Certain people who knew her better than others said that she had evolved into an affable, generous, and profoundly capable of feeling compassionate toward people who needed her care and what they called grace tied to the gift of healing that she had received. Lucienne often prayed to the Holy Spirit in order to receive from him a better understanding of things that others understood more easily. On the other hand, she understood certain things that surpassed the comprehension of others. Lucienne was one of these rare creatures who appear to be simple-minded but who in reality are not. Is it a trick on the part of nature or the Creator who works in the Infinite on his own plans and his own adventures with human beings. We know nothing about it or hardly know if we know something.

Lucienne took very good care of her three children, Célie, Thomas Marjolain and the little one, Marie Félicité. This "petite" was incredibly endowed with a rare intelligence. She learned very fast and spoke like a grown-up. Lucienne was so proud of her that she could not stop talking about her and thanked *le Bon Dieu et la Vierge Marie* for giving her such a child that made her life complete as a woman. Not that Lucienne did not recognize the qualities of the other two children but she saw that one day a child of hers would grow up and become the thrill of many, a recognized celebrity for her talents, her success in life, perhaps an outstanding healer with a diploma and sought after by many. "Is it a misplaced or deceiving pride?" she asked herself. "No, dreams do not deceive, I'm convinced of that."

Lucienne continued the pace of life filled with joy for rendering services to others and sometimes undercut by some hitches, but she kept thinking that one day she would have grandchildren and that she would get to be a grandmother. That one day she would follow in the steps of her mother and her grandmother and hand down the heritage so appreciated by the ancestors and the descendance of her children and grandchildren. However, she recognized the fact that she had not thought very often of her heritage nor had she affirmed the fact that she descended from the Lanouettes by instructing her children about their québécois heritage. Probably she had not cultivated enough interest in it, a fruitful interest enough to give the cultural push. Evidently the three children were of a mixed heritage but this did not lend a negativity to the fact that they were part of the heritage of the Lanouettes rich in values and soaked in traditions, a heritage that was worthwhile cultivating. The simple-minded had turned around the negligence by replacing it with a new and revived interest. Héloïse's daughter had arrived at the summit of her alliance with the past, a past that gave her one more reason to live in harmony with her intellectual capacities, sometimes said to be limited, and recognize that the past for her and her children was not a handicap but a trump card. What was called old fashion no longer applied to Lucienne once out of her naive self.

Meanwhile Lucienne took care of those who needed her as well as her parrot Loulou that she adored and spoiled. It was the color emerald green with touches of yellow. It was not as striking as other parrots with brilliant colors but Loulou had become Lucienne's *chérie* and her pastime when she felt lonely. Loulou had become her constant companion of sweet murmurs and little songs mixed with the sounds of a parrot speaking in parrot talk. Lucienne and Loulou were two beings inseparatively linked by a heartfelt simplicity. Neither the woman nor the parrot were affected by a distressing hypocrisy or a false mark of insincerity.

One autumn day, Lucienne found her Loulou dead in its cage. Contrary to the Félicité of Flaubert's tale, Luciennne did not want to have her Loulou stuffed by a taxidermist, She would keep it locked in her memory among her cherished souvenirs. After all, it was but a bird and not a Holy Spirit she read in the tale. The simple-minded had surpassed the limits of a bewitching mysticism that comes to blur the thoughts and put them over and above daily reality. Lucienne took the birdcage and brought it in the attic. She thought of buying a little dog. She would call it Moxie after the well-known soft drink that she liked once in a while. The little dog ended up being named Timiskamengo. Sometimes memory plays tricks on us and teases us with indelible souvenirs. The children loved to play with the little dog. However, they wondered why their mother had given the dog that name. As for the boys of the street gang, they started calling the dog *Tit-Criss-de-mango*, little christ-de-mango. Lucienne did not like that but she accepted it with an open mind disposed to pleasantries. This was part of the fact that Lucienne had remained an adherant to natural healing. Lucienne the simple-minded had without a doubt surpassed the limits of retardation and had found herself finally in the pasture of real and genuine human simplicity that endorses normality.

Gaétane goes and visits her from time to time. The two friends love to tell stories and tales to Lucienne's children. She has three of them as everyone knows.

Unfortunately, they all have Irish last names due to marriage and a sign of anglicisation and assimilation. The Lanouette heritage is lost for these descendants of the québécois race. At the very least, they are remitted to the corners of a facility for genealogical research that will be most probably useful for future generations of the Lanouette clan. Héloïse-Lanouette-Charbonneau must be turning over in her grave as those people say and who know very well the hidden corners of this heritage. Lucienne anticipates returning to Batiscan some day. She wants to go and pray at the gravesite of a lady whom she assumes was dead after so many years ago. However this lady who is a healer is quite alive in Lucienne's memory and will remain there just like her mother, Héloïse, as well as Célie and her Timiskamengo. Without forgetting the father, Alexis Charbonneau who burns in her memory like a votive candle.

Lucienne has just bought a parrot that she calls Froufrou the simple-minded because it's not very much alert and he hardly reacts to her words and little songs. It is not normal for a parrot of this race and species, she said. Lucienne loves parrots since they are a good sight and they're usually good company. Froufrou fills the empty spaces now that she is alone. One of her neighbors, Vézinalda Lapointe, a former friend who does not have her tongue in her pocket as the Québécois say, *n'a pas sa langue dans sa poche*, loves to make reproaches to Lucienne about her parrot each time she sees her.

—Why do you keep this damn little beast, a bundle of feathers. It's a dumb and retarded bird.

And Lucienne replies,

—It's exactly for that reason, Vézinalda, it's because I love him like that. Froufrou is simple-minded and deserves to be as it is.

—*Bonne Sainte Viarge,* you're hard to be understood sometimes, Lucienne. You're not like the others. It makes no sense at all. *Pantoute.*

—I know, Vézinalda. I wouldn't like to be either.

A light nodding of the head followed by a slightly hoarse cough. Then a long moment of silence.

—Will it rain tomorrow, Lucienne?

—I don't know Vézinalda, maybe.

—I sure hope so. Everything is so dry. It's dangerous for the fire.

—You must not worry about things like that, Vézinalda. Things take care of themselves. My mother used to say that we must not make a big deal wih things like that. Things arrange themselves without preoccupying yourself with their fate.

—Your mother had a good head on her shoulders, Lucienne.

—Yes, a very good head.

—And, she had *du casque,* some daring, your mother.

—Yes but daring that came from an iron will. No one dared to step on her toes, I assure you.

—Yes, a woman of brains and gohead.

—I don't know if God makes anyone like her today.

—It would be hard to reproduce. And then would anyone want a woman like that.

—Me, I would want one.

—Yes, you're her daughter.

—Yeah, Lucienne the simple-minded. And a mother who always loved her.

—The mother à vache, the parcheesi mother. Do you remember when your mother played parcheesi with you? Your mother loved to tell me everyting about those episodes. [the game was called *jouer à vache*].

—Yes, maman always fixed it so I might go to heaven.

—Without that you would have cried for having lost the game, I'm sure.

—I was young then.

—Young enough to cry but not too young not to remember it. I will always remember when my mother used to tell me the little delights of Lucienne.

—Poor maman. Poor her who had wished so much to see me sane of spirit.

—But you are my *chouette*.

—Yes, I did obtain my healing by means of my gifts of healing.

—It's so marvelouss what happens when we have faith in the Holy Spirit.

—Not only in the Holy Spirit but faith in oneself.

—That's really a gift.

—Yes, I know. A gift that is given without having merited it.

—You did merit it by your life and your abundance of love. You have a heart that loves and knows how to love. That's what living fully is. It's done in spite of the adversities and the traps that we get from God.

—Traps?

—Yes, traps like the intellectual limitations.

—As for the intellectual limitations, I have crossed them and I was able to conquer my doubts and my losses of hope. Everything is possible, Vézinalda, everything is possible. Nothing is impossible. It's possible if we start going on top of the obstacles that scare us and betray us by their prevarications.

—You had *casque, ma chouette.*

—I always had some and I will have some until I die. It didn't always come out but I had some.

—Live when we have some is my motto. Me, I have some. I'm timid and I have a head full of little fears that come to bother me and put me in discomfort.

—We must not get discouraged, Vézinalda. With that we make jam, *des confitures.* Bursts of laughter. Bursts of the heart.

Then a very long silence followed by movement of trailing chairs and the clacking closing of doors afterwards. Silence. Lucienne the simple-minded has nothing more to say. Silence and quietude. The story of Célie, Héloïse and Lucienne has ended. A story that is intertwined stitch by stitch, brand by brand like the seductive brands of a tapistry well woven, well done by workers, toilers and artists who know how to put together a masterpiece. It's the heritage at work.

The Lanouette tapistry whose colors most probably will lose their brightness and splendor with the years. Everything loses something with age it seems. However, the design will not be erased or diminished to a point of no return due to the tenacity and the permanence of the very good if not excellent weavers of Batiscan.

www.ingramcontent.com/pod-product-compliance
Lightning Source LLC
Chambersburg PA
CBHW030148100526
44592CB00009B/179